Segregation and Mistrust

Generalized trust – faith in people you don't know who are likely to be different from you – is a value that leads to many positive outcomes for a society. Yet some scholars now argue that trust is lower when we are surrounded by people who are different from us. Eric M. Uslaner challenges this view and argues that residential segregation, rather than diversity, leads to lower levels of trust. Integrated and diverse neighborhoods will lead to higher levels of trust, but only if people also have diverse social networks. Professor Uslaner examines the theoretical and measurement differences between segregation and diversity and summarizes results on how integrated neighborhoods with diverse social networks increase trust in the United States, Canada, the United Kingdom, Sweden, and Australia and how they increase altruism toward people of different backgrounds in the United States and the United Kingdom. He also shows how different immigration and integration policies toward minorities shape both social ties and trust.

Eric M. Uslaner is a Professor of Government and Politics at the University of Maryland, College Park. He is also a Senior Research Fellow at the Center for American Law and Political Science, Southwest University of Political Science and Law, Chongqing, China, and an Honorary Professor of Political Science at Aarhus University, Denmark. He is the founding editor of the *Sage University Papers on Quantitative Applications in the Social Sciences* and has served on the editorial boards of the *Journal of Politics*, *American Politics Quarterly*, *Social Science Quarterly*, *Political Research Quarterly*, and the *Journal of Trust Research*. Professor Uslaner is author or editor of twelve books, including *Corruption, Inequality, and the Rule of Law* (Cambridge University Press, 2008) and *The Moral Foundations of Trust* (Cambridge University Press, 2002). He received his PhD from Indiana University.

Segregation and Mistrust

Diversity, Isolation, and Social Cohesion

ERIC M. USLANER
University of Maryland, College Park

CAMBRIDGE UNIVERSITY PRESS
Cambridge, New York, Melbourne, Madrid, Cape Town,
Singapore, São Paulo, Delhi, Mexico City

Cambridge University Press
32 Avenue of the Americas, New York, NY 10013-2473, USA

www.cambridge.org
Information on this title: www.cambridge.org/9780521151634

First published 2012

Printed in the United States of America

A catalog record for this publication is available from the British Library.

Library of Congress Cataloging in Publication data
Uslaner, Eric M.
Segregation and mistrust : diversity, isolation, and social cohesion / Eric M. Uslaner, University of Maryland, College Park.
p. cm.
Includes bibliographical references and index.
ISBN 978-0-521-19315-3 (hardback) – ISBN 978-0-521-15163-4 (paperback)
1. Race relations. 2. Trust. 3. Segregation. 4. Multiculturalism.
5. Cultural pluralism. I. Title.
HT1521.U85 2012
305.8–dc23 2012013660

ISBN 978-0-521-19315-3 Hardback
ISBN 978-0-521-15163-4 Paperback

Contents

Preface

This is an accidental book. In 2002 I published *The Moral Foundations of Trust*. I thought I was done with trust as the major focus of my research. I was asked to give talks on trust well after that, and my next book, *Corruption, Inequality, and Trust* (2008), was mostly about corruption, but trust reappeared as a "supporting actor" in the story of what makes for honest governance.

The idea for this book came when I received notification of a conference to be held in Milan, Italy, in January 2006. I wanted to go to the conference, but the conference topic was "Understanding Diversity." I didn't know too much about diversity, but I had read papers in which authors such as Alberto Alesina attributed many ills of modern society – including low trust – to the reluctance of people to engage with people unlike themselves. Since the sort of trust I believed (and still believe) to be important is faith in people unlike yourself, I proposed to see whether it was really true that diversity drives down trust. I proposed a paper for the conference, it was accepted (a paid trip to Milan and shortly afterward another to Norway), and I started my analyses. All sorts of negative things began to happen. It snowed in Milan; I slipped and almost hurt myself on the icy road on the way to a restaurant. It poured in Norway, so a boat trip to the fjords was literally a washout. And the correlations across countries and American states between trust and all sorts of measures of diversity were about as close to zero as one can imagine.

I wasn't happy about the weather in either Milan or Norway, but I was delighted that living among people who are different from yourself didn't make you less trusting in people who are different from yourself. But that left me with a quandary: Does the composition of where you live not matter at all for trust in people unlike yourself? I had no ready answer, but going through the cross-national data set I had constructed, I found a variable that seemed remotely relevant: a crude ordinal measure (from the Minorities at Risk Project at my own university, indeed just one floor below my office) of whether minorities lived apart from the majority population. I found a moderately strong correlation with trust across nations – a relationship that held even controlling for other factors in the trust models I had estimated in my 2002 book. It wasn't diversity but segregation that led to less trust. I had an argument. But I put it aside as I turned my attention to corruption.

After my corruption book was published, I looked around for another project. Once again, travel was the mother of invention. I received a series of invitations to conferences in Denmark and Sweden, the first at Aalborg University on "The Social Differentiation of Trust and Social Capital" (where even in June the weather was cold). This invitation renewed my interest in segregation and trust and I was off to a new project, which turned into this book. The opportunity to work with colleagues in Sweden on a social capital survey heightened my interest in diversity, since I knew from my friend Bo Rothstein that Sweden has remained a high-trusting society even as it has become more diverse.

I knew about the legacy of segregation in the United States, so that is where I began, although I knew little of the segregation literature at the time. A lot of hard work was before me. I wanted to extend my work beyond the United States. The opportunity to work with my Swedish colleagues provided a natural comparison. I also had written a fair amount on Canada, so that country seemed to be another place to study. At a conference in Paris in late 2008 where I was the only political scientist in a sea of economists, I met an English economist, Alan Manning, who was examining Muslims' sense of belonging using the United Kingdom Citizenship Survey. I was intrigued with the survey. I knew of issues of immigration and multiculturalism in Britain through the news and I felt that I understood a bit about England since my wife was born and raised in London. I had a lot of work to do, since I didn't know enough about residential patterns in Sweden or Canada to make reasonable arguments. I barely knew enough about the United Kingdom to write anything worthy of an academic paper (much less a book). And the notion of reading a few papers on segregation to set me on my way was way too optimistic. Every paper I read had many more citations. When I reached the electronic journal *Urban Studies*'s Web site and entered "segregation" in the search box, I was stunned at the sheer volume of papers in just that journal.

Yet I persevered and started working on the project. Reasonably early on, I posted a paper or two on my Web site, and I received an e-mail from an older scholar who had found the papers and wanted to start a conversation. It was Thomas Pettigrew, who with his mentor, Gordon Allport, were the major figures in contact theory. Tom kept encouraging me, ultimately calling me a "social psychologist in political scientist's clothing," which I took as a compliment but didn't advertise too much among my colleagues in my own discipline. The continued encouragement of Tom Pettigrew led me to continue with this project.

The literature on segregation turned out to be a natural fit for my interests – it is strongly linked to inequality, which I have long argued is the major factor leading to low trust. My selection of cases turned out to be more than fortuitous. And then I went away for four months – to Australia. The Fulbright grant I received had no teaching responsibilities, but I was expected to extend my research on segregation and trust to Australia and I was also expected to talk on this research throughout Australia. I found very receptive audiences throughout Australia, including government officials. And the new case seemed to fit in very well with the other four countries – the United States, the UK, Canada (which is culturally very similar to Australia, but with worse weather), and Sweden (more of a surprise). The topic intrigued me more and more as I progressed, and it brought me back to the arguments I had made in my 2002 book.

I am grateful to many colleagues (all listed alphabetically) who read the manuscript in draft, most notably Peter Thisted Dinesen, Miles Hewstone, Bo Rothstein, and Kim Mannemar Sonderskov, who read the manuscript in its entirety. Peter and Kim forced me to recognize that segregation doesn't just happen – it reflects where people want to live (so Chapter 8 stems from their early criticisms). Bo forced me to think more like a political scientist at the end: What are the policy implications of all of this? And Miles told me I thought too much like a North American political scientist and pushed me to broaden my notion of contact.

Others who generously gave their time and expertise to portions of the book are Barbara Arneil, Ernesto Calvo, John Helliwell, Patrick James, Staffan Kumlin, Andrew Mason, Brian McKenzie, Jonathan Rothwell, Kim Rubenstein, Stuart Soroka, Dietlind Stolle, and Dag Wollebak. Susanne Lundåsen, my co-author on part of Chapter 6, was wonderful to work with and made it possible to extend my argument beyond English-speaking countries. She and Lars Svedberg and Lars Trägårdh of Ersta Sköndal University College in Stockholm have taught me much about Swedish political and social life – and about trust more generally – and have served on multiple occasions as most gracious hosts at their institution (as have so many others, most notably Bo Rothstein of Goteborg University and Kim Mannemar Sonderskov of Aarhus University – where I am now Honorary Professor of Political Science).

All of these great people have helped me with my arguments. The arguments rest upon data, and much of the data were either proprietary or not readily accessible (at least to me). Susanne Lundåsen, Lars Svedberg, and Lars Trägårdh made the Swedish Social Capital survey from Ersta Sköndal University College available to me (and Susanne calculated the segregation indices). Andrew Markus of Monash University made the Australian data (the 2007 Scanlon Social Cohesion Survey) available to me; Mike Poulsen of Macquarie University provided the segregation measures; Steve McEachern and Andrew Leigh of Australian National University (Leigh is now a member of parliament for Canberra) provided data on diversity. Feng Hou of Statistics Canada graciously (and at short notice) calculated diversity and segregation measures for Canada; Isabelle Cadieux, Matthieu Ravignat, and Frank Larouche expedited my visit to the Centre Interuniversitaire Québécois de Statistiques Sociales/Quebec Inter-University Centre for Social Statistics to use the 2008 Canadian General Social Survey.

John Iceland, one of the gurus of measuring segregation in the United States, provided the data on segregation in the United States that I use for most of my analyses; John Logan helped me understand other measures (which he also provided). Doug Goldenberg-Hart of *Congressional Quarterly* helped me obtain the American City Crime data for the United States (after I won a lottery at the American Political Science Association in 2009). Alberto Alesina and Ekaterina Zhuravskaya shared their national-level data on segregation; Eliana La Ferrara provided community-level Gini indices for the United States. Nathan Dietz of the Corporation for National and Community Service and Thomas Pollak and Katie Uttke of the Urban Institute provided the data on volunteering and charitable giving I use in Chapter 7, and Dale Jones of the Global Ministry Center helped to estimate community-level membership in religious denominations.

I am also grateful to the Inter-University Consortium for Political and Social Research, which made the General Social Survey for the United States available; to Robert Putnam for the Social Capital Benchmark Survey; to the UK Data Archive for the 2007 United Kingdom Citizenship

Survey; and to Richard Johnston and Stuart Soroka for making the Equality, Security, Community survey available.

Not only did I get many comments from individuals who read the draft – all or chapters – but I also benefited from comments at conferences where I presented my work, as either a keynote speaker or a paper giver. I single out several friends for their great hospitality in hosting me for a week each: Ola Bergstrand of the University of Goteborg (Sweden); Ali Carkoglu at Sabanci and Koc Universities (Istanbul, Turkey); Ed Fieldhouse at the Institute for Social Change at the University of Manchester (United Kingdom); Kimmo Gronlund of the Centre of Excellence: Democracy – A Citizen Perspective, Åbo Akademi University (Turku, Finland); Yoji Inaba at the School of Law, Nihon University (Tokyo, Japan); Bo Rothstein at the Quality of Government Institute, University of Goteborg (Sweden); and Eskil Wadensjö at Stockholm University (Sweden).

I am particularly grateful to the U.S.-Australia Fulbright Commission for the opportunity to spend the fall 2010 semester as the Fulbright Australian National University Distinguished Chair in American Political Science at the Australian National University (ANU). In Australia, I was particularly grateful to the wonderful Fulbright staff: Acting Director Lyndell Wilson, Natalie Collins, Kate Lyall, Rosemary Schmedding, and Jenny Street – especially to my hosts at ANU. John Hart, who was responsible for my well-being there, went well beyond what anyone might expect to make me feel welcome in one of the most beautiful (and now diverse) countries in the world.

While in Oz (as the locals call it), I had great colleagues at ANU: John Dryzek and Bob Goodin, both of whom I knew from their days at Maryland, as well as Kizzy Gandy, Kim Huynh, Bora Kanra, Kim Rubenstein, Meg Russell, Tetsuki Tamura, and Helen Taylor; a former ANU faculty member (Andrew Leigh, with whom I was going to do joint research before he became professionally unavailable due to his election to parliament); Geoff Woolcock and Jenny Wilson at Griffith University; Benno Torgler at the Queensland Institute of Technology; Robert Tanton of the University of Canberra; David Brown at Murdoch University; Mike Poulsen at Macquarie University; and Jenny Onyx at the University of Technology Sydney – all of whom arranged talks at their universities for me. I am grateful to Paul Ronalds of the Office of the Prime Minister for coming to hear me talk on my research.

I am also grateful to the Embassy of Canada and the Association for Canadian Studies in the United States for a Faculty Research Award for support for my research on trust among different ethnic groups in Canada.

And, of course, I express my deepest appreciation to the Graduate School of the University of Maryland, College Park, for a Research and Support Award in 2011 that gave me a semester free of teaching so that I could travel to present my work and write most of the rest of the first draft.

I have had wonderful opportunities to present my work throughout the world. I was a keynote speaker at the following conferences:

Conference on "The Social Differentiation of Trust and Social Capital," Aalborg University, Denmark, June 6–9, 2009; Conference on "The Politics of Social Cohesion," Centre for the Study of Equality and Multiculturalism (CESEM) at the University of Copenhagen, September 9–12, 2009; the 2009 Sweden Conference on Urban Policies and Social Capital, Lidkoping and Gothenburg, September 24–6, 2009; the EURODIV 5th Conference "Dynamics of Diversity in the Globalisation Era," Milan, Italy, October 22–3, 2009; the Inaugural Colloquium for Research Higher Degree Students, Griffith Institute for Social and Behavioural Research, Griffith University, Brisbane, Australia, November 11, 2010; the 2011 President Mauno Koivisto Lecture, Abo Akademi University, Turku, Finland, May 10, 2011; and the Asia Science Seminar, sponsored by the National Research Foundation of Korea and the Japan Society of Promotion of Science, Nihon University, Tokyo, Japan, September 16, 2011.

I also presented this work at:

The Diversity and Democratic Politics Workshop, Queens University, Kingston, Ontario, May 7–9, 2009; the Stockholm University Linnaeus Center for Integration Studies, March 16, 2010; the University of Oxford, April 13, 2010; the Conference on "'People Like Us': The Impact of Ethnic Concentration in Diverse Societies," University of Manchester (UK), April 16, 2010; Chuo University, Tokyo, Japan, May 25, 2010; School of Politics and International Relations, Australian National University, Canberra, Australia, October 11, 2010; an informal seminar with faculty from the School of Law, the Department of Immigration and Citizenship, and the Office of the Prime Minister, Australian National University School of Law, October 20, 2010; University of Melbourne, School of Social and Political Sciences, November 1, 2010; Department of Environment and Human Geography, Macquarie University, Sydney, Australia, November 15, 2010; External Seminar at NATSEM (National Centre for Social and Economic Modeling), University of Canberra, Canberra, Australia, November 22, 2010; Cosmopolitan Civil Societies Research Centre, University of Technology Sydney, Sydney, Australia, November 17, 2010; Research School of Social Sciences, Philosophy Program, Australian National University, December 3, 2010; the Quality of Government Institute, University of Gotenborg (Sweden), January 24, 2011; Department of Political Science, Koc University (Istanbul, Turkey), February 22, 2011; Abo Akademi University (Turku, Finland), May 11, 2011; the European Consortium for Political Science General Conference (Reykjavik, Iceland), August 26, 2011; Workshop on Trust, Aarhus University (Denmark), October 27, 2011; Sabanci University (Istanbul, Turkey), January 4, 2012; and

Workshop on Trust and Computational Models, University of Manchester (UK), January 18, 2012.

I am grateful to the many colleagues and new friends who commented on my work and were uniformly supportive. I presented an early version of my work at the American Politics Workshop at the Department of Government and Politics at my own university, the University of Maryland, on March 12, 2010. As usual, I got great feedback from my colleagues and graduate students. We never spare each other criticism, but we always do it in a supportive manner and we always remain good friends afterward. Masamichi Sasaki of Chuo University solicited a paper from the project and it was published as "Trust, Diversity, and Segregation in the United States and the United Kingdom," *Comparative Sociology*, 10 (2011): 221–46. An expanded version appeared in Masamichi Sasaki and Robert M. Marsh, eds., *Trust: Comparative Perspectives*, Leiden, the Netherlands: Brill Publishers. Nils Holtug of Copenhagen Business School invited me to be a keynote speaker at a conference on "The Politics of Social Cohesion" at Copenhagen in September 2009 and invited me to publish a nontechnical summary of the paper in a special issue of *Ethnicities*; the paper, "Segregation, Trust, and Minorities," appeared in volume 10 (2010): 415–34.

I have received strong support over the years from the Department of Government and Politics at the University of Maryland, College Park, especially from my department chair, Mark Lichbach. More recently, I have been fortunate to be Senior Research Fellow at the Center for American Law and Political Science at the Southwest University of Political Science and Law, Chongqing, China, since 2006, with strong support from President Zitang Fu as well as Secretary Zhan and Larry Li. Eric Crahan at Cambridge University Press has been very supportive as my editor in this and my previous book (and Lew Bateman was in my first book and continues to support me).

But the real support lies at home, where I am fortunate to have a son who is sometimes cynical, but always very bright and very humorous. After four years of a very demanding academic regimen at Colorado College, Avery better appreciates academic arguments and makes some strong ones himself. And I am more than fortunate to have in my life Debbie, my loving wife. She never doubted me or the worth of this project because she is a true generalized truster who always has contacts with people of different backgrounds.

1

Trust, Diversity, and Segregation

> Walid was born in France and went to a French high school. He will show you his French driving license and even his French identity card. But ask him what his identity is and he will say "93." ... "Nine Three" – the first two digits of the postal code spanning the roughest suburbs on Paris's northeastern fringe – stands for unemployment and endless rows of housing projects. It stands for chronically high crime rates, teenage gang wars and a large immigrant community.... "The question of being French is irrelevant – what's in a piece of paper?" said Walid, 19, who is of Algerian descent, dismissively putting his identification card back into his jeans pocket. "I'm from the ghetto, I'm from 93, end of story." ... "We are French, but we also feel like foreigners compared to the real French," said Mamadou, whose father came to France from Mali decades ago and married his mother, a French woman. Who, according to him, are the "real" French? The answer comes without hesitation and to vigorous nodding by a group of his friends: "Those with white skin and blue eyes."
>
> Bennhold (2005)

> Whence all this passion toward conformity anyway? – diversity is the word. Let man keep his many parts and you'll have no tyrant states. Why, if they follow this conformity business they'll end up by forcing me, an invisible man, to become white, which is not a color but the lack of one. Must I strive toward colorlessness? ... America is woven of many strands. I would recognize them and let it so remain.
>
> Ralph Ellison (1952, 499) *Invisible Man*

When our son was six years old, my wife and I took him to spend a weekend on a farm in Pennsylvania Dutch country, just outside the city of Lancaster. We woke up early in the morning so that he could help milk the cows. The evening before, at dinner, the farmer told us that his daughter had made a new friend at school that day. "Is she black or is she white?" the farmer asked his daughter and the girl replied, "I don't remember. I'll look tomorrow."

The farmer's daughter was color-blind: the background of her new friend didn't matter to her. She seemed unconcerned, but was unlikely to report back that her new friend was an African-American. Only 3 percent of Lancaster's population is African-American. The metropolitan area is mostly white and African-Americans are far less likely to come into contact with whites in Lancaster than in most metropolitan areas. The elementary schools are at least as segregated as the larger community.[1]

I grew up in the 1950s and 1960s in a more diverse city – Paterson, New Jersey. Paterson's African-American population grew from 6 percent in 1950 to 15 percent in 1960, increasing dramatically thereafter (New Jersey Office of State Planning, 1988, 41). I remember only one African-American student among the 600 or so students in Public School 26, which I attended in the 1950s.[2] My high school, Eastside High School (which featured a principal named Joe Clark who kept order with a baseball bat in both real life and the 1989 movie *Lean on Me*), was far more diverse. African-Americans comprised 46 percent of the school's 2,100 students in the late 1960s, but whites and blacks mostly passed each other in the halls. Classes were largely segregated in tracks supposedly determined by ability, though African-Americans saw such divisions as a method of enforcing segregation (Norwood, 1975, 188). Paterson's schools in the 1970s were highly segregated: three-quarters of American

[1] The percent of African-Americans ranks 49th of 237 metropolitan areas (data from Echenique and Fryer, 2007, available at http://www.hss.caltech.edu/~fede/segregation/). Lancaster's diversity score is .469, ranking 63rd of 325; its segregation measure (multigroup entropy) is .227, ranking 234th of 325 areas (from Iceland and Weinberg with Steinmetz, 2002; see Chapter 2, n. 11 for the data link). The probability of interaction between groups (here whites and African-Americans) is measured by P*, which estimates the likelihood that two randomly selected people come from the same group (Lieberson, 1961). The Lancaster area has a P* for blacks and whites of .627, which ranks 176th of 239 areas (with higher scores indicating greater isolation). The data are available at http://www.s4.brown.edu/cen2000/WholePop/WPdownload.html. Lancaster ranks 81st of 329 areas in black-white school segregation, with an index of dissimilarity (see Chapter 2) of .655, which is nevertheless very high and considerably above the median of .53 (see Cutler, Glaeser, and Vigdor, 1997, 462 on the range of the index and http://www.s4.brown.edu/cen2000/SchoolPop/SPsort/sort_d1.html for the metropolitan area rankings); 2.9 percent of white students are exposed to African-Americans. Slightly less than half of African-Americans are exposed to whites, down from 63 percent in 1970 (http://www.s4.brown.edu/schoolsegregation/schoolsegdatapage/codes/msaschseg.asp).

[2] The figure comes from the school, which I called on August 16, 2011. The administrator said that the figure has remained mostly constant over time.

schools had more racial diversity than did Paterson's.[3] This reflected the continuing racial tensions in this mid-sized American city of 150,000 people, conflicts that spilled over into the school system (Norwood, 1975, chs. 9–10).

The farmer's daughter was far more likely to see an African-American on television than at school. Kids' television programming has become a virtual rainbow.[4] This is a sea change from the 1950s and 1960s, when children's programming was far more central to television in the United States (and elsewhere). The airwaves were filled with lots of smiling hosts and child actors – and virtually all of them were white.[5] Occasionally I wondered why our school and neighborhood was almost completely white, but our lower middle-class neighborhood didn't seem so different from what I saw in the early days of television. What we see on television today – and in the entertainment world more generally and in sports – has become a vision of what we think we ought to be.

American society has grown more diverse: minorities made up barely more than 10 percent of Americans in 1950. Today more than one-third of Americans are non-whites. American cities have become less racially

[3] The diversity index (see n. 1) between whites and minorities for 1970 is .626 for the Paterson school system, slightly lower than that for contemporary Lancaster but still greater than three-quarters of other municipalities for more contemporary data from 1989 (see n. 1 for the comparative data and http://www.s4.brown.edu/schoolsegregation/schoolsegdatapage/codes/schoolseg.asp for the Paterson data). No data are available prior to 1970. Paterson's school segregation is lower than larger cities in the 1960s (Farley and Tauber, 1974, 895–6). This may reflect the smaller number of public schools in the city rather than real interaction between people of different races and ethnicities.

[4] The *Mickey Mouse Club* of the 1970s included several minority cast members (http://www.retrojunk.com/details_tvshows/2865-new-mickey-mouse-club-70s-series/). The major contemporary program in the United States is the Public Broadcasting System's *Sesame Street* (http://www.sesamestreet.org/onair/cast), which likely has the most diverse cast of any television program in the United States. Primetime programming also has far greater diversity.

[5] The most famous in the United States was the *Mickey Mouse Club*, aired daily on the ABC Network. The adult hosts and the young "Mousketeers" were all white (see http://www.tvacres.com/child_mouseketeers.htm and http://www.originalmmc.com/cast.html). Minorities who did get on these shows were classic stereotypes such as "Gunga Ram," a young Indian elephant trainer on NBC's *Andy's Gang* (http://www.bygonetv.com/shows/andys_gang/index.htm) and the American Indian "Princess Summerfallwinterspring" on NBC's *Howdy Doody Show*. Even more "mainstream" minorities such as Jews took on Anglicized names for their children's shows (Irving Pincus was "Pinky Lee," "Andy Devine" was actually on Jeremiah Schwartz, both on NBC, which was owned by the Sarnoff family, themselves Jewish). Adult programming was not much more diverse: The only African-American with a primetime network show was singer Nat "King" Cole, whose NBC series lasted one year because it could not find sponsors (http://www.jazzonthetube.com/videos/black-history-month/the-nat-king-cole).

segregated in the past few decades, but the gains have been small since the 1950s (Lichter, 1985).[6]

Our children are especially likely to see people of different backgrounds primarily on television (or in other forms of entertainment and sports) than in daily life: 44 percent of students in American public schools are minorities. Yet "our two largest minority populations, Latinos and African Americans, are more segregated than they have been since the death of Martin Luther King more than forty years ago [in 1968]" (Orfield, 2009, 6). There are more and more minorities all around us, but we are more likely to see them on the wide screen than in our neighborhoods.

When we live apart from people who are different from ourselves, we are unlikely to trust them – or to trust people more generally. When you live apart from people of different backgrounds, you are more likely to develop negative stereotypes of "other groups" than to trust people who are more likely to be strangers than close friends. Contact with people of different backgrounds can lead you to a broader sense of trust – generalized trust – but simple contact is not enough. You must interact with people of different backgrounds on the basis of equality (which children generally do), and do so often. Frequent contact, in turn, depends upon where you live. If you live apart from people of diverse backgrounds, you are unlikely to develop the strong ties needed to build trust. Segregated communities separate people and breed mistrust. A Patersonian said of the city in the late 1960s: "It don't matter, white, black, or Puerto Rican, there's no unity. Nobody sees nothing, nobody helps nobody, nobody trusts nobody" (quoted in Norwood, 1975, 68).

The farmer's daughter was a prototypical generalized truster. It didn't matter to her whether her new friend was black or white. Even when she would notice her friend's race the next day, it would not make any difference. Yet she is an anomaly – living apart from minorities didn't shape her worldview. And if her friend turned out to be African-American, she would be an anomaly in another sense: our friends tend to look like (and have interests) very much like ourselves. Whites hang out with whites, blacks with blacks, Jews with Jews, Muslims with Muslims. So our contacts largely reinforce our sense of in-group identity.

Believing that "most people can be trusted" is atypical – at least in most countries. For some, it seems strange that we might ever consider

[6] See http://articles.latimes.com/2010/jun/10/nation/la-na-census-20100611, http://www.brookings.edu/opinions/2010/1216_census_frey.aspx, and for data on racial diversity, http://www.census.gov/population/www/documentation/twps0056/twps0056.html.

trusting people we don't know, at least until we have substantial evidence that they are trustworthy (Gambetta, 1988, 217; Hardin, 2004). Even the late President Ronald Reagan was too forgiving when he said of the former Soviet Union "trust but verify." Most of us are not willing to make the inferential leap of faith that "most people can be trusted." Across 69 countries in the 1981, 1990, and 1995 World Values Surveys,[7] only 30 percent of respondents agreed with this statement. In only five countries (Norway, Sweden, Denmark, Finland, and Canada) did a majority of respondents give a trusting response.

As far back as Virgil, Trojans were warned to "beware of Greeks bearing gifts."[8] Our parents told us not to take candy from strangers. We feel more comfortable with people like ourselves. African-Americans call each other "brothers" and "sisters." Jews refer to each other as "members of the tribe." The Mafia calls its members "the family." Outsiders are "the other," not part of our community.

We are programmed to look out for our own kind first and to be wary of others (Brewer, 1979). Messick and Brewer (1983, 27–8, italics in original) review experiments on cooperation and find that "members of an in-group tend to perceive other in-group members in generally favorable terms, particularly as being *trustworthy, honest, and cooperative*." The Maghribi of northern Africa relied on their extended Jewish clan – and other Jews in the Mediterranean area – to establish a profitable trading network in the twelfth century (Greif, 1993). Models from evolutionary game theory suggest that favoring people like ourselves is our best strategy (Hamilton, 1964, 21; Masters, 1989, 169; Trivers, 1971, 48). For most of us, the default position is to put our trust *only* in people like ourselves – what Yamigishi and Yamigishi (1994) call *particularized trust*.

Why, then, do almost a third of people throughout the world throw caution to the wind and trust others? What does it mean to say that "most people can be trusted"? Where does trust come from and why are we so reluctant to put our faith in people unlike ourselves? I consider

[7] I don't use later WVS modules because of some puzzling results for trust and other variables. Most notably, the 2000 wave shows that 39 percent of Canadians believe that most people can be trusted, compared to 54 percent in 1995 – and in three other surveys conducted in Canada in 2000 (the Canadian National Election Study, the Quebec Referendum Study, and the Economy, Security, Community Survey). Iran has a higher level of trust than almost any other nation – tied with Norway – and Indonesia, Vietnam, and Belarus (among other nations) have higher levels of trust than the United Kingdom, Belgium, and Germany. Details of other anomalies are available on request. I also exclude China (see Uslaner, 2002, 226, n. 8).

[8] See http://german.about.com/library/blidioms_greeks.htm.

these questions, discussing different conceptions of trust, the foundations of each type of trust, and the relationship of faith in others to diversity and to residential segregation. I then consider the cases I examine and discuss the route ahead.

In contrast to the view that contact with people of different backgrounds leads to greater trust, some argue that we turn away from people who are different from ourselves because we fear that increasing diversity threatens social cohesion. Living among people who are different from ourselves leads us to be less likely to trust others and to have lower levels of civic engagement – not just in the United States, but throughout the West and elsewhere. Walid and Mamadou may express their thoughts more forcefully than many, but they are not atypical.

Which perspective is correct? Does living among people who are different from yourself make you more or less likely to trust people more generally? I present evidence supporting the former view and suggest that the two perspectives are inherently contradictory. If you live among people who are different but don't have close contact with them, you are more likely to become (or remain) a particularized truster. But people don't just find themselves living among people who are different from themselves in some random order. Where you live often reflects whom you want your neighbors to be.

Trust: A Multi-Headed Hydra[9]

The standard view of trust is a story of reciprocity: we learn to trust each other by our daily interactions. If I loan you five dollars and you pay me back, I will trust you. But trust is always conditional. Paying back a loan is not a good basis for trusting you to paint my house or to perform open heart surgery on me. This "knowledge-based trust" (Yamigishi and Yamigishi, 1994) reflects Offe's (1999, 50) observation that trust in persons results from "continued interactions with concrete persons whom we typically know for a considerable period of time." Hardin (2004, 10) is even more emphatic: "My trust of you must be grounded in expectations that are particular to you, not merely in generalized expectations."

Of course, much trust is based upon experience. There is also another form of faith in others, called "altruistic" trust by Mansbridge (1999) and which I call "moralistic trust" (Uslaner, 2002, 2–3, 17–21). The belief that people can be trusted stems from a moral argument that *we ought to trust*

[9] This section is largely drawn from Uslaner, 2002, chs. 1 and 2.

most people, that we would be better off taking the risk to trust strangers, including people who look and think differently from ourselves. Since many, if not most, people in Western societies are likely to be different from yourself, moralistic trust is both a leap of faith and a commitment to the belief that people from diverse backgrounds can still be part of your "moral community." Moralistic trust is the belief that others share your fundamental moral values and therefore should be treated as you would wish to be treated by them. What happens to them affects you. Walid and Mamadou should be seen as "real French," as part of the greater community rather than known by their ethnicity or where they live.

The scope of our moral community is key to understanding moralistic trust. Particularized trust is restricted to people like yourself – however defined, by race, class, ethnicity, or whatever is most salient, including people in your neighborhood. Generalized trust is the belief that "most people can be trusted" (as opposed to "you can't be too careful in dealing with people," in the standard survey question).

We don't learn to trust "most people" by evidence. We can't meet most people. Nor can we generalize from the people we know to "most people." Generalized (moralistic) trust is *not* trust in Walid or Mamadou, but of people in general, especially people who are different from ourselves, as are most people we don't know. And it is not specific to one domain such as loaning money, painting a house, or performing surgery. Nor is it a judgment that others are trustworthy, but rather that we should treat strangers *as if they were trustworthy*. Generalized trust does not depend upon reciprocity. It may seem foolhardy for people to place confidence in people generally or to think that they might do so.

Perhaps the best reason for people to "invest" in moralistic trust is that faith in others has many positive consequences. Trust is not a magical cure-all for collective action, as Putnam suggests (1993, 170–2). It does not lead us to join more voluntary organizations, to socialize more with our friends, to participate more in politics, or even to vote. Nor does it make us more likely to help people we know – or even make us more willing to pay our taxes (Uslaner, 2002, ch. 5; Uslaner, 2007a). These are all activities in which we interact with people we know or who are very much like us. You don't need trust to cooperate with people who are like you. You don't need trust in other people to participate in politics where the goal is to defeat the other side. And you don't need trust in people to do your duty to your government.

Generalized trust does connect us to people who are different from ourselves: Trusters are more likely to be tolerant of minorities and supportive of equal rights for blacks, gays, and women (among other groups). They give more to charities and volunteer more for causes that link them to people who are different from themselves. High-trust societies have higher growth rates and less corruption and crime, and are more likely to redistribute resources from the rich to the poor. Generalized trust leads people of different backgrounds to work with each other, to less polarization in our political life, and to greater legislative productivity over time in the United States.

Trust makes people less likely to see risks wherever they turn – in their own neighborhoods when they walk at night or when they come into contact (or consider coming into contact) with people unlike themselves. If you believe that "most people can be trusted," you are more likely to hold that people of different backgrounds share the same fate. This leads to a more inclusive identity encompassing diverse groups in a society rather than seeing ourselves as members of different ethnic and racial groups – and to expect our leaders to represent all of us rather than just their "tribes." Trusters are more willing to admit immigrants to their countries, and are less worried that immigrants will take their jobs. This sense of unity of identity underlies the provision of universal social welfare benefits, where all are entitled to receive benefits such as education from the state *simply because they are members of a political and social community*. Governments in highly trusting societies also have greater commitments to policies that promote equality among their publics (Algan and Cahuc, 2010; LaPorta et al., 1999; Rothstein and Uslaner, 2005; Uslaner, 1993, 2000, 2002, chs. 5, 7, 2007b).

The best evidence for believing that people have faith in others more generally is that they say they do. When asked what the standard trust question means to them, the overwhelming majority of respondents to a pilot survey for the 2000 American National Election Study gave responses that reflected general moral concerns rather than specific incidents (Uslaner, 2002, 72–4). The question "most people can be trusted" forms a scale with trust in strangers (people you meet on the street, clerks in stores) rather than with people you know (friends, family, co-workers; Uslaner, 2002, 52–5). People interpret the standard trust question as faith in people they don't know.

If the only basis for trust is experience, we would expect trust to be fragile (Bok, 1978, 26; Dasgupta, 1988, 50), but it is not. Trust is among the most stable values over time across a wide range of attitudes (Uslaner, 2002, 68–75). If trust were based upon experience, it should reflect life events such as being helped by others, joining civic groups, and our confidence in people we know. But it is not (Uslaner, 2002, ch. 5).

Instead, we learn to trust at an early age, mostly from our parents but also from experiences at schools and with friends. Once formed, trust remains stable from youth to adulthood (Uslaner, 2002, ch. 6). We can even trace the roots of trust back further. We "inherit" a substantial share of our trust from where our ancestors came from. If our grandparents came from the Nordic countries, we are more likely to believe that "most people can be trusted," while people whose background is from low-trusting places (Africa, Spain, Latin America) will be less likely to place faith in others (Uslaner, 2008b; cf. Algan and Cahuc, 2010).

People who trust others are optimists: they believe that the world is a good place, it is going to get better, and they can shape their destiny. Thus they can wave away bad experiences as exceptions to the general rule that things will go well, so that trust doesn't seem quite so risky. Yet trust is not divorced from the "real world." Across nations without a legacy of communism, over time in the United States, and across the American states, the consistently best predictor of trust is the level of economic inequality: in an unequal world, those at the bottom will have little basis for optimism. People at the bottom and the top will not see each other as having a linked fate – as part of each other's "moral community" (Uslaner, 2002, chs. 2, 6, 8; Uslaner and Brown, 2005). This tight connection with inequality explains why generalized trust is rare. Inequality is widespread in the world, especially in the developing countries of Latin America and Africa. High levels of inequality breed greater in-group trust at the expense of trusting strangers because inequality is often overlaid with group tensions (Baldwin and Huber, 2010; Uslaner, 2008a, 52).

In-Group Trust, Out-Group Trust, and Diversity

High in-group trust does not automatically lead to low generalized trust. You are unlikely to have positive feelings toward others if you don't like your own kind. But particularized trust is having faith *only* in people like yourself and such sentiments can lead to intolerance and withdrawal from participation in more broad-based civic activities (Uslaner, 2001; Wuthnow, 1991).

The more you are surrounded by people like yourself, the more likely you are to become a particularized truster. Alesina and LaFerrara elaborate on how in-group preference leads to demobilization and to negative social attitudes toward minorities:

> [I]ndividuals prefer to interact with others who are similar to themselves in terms of income, race, or ethnicity ... diffuse preferences for homogeneity may decrease total participation in a mixed group if fragmentation increases. However, individuals may prefer to sort into homogenous groups.... For eight out of nine questions concerning attitudes toward race relations, the effect of racial heterogeneity is strongest for individuals more averse to racial mixing. (2000, 850, 889)

Putnam makes an even stronger claim. When you live among people like yourself, you will be less trusting of *everyone*:

> Rather, inhabitants of diverse communities tend to withdraw from collective life, to distrust their neighbours, regardless of the colour of their skin, to withdraw even from close friends, to expect the worst from their community and its leaders, to volunteer less, give less to charity and work on community projects less often, to register to vote less, to agitate for social reform more, but have less faith that they can actually make a difference, and to huddle unhappily in front of the television ... this pattern encompasses attitudes and behavior, bridging and bonding social capital, public and private connections. Diversity, at least in the short run, seems to bring out the turtle in all of us. (2007, 150–1)

This is a dire set of results. If trust connects us to people who are different from ourselves, but living among them leads to less trust, then what good is trust?

Diversity is not the culprit driving down trust. Instead, it is residential segregation. When people live apart from one another, they will not develop the sort of bridging ties that promote tolerance and trust. Living in integrated communities is not sufficient to boost trust: you must also have friends of different backgrounds, as Allport (1958), Pettigrew (1998), and Marschall and Stolle (2004) have argued.

This is the core argument to come. I develop the theory and the framework for analyzing diversity, segregation, and trust in Chapter 2. I show why diversity is not the key problem: it is largely a proxy measure for the percent of nonwhites in a community and we know that minorities are less trusting. And I show that diversity and segregation are not the same thing; they are only modestly correlated.

I then move to examinations of how living in diverse and integrated communities and having friends of different backgrounds leads to greater trust in the United States (Chapter 3), Canada (Chapter 4), the United Kingdom (Chapter 5), and Sweden and Australia (Chapter 6). I also show that people living in integrated and diverse communities with heterogenous social networks do more altruistic deeds helping strangers rather than members of their own communities (Chapter 7). I end on a less optimistic note when I show (Chapter 8) that the positive effects of what are called Allport's "optimal conditions" may be overstated. People just don't live anywhere randomly. Instead the choice to live in integrated communities (and to have friends of different backgrounds in the United Kingdom) depends on trust as much as it leads to greater faith in people. When I allow for simultaneous causation between residential choice and trust, most of the positive effects of Allport's optimal conditions grow very small. Finally, I consider whether housing policies that promote integration can build trust.

There is, however, a seeming contradiction between my arguments on the roots of trust and the impact of either diversity or integration with diverse friendship networks. If trust does not reflect experience, if trust is formed early in life and largely remains stable, why should diversity, segregation, or the heterogeneity of friendship networks matter?

First, greater diversity of your social network doesn't by itself lead to greater trust (see Chapter 2). It does foster greater tolerance (Pettigrew and Tropp, 2006, 757–8), primarily for whites (Pettigrew and Tropp, 2011, 133, 139). But trust is more resistant to change than is tolerance.

Second, the effects of diversity seem weaker than Putnam (2007) has argued, and the interpretation is open to debate. Third, trust may largely be stable, but it is hardly set in stone (Uslaner, 2002, chs. 3, 6). It does change even for adults. Major events in society, such as the Watergate scandal and the civil rights movement, can lower or increase trust (Uslaner, 2002, 165–83). Context can shape values such as trust. A key reason I did not find such effects (Uslaner, 2002, chs. 4, 5) is that *most people don't have the types of social networks conducive to building trust.* We hang out with people like ourselves; we join groups with people of similar interests. In the end, however, our choice of where to live depends on how trusting (and tolerant) we are. So the giddy optimism of findings I report in Chapters 3 and 5 (in which I discuss the United States and the United Kingdom) leads to a more sober reassessment of what housing policy can do – and to a renewed emphasis on examining where *children* live rather than where their parents reside.

The Five Countries

I examine the link between trust and integrated communities with diverse friendship networks in five countries: the United States, Canada, the United Kingdom, Australia, and Sweden.

Why these five nations? As always, opportunity is the mother of invention. The availability of data makes these countries suitable for study. But that is not the key reason for my selection of these five countries. The United States has a long history of racial divisions – with persistent segregation for African-Americans. One can't study segregation without considering the United States. None of the other four countries has high levels of segregation. However, the English-speaking countries all have histories of racial or ethnic (or both) tensions. Lack of segregation does not automatically mean that minorities are strongly integrated into white society. In Canada and the United Kingdom, minorities have lower levels of trust than do whites; they also say that they face discrimination. So the question of whether integrated neighborhoods with diverse friendship networks can lead to more trust is hardly moot. In Sweden and Australia, minorities do report discrimination but have relatively high levels of trust – far closer to the majority white populations than in the other nations.

Sweden, Canada, and Australia are distinctive in two ways. They have high levels of trust. (Australia is a recent addition to the small core of high-trust countries.) They also have low levels of inequality. Segregation is not strongly correlated with inequality, as it is in the United States and to a lesser extent in the United Kingdom. The United States has the lowest level of trust, though the United Kingdom's share of trusting citizens is only modestly higher. Both countries have higher levels of inequality (the United States by a lot) than the other countries.

The United States stands out on another dimension. American culture emphasizes assimilation rather than division. Ralph Ellison's *cri de coeur* in favor of diversity and against integration is a protest of the American model of assimilation. The United Kingdom emphasizes multiculturalism – the idea that minorities should retain and celebrate their separate identities. The idea of multiculturalism began in Canada, ironically as part of an effort to define a national identity. It spread to other Western nations, including Sweden and Australia. Both now pay homage to multiculturalism, but have largely abandoned it in favor of a more assimilationist model. The high levels of trust among minorities reflect their sense of belonging as well as the higher socioeconomic status of minorities in these countries, in part shaped by who can immigrate (Australia) and by a strong welfare state (Sweden).

For these five nations, there are different levels of segregation, diversity, trust, and inequality – ranging from the most equal and trusting Sweden to the least equal, least trusting, and most segregated United States. The countries have different histories in terms of accepting and integrating minorities. The United States long has had more diverse immigrants than any of the other countries – two of which (Sweden and Australia) restricted entrance for many years for people unlike themselves, though both now welcome immigrants from diverse backgrounds. The five countries have different patterns of immigration today: Canada and Australia have strict requirements on who may enter based upon skills, education, and language fluency. Immigration has been increasing dramatically in all five countries, even with different policies – but who comes to each country and the policies of each country toward immigration lead to different levels of trust, segregation, and inequality. Canada was the home of multiculturalism, where it still prevails, as it does in the United Kingdom. Sweden and Australia adopted multiculturalism as official policy, but have since retreated from it. The United States has always had a very different approach to integrating minorities – assimilation to a common identity. The five countries, even as four of them have Anglo-American heritage, constitute a considerable range of the conditions I believe underlie the relationships among segregation, diversity, and trust.

Trusters believe in a common culture and argue that ethnic politicians should not primarily represent their own communities (Uslaner, 2002, 197). They are thus strongly assimilationist even as they are supportive of minorities and immigrants. Multiculturalism may promote particularized trust and inadvertently lead to lower generalized trust by emphasizing the right of minorities to maintain their own identity. The irony for the United States is that the cultural approach – assimilationism – that should promote high levels of trust seems undermined by high levels of inequality and segregation.

The Plan of the Book

I begin (Chapter 2) with an examination of contact theory – the idea that if we get to know people who are different from ourselves, we will become more tolerant of others of their background. The evidence on "simple" contact is mixed. Context matters and so does the equality of contacts (Allport, 1958, 251, 260, 267). Segregation, far more than diversity, leads to greater inequality, and I show that this is the case in both American communities and across nations. There is some evidence that diversity may drive down trust, but its effects are not as powerful as those for segregation together with having friends of different backgrounds. Much of the time, diversity doesn't matter at all, and, in some cases, living in a diverse community leads to *more* trust. And segregation (interacted with diverse contacts) does not always boost trust – but the patterns of when it does and does not reflect the experience of minority groups (and immigrants) in different countries and the levels of segregation and inequalities in the five countries I examine. A key consideration is that diversity and segregation are *not* the same thing, either theoretically or in terms of measurement.

Segregation leads to negative outcomes across American communities: higher rates of violent crimes, lower levels of well-being. Across American communities and across nations, segregation is a key determinant of inequality. Across countries, there is a chain from segregation to inequality to low trust. I end Chapter 2 with an examination of attitudes toward multiculturalism and trust arguing that strong ethnic identities (in the United States and Canada) as well as support for policies maintaining separate identities (cross-nationally) are associated with lower levels of trust.

I turn next to case studies of the United States, Canada, the United Kingdom, Sweden, and Australia (Chapters 3, 4, 5, and 6) and an analysis of the roots of secular and religious charitable giving and volunteering (Chapter 7). The central results are:

- Living in an integrated community *and* having friends of diverse backgrounds leads to increased trust.
- The effects are greatest when there is less trust and more segregation in the United States.
- The effects are generally greater for the white majority than for minority groups – especially in the cases of Canada and Australia, where minorities have high levels of education (and trust) because of a "point system" that limits who may immigrate to these countries.
- The effects are powerful for minorities, but insignificant for the majority, as in Sweden, where both native Swedes and immigrants have high levels of trust (cf. Dinesen, 2011a, 53). Unlike Canada and Australia, the high-trusting minority respondents are not selected on the basis of their education, language familiarity, or skills. Most immigrants to Sweden come as refugees from strife-torn places. They *should be* low in trust, but Sweden's universalistic social welfare regime builds equality and trust.
- In the United States and the United Kingdom, people who live in integrated communities with friends of different backgrounds are more likely to give to and volunteer for secular causes and generally are *less* likely to give their time and money to religious charities. Allport's optimal conditions promote reaching out to help people different from yourself rather than people of your own background and faith. Data on the sources of volunteering and charitable giving are only available

for the United States and the United Kingdom. Religion plays a much stronger role in public life in the United States than in any of the other countries I examine, including the United Kingdom. So the similarity of results for the United States and the United Kingdom indicates that the argument is *not* simply a result of the centrality of religion to much of altruism in the United States. Whether the logic extends to the most secular of the five countries I consider – Sweden – is unclear and not testable with available data.[10]

- Segregation rather than diversity drives down trust and altruism. Diversity does lead to less trust in some estimations, but the positive effects of living in an integrated community with friends of diverse backgrounds outweigh any negative impacts of heterogeneity.
- We cannot simply build trust by creating integrated communities. First, integrated areas do not guarantee social interaction, much less the strong ties underlying Allport's optimal conditions. But beyond that, data from the United States and the United Kingdom (Chapter 8) point to a deeper problem: residential choice is not random. Low-trusting people (as well as people holding negative racial stereotypes) are less likely to want to live in integrated neighborhoods (with diverse friendship networks in the United Kingdom). Once I take this into account statistically (by estimating simultaneous equation models for trust and residential choice), the positive effects of Allport's optimal conditions either vanish or become far weaker. Housing policy is not a quick fix to increase trust, and experimental programs in the United States to develop integrated communities and improve housing for the poor have had mixed success (Chapter 9).

Ultimately, the problems of segregated communities come back to the larger problem of inequality. Diversity is also a culprit, but the problem is *not* with minorities, but rather with majority groups' unwillingness to live in integrated neighborhoods. Tackling inequality is critical to developing more trust, but it does not seem to be on most political agendas except in Sweden. In the absence of policies that would limit segregation and combat inequality, the focus should shift to people who have more favorable impressions of minorities and who don't choose where they live based upon race: young people like the farmer's daughter.

[10] It makes less sense to ask about religious volunteering and charitable giving in a country where so few people consider themselves religious, although the increasing number of Muslims in Sweden would make for an interesting comparison (and this is likely why the Swedish survey asks if people have friends of different religions).

A note on presentation: the evidence on diversity, segregation, and optimal contacts comes from statistical analyses. The major dependent variable is trust, with measures of altruism (charitable giving and volunteering) the focus of Chapter 7 and residential preference the subject of Chapter 8. My concern is how Allport's optimal conditions and diversity shape trust and altruism, not simply what determines who trusts or who gives to charity or volunteers time. So I focus on what is essential and leave discussions of other determinants to brief textual discussions or, more commonly, to endnotes. This is *not* a book on what shapes trust. Been there, done that (Uslaner, 2002, ch. 4) – and my earlier work shapes what I do here. Focusing on just those results that are relevant to the core arguments also suggests a different form of presentation. Instead of taxing the reader with endless tables of all of the variables considered, I present figures showing the relative impact of each variable (see Chapter 3 for the discussion of the measure of "effects," or changes in probability of trusting or doing altruistic deeds). Graphical presentations are more common these days.[11] They make comparison of the impacts of variables easier to see and reduce clutter. For some estimations with few predictors (especially in Chapter 2), I present the full estimations in tables.

A word of caution as I proceed: the inferences I draw come from surveys that are not linked in any way, so the questions about friendship networks vary considerably from one survey to another. The trust questions are all identical (the essential requirement). The diversity measures are identical across countries and the segregation measures are as close as possible to being equivalent. The major exception is for the United Kingdom, where I could not get "geocodes" for survey respondents to merge with the survey data and had to rely upon peoples' estimates of the level of segregation of their neighborhoods.[12] Am I comparing the incomparable? I don't think so. The patterns I uncover make sense given the cultures and levels of segregation and inequality in the five countries. And the story they all tell is that segregation plays a more important role in depressing trust than does diversity.

[11] The *American Journal of Political Science*, one of the leading journals, states in its guidelines for manuscripts (see http://www.ajps.org/manu_guides.html): "The use of figures that demonstrate an argument or a finding is strongly encouraged. The extensive use of tables is discouraged in the main text." One also learns this from his/her graduate students. The full estimations are available on request.

[12] Geocodes are variables indicating the geographic area (neighborhood, community, metropolitan area) where each respondent lives. For the United States, Canada, Sweden, and Australia, the surveys include geocodes that I merge with aggregate data.

2

Contact, Diversity, and Segregation

"The more we get together, the happier we'll be."

Children's song by Jim Rule

"Good luck will rub off when I shakes [*sic*] hands with you."

The chimney sweep in *Mary Poppins*

"To know, know, know him is to love, love, love him."

Phil Spector[1]

"Familiarity breeds contempt."

Alternatively ascribed to Aesop, *The Fox and the Lion*, to Mark Twain, and to a Nigerian proverb.[2]

Contact is both the great hope and the great fear of liberals who work to make people more accepting of those from different backgrounds. *Contact theory*, which Pettigrew and Tropp (2006, 751–2) trace back to the 1940s, especially to the summary by Williams (1947), is the claim that exposure to people of different backgrounds leads to less prejudice. The greater your opportunity for interacting with people different from yourself, the more likely you are to hold positive attitudes toward them.

Conflict theory, the argument that interactions among people of different backgrounds is likely to lead to more hostility, dates back even

[1] Lyrics available at http://www.songsforteaching.com/jimrule/themorewegettogether.htm, http://www.disneyclips.com/lyrics/lyrics98.html, and http://www.risa.co.uk/sla/song.php?songid=15566.

[2] See http://www.aesops-fables.org.uk/, http://www.quotedb.com/quotes/1806, and http://www.dictionary-quotes.com/nigerian-proverb-familiarity-breeds-contempt-%E2%80%A6/.

further (Baker, 1934). Key argued that Southern whites in the United States were most likely to support racist candidates for office in areas with large populations of African-Americans (1949, 666).

These two conflicting theories of attitude formation toward "the other" – people who are different from yourself – have dominated arguments about how majorities and minorities relate to each other. Advocates of each perspective claim greater support for their argument. This standoff leads many to wonder how both sides could possibly be correct. Could there be nuances – or more fundamental issues – that have been overlooked? Are there common elements underlying these conflicting arguments? Have we been too quick to presume that these two simple arguments lead to starkly different outcomes for all sorts of attitudes and outcomes?

I review some of the arguments and evidence for each approach here. There are too many studies across different disciplines to summarize them (but see Pettigrew and Tropp, 2006). And, as Mark Antony said in Shakespeare's *Julius Caesar*, I come to bury both arguments, not to praise them – or at least to suggest that they need reformulation. Alas, I cannot claim to have uncovered a new framework to supplant the old ones: Gordon Allport (1958, originally published in 1954) beat me to it by more than half a century and did it with elegance. Others have refined Allport's thesis (Forbes, 1997; Pettigrew, 1986, 1998).

My contribution is to highlight the contributions of Allport, Pettigrew, and Forbes and to bring to the forefront an aspect of their work often overlooked in the literature: residential segregation. I argue that this framework is more powerful than conflict theory – the foundation of the arguments about the negative effects of diversity – in explaining why trust is lower among some people, neighborhoods, or countries.

Segregation is not the same thing as diversity, as I shall demonstrate. The presumed negative effects of diversity occur when people of different backgrounds live among each other. Segregation is all about isolating people of diverse ethnicities and races from each other. The key distinction is being too far away rather than too close. There is more agreement on the negative consequences of segregation than on whether diversity brings more harm than good – although segregation does have its defenders. While most recent discussions of contact and diversity have ignored segregation, many of the initial formulations and tests of contact theory – notably Allport's – put residential isolation at the forefront.

There is a wide-ranging literature on the good and bad effects of contact and diversity. Even if diversity does have perverse effects for many outcomes, it may not have negative consequences for trust. The theoretical link between segregation and mistrust is much stronger than that for diversity and mistrust. While there is a considerable literature positing a link between contact and trust, it is based upon shaky empirics and even weaker theory, as I shall discuss later in this chapter.

I examine the linkages among segregation, diversity, inequality, and trust across American communities and cross-nationally as well as other consequences of segregation – overall well-being and crime. The back story is that segregation matters – for trust and for other indicators of social life, and much (though not all) of its impact comes from the effects of segregation on inequality. Segregation leads to outcomes (more crime and less well-being) that make trust more difficult to attain, while diversity has much smaller effects.

The converse of segregation is, of course, integration. How one integrates people of different backgrounds into a common culture – or, if one tries to do so at all – is a central question underlying trust in people of different backgrounds and a key issue of public policy. Multiculturalism reinforces a sense of in-group identity. I argue and present evidence that regimes emphasizing multiculturalism may inhibit the development of trust.

Diversity: The Downside and the Upside

Long before Putnam, scholars and political leaders recognized that diversity can have negative effects on a variety of outcomes. Key (1949) made one of the most famous arguments in what came to be known as the "racial threat" hypothesis: the long and bitter history of racial conflict in the American South was most pronounced where the African-American population was greatest. Whites felt most threatened when blacks were numerous and nearby. Key's argument is a natural extension of what came to be known as "social identity" theory: we are predisposed to trust our own kind more than out-groups (Brewer, 1979). Messick and Brewer review experiments on cooperation and find that "members of an in-group tend to perceive other in-group members in generally favorable terms, particularly as being *trustworthy, honest, and cooperative*" (1983, 27–8, italics in original). The Maghribi of northern Africa relied on their extended Jewish clan – and other Jews in the Mediterranean area – to establish a profitable trading network in the twelfth century (Greif, 1993). Models from evolutionary game theory suggest that favoring people like ourselves is our best strategy (Hamilton, 1964, 21; Masters, 1989, 169; Trivers, 1971, 48).

Alesina and LaFerrara elaborate how in-group preference leads to demobilization and to negative social attitudes toward minorities:

> [I]ndividuals prefer to interact with others who are similar to themselves in terms of income, race, or ethnicity ... diffuse preferences for homogeneity may decrease total participation in a mixed group if fragmentation increases. However, individuals may prefer to sort into homogenous groups.... For eight out of nine questions concerning attitudes toward race relations, the effect of racial heterogeneity is strongest for individuals more averse to racial mixing. (2000, 850, 889)

A mini industry among academics has developed to show how widespread the negative effects of diversity are. The negative consequences of racial and ethnic diversity include:

- greater corruption, infant mortality, illiteracy, and lower rates of governmental transfers (Alesina et al., 2003, 171);
- lower long-term growth (Alesina and LaFerrara, 2004);
- less support for racial integration among Americans in the early 1970s as well as perceptions of threat (Fossett and Kielcolt, 1989) and anti-black sentiment (Taylor, 1998);
- less favorable views of neighborhoods and lower levels of participation in community improvement projects (Guest, Kubrin, and Cover, 2008, 512; Rice and Steele, 2001);
- lower rates of voting and participation in civic organizations for whites and African-Americans (but not Hispanics) across American cities (Oliver, 2001, 120); and
- higher rates of civil conflict (Matuszeski and Schneider, 2006).

Since minority groups everywhere, especially blacks in the United States and immigrants in other Western countries, are far more likely to be poor and to receive government assistance than are the majority (white) populations, greater minority populations may lead to less support for public spending, especially on welfare. Joppke (2007, 18–19) argues that diversity strains the welfare state in Europe (see also Burns, 2010, quoted in chapter 5):

> Because a majority of ... migrants are unskilled and (with the exception of France) not proficient in the language of the receiving societies, and often directly become dependent on welfare, they pose serious adjustment problems.

Greater diversity is linked to lower levels of support and provision of collective goods:

- lower levels of transfer payments adjusted for gross domestic product across nations (Alesina et al., 2003, 171) but more transfer payments in American municipalities (Alesina, Baqir, and Easterly, 1999, 1264);
- less spending on welfare and on roads in American municipalities (Alesina, Baqir, and Easterly, 1999, 1259, 1263);
- less support for public education in more heterogenous urban areas in the United States from 1910–28 than in more homogeneous small towns (Goldin and Katz, 1999, 718);
- lower public goods production across a wide variety of measures (Baldwin and Huber, 2010);
- lower support for school funding, the quality of school facilities, and ownership of textbooks across Kenyan communities as well as for the maintenance of community water wells and fewer threats against parents who do not pay their school fees or participate in school projects (Miguel and Gugerty, 2005); and
- the failure to maintain infrastructure in Pakistan (cited in Putnam, 2007, 143).

If diversity leads to less favorable attitudes toward out-groups and to an unwillingness to provide benefits for minorities, the claim that diversity leads to less trust makes sense. Or does it? I discuss the evidence – pro and con – after I present a more general framework for trust.

The evidence on diversity and poor outcomes is not universal. Woolever (1992) finds no connection between neighborhood diversity and community attachment or participation in Indianapolis in 1980. Collier, Honohan, and Moene (2001) find that ethnic group dominance, but *not* simple ethnic diversity, leads to a greater likelihood of civil conflict (cf. Bros, 2010). Even in the very diverse society of Uganda, ethnicity had only minimal effects on how people valued the welfare of others in experimental games (Habyarimana et al., 2009, 23).

Nor is there universally a negative relationship between diversity and support for the welfare state. Sweden is particularly generous to refugees (Jordan, 2008, A14):

> [Forty thousand] Iraqis are lured by ... Sweden's famous social welfare system. The national government budgets $30,000 to help settle each person granted asylum. It pays for Swedish language classes, helps with housing and job training and pays a monthly allowance for living expenses.

Even as Swedish policy makers realized that such generosity could lead to resentment, they redoubled their efforts to integrate immigrants into

Swedish society through the welfare state – and support for welfare programs remained high (Crepaz, 2008, 225–6; Kumlin and Rothstein, 2010, 12–13).[3] There was a reaction in the 2010 election when support for the anti-immigrant Swedish Democrats reached an all-time high – but it was still less than 6 percent. In Canada, diversity seems to increase, rather than decrease, support for the welfare state (Soroka, Johnston, and Banting, 2007). Finseraas (2009) finds no support for the argument that increasing diversity leads to less support for redistribution in a cross-national analysis of European Social Survey data.

The effects of diversity on prejudice and outcomes do not seem to follow a single pattern. Forbes (1997, 58) argues: "Social scientists have always recognized ... that contact is a condition for conflict as well as for cooperation. Two groups must be in contact before they can fight or compete." Yet there is little evidence of actual contact between members of different groups in the studies showing the negative effects of diversity. The aversion to people of different backgrounds *reduces civic participation in many different areas*. Forbes (1997, 101, italics added) summarizes Key's argument that Southern whites sought "to *exclude* blacks from politics, to *isolate* them socially, and generally to keep them subordinate to whites." Putnam, some 60 years later, argued that "inhabitants of diverse communities tend to withdraw from collective life" (2007, 150).

Aversion to diversity discourages contact. When people of different backgrounds get together, the results are remarkably different. Forbes argues that "[t]he more frequent and the more intimate the contacts among individuals belonging to different tribes or nations, the more these groups come to resemble each other culturally or linguistically.... Isolation and subordination, not gore and destruction, seem to be the main themes in ... conflict" (1997, 144, 150). Heterogeneous networks lead to positive outcomes such as more productive job searches (Granovetter, 1973; Loury, 1977) and more creativity (Burt, 2000). Such outcomes are more consistent with contact theory than with the claim that interaction with people of different backgrounds leads to conflict. Some aggregate results show positive relationships between diversity and economic outcomes. Diversity is associated with increased wages and higher prices for rental housing (Ottaviano and Peri, 2005), greater profits and market share for firms that have more diverse work forces (Herring, 2006), and greater problem-solving capacities (Gurin, Nagda, and Lopez, 2004). Florida,

[3] Bay, Hellenvik, and Hellevik (2009) find no support for a link between diversity and support for the welfare state in another Nordic nation, Norway.

Mellander, and Rentfrow (2009) find higher levels of overall well-being in more diverse states.

The connection between diversity and negative outcomes does not receive unequivocal support – and this will become evident when I examine trust. I cannot hope to resolve all of the issues involved. Some results stem from the confounding of measures of diversity and the size of the minority population. Equally important is the argument that diversity may lead, under some conditions, to isolation (as Forbes has argued). When does diversity isolate people and when does it bring them together? To resolve this question, I turn first to contact theory and then to "refinement," stressing the role of residential segregation in restricting contact among people of different backgrounds.

Contact Theory

When you get to know people of different backgrounds, negative stereotypes will fade away. And there is considerable evidence to support this claim – though many doubters wonder if prejudice could fade so easily.

There is a voluminous literature on contact theory, most of it supportive (Pettigrew and Tropp, 2006). However, not just any contact is sufficient to overcome prejudice. Superficial contact is likely to reinforce negative stereotypes; "[o]nly the type of contact that leads people to *do* things together is likely to result in changed attitudes" (Allport, 1958, 252, 267). Allport formulated conditions of "optimal contact": equal status between the groups, common goals, cooperation between the groups, and a supportive institutional and cultural environment (Allport, 1958, 263, 267; Pettigrew, 1998, 66). In a meta-analysis of 513 studies of contact theory, Pettigrew and Tropp (2006, 760) found that *any* contact was likely to reduce prejudice (cf. Dixon, Durrheim, and Tredoux, 2005, 2007), but that optimal contact had considerably greater effects. Williams (1964, 185–90), Ihlanfeldt and Scafaldi (2002, 633), Dixon (2006, 2194–5), and McClelland and Linnander (2006, 107–8) find that whites develop more favorable attitudes about minorities only if they know and feel close to a minority group member.

Hewstone (2009) summarizes a large body of research demonstrating that *contact alone* (regardless of the context) will lead to a reduction in prejudice, but interactions must be "sustained, positive contact between members of the two previously antipathetic groups." Since trust is more demanding than mere prejudice reduction, so will be the conditions of boosting this stable value that doesn't change much over one's lifetime. Here context matters, as I shall argue and support.

What constitutes a positive environment? Context is critical – and the most important context is your community. Residential segregation leads to isolation, "exaggerate[s] the degree of difference between groups," and makes the out-group "seem larger and more menacing than it is" (Allport, 1958, 18–19, 256). Contacts in segregated communities are most likely to be "frozen into superordinate-subordinate relationships" – exactly the opposite of what is essential for the optimal conditions to be met (Allport, 1958, 251). Integrated neighborhoods "remove barriers to effective communication" (Allport, 1958, 261) and may lead to more contact with people of different backgrounds, especially among young people (Phinney et al., 2006, 94; Quillian and Campbell, 2003, 560). Forbes goes further, arguing – "[D]ifferent languages, religions, customs, laws, and moralities – in short, different cultures – impede economic integration, with all its benefits...." (1997, 144,).

The Allport argument has garnered considerable support and, ironically, some of it came before he refined contact theory. Deutsch and Collins (1951) surveyed occupants of public housing in four projects in New York City and Newark, two integrated and two segregated. "Neighborly contacts" between whites and blacks were almost nonexistent in segregated projects but were common in integrated units – and contact in integrated units led to less prejudiced racial feelings among both whites and African-Americans regardless of their levels of education, ideology, or religion (Deutsch and Collins, 1951, 57, 86, 97). A similar design in cities in the Northeast in 1951 also found that respondents (all white women) in integrated housing projects had far more contact with African-Americans, were far more approving of integrated housing than those in segregated units, and were more likely to report that their views toward blacks had grown more positive (Wilner, Walkley, and Cook, 1955, 86, 92, 99).

Many studies have provided support for the argument that contact with people of different backgrounds leads to less prejudice in neighborhoods that are integrated or even simply diverse. Anglos living in integrated neighborhoods have more favorable attitudes toward Latinos (Rocha and Espino, 2009). There is also evidence that more intimate contact with people of different backgrounds – approximating Allport's optimal conditions – leads to more favorable attitudes toward out-groups (McClelland and Linnander, 2006, 108; McKenzie, 1948), especially if that contact occurs in more diverse and integrated neighborhoods (Dixon, 2006, 2194–5; Stein, Post, and Rinden, 2000, 298–9; Valentova and Berzosa, 2010, 29; Wagner et al., 2006, 386). In surveys conducted in Elmira, New York between 1949 and 1951, more "intimate" ties between Jews and African-Americans with people of different backgrounds led to more positive views of the other (Williams et al., 1964, 185).

Contact, Diversity, and Trust

Contact may lead to less prejudice. What about trust? Putnam sees contact and trust as interconnected:

> [N]etworks of civic engagement foster sturdy norms of generalized reciprocity and encourage the emergence of social trust.... Across 35 countries social trust and civil engagement are strongly correlated; the greater the density of associational membership in a society, the more trusting its citizens; trust and engagement are two facets of the same underlying factor – social capital.... The causal arrows among civic involvement, reciprocity, honesty, and social trust are as tangled as well-tossed spaghetti. (2000, 67, 73, 137)

The idea that contact can boost trust is that interactions with people of different backgrounds will lead to greater understanding of people of different backgrounds and will make them seem more like us. Contact could thus build trust as well as reducing prejudice. Yet most of the evidence on contact and trust is *not* supportive because: (1) most of our contacts are with people like ourselves; (2) trusting people like yourself does not mean that you will trust people from different backgrounds; and (3) when we do have contact with people of different backgrounds, our connections may not meet Allport's optimal conditions – social ties on the basis of equality in a supportive context. Since trust is formed early in life, casual contact with people of different backgrounds may lead to more positive views of some individuals or even to less prejudice. But trust is more than the absence of negative stereotypes. It is viewing others as part of our moral community.

As Allport argues, we socialize and form groups with people like ourselves (cf. Uslaner, 2002, 40). Putnam (and others) assumes that trust can spread from people you know – and who are like yourself – to people you don't know and who may be different from yourself (Clark, Putnam, and Fieldhouse, 2010, 143). Yet once confronted with diversity, people tend to shy away from them and to mistrust them (Putnam, 2007, 142, 148, 158).

There is reason to doubt both claims – that we learn to trust strangers by putting faith in people we know and that diversity drives down trust. Simple contact with people who are different from yourself is insufficient to boost trust. The evidence linking trust to social contacts, formal or informal, is weak, even with people of diverse backgrounds. There is also scant support for the link between diversity and trust.

The bulk of the evidence does not support a link between contact and trust (Claiborn and Martin, 2002). I take Putnam's argument that trust and social ties reinforce each other seriously, and test to see if there are indeed reciprocal relationships between group membership and trust (Uslaner, 2002, ch. 5). I estimate a simultaneous model where trust and group membership shape each other – and find no significant relationships *in either direction*.

Stolle (1998) shows that long-standing membership in voluntary associations leads to greater trust, but only for members of the group and not to the larger society. She (1998, 500) argues that the extension of trust from your own group to the larger society occurs through "mechanisms not yet clearly understood." An even more skeptical Rosenblum (1998, 45, 48) calls the purported link "an airy 'liberal expectancy' that remains 'unexplained.'" Its proponents believe that if you develop trust in one sphere, it extends automatically to another. I show that in-group and out-group trust form distinct clusters in people's minds and that trust in people you know does not lead to trust in strangers (Uslaner, 2002, 52–6, 142–8).

It may be naive to expect any link between civic engagement or other forms of social contact and trust. Many groups we join don't require trust at all. We come together with others because of common interests, not to establish long-lasting ties. Yet, even when we do establish enduring ties, our fellow group members and our friends are likely to be very much like ourselves, even if they don't look the same as we do. We choose people very much like ourselves to form our social networks (Marsden, 1987; McPherson, Smith-Lovin, and Cook, 2001). As Allport argues:

> People mate with their own kind. They eat, play, reside in homogenous clusters. They visit with their own kind, and prefer to worship together. We don't play bridge with the janitor. (1954, 17–18; cf. Uslaner, 2002, 40–2)

So the notion that we transfer any trust we develop in group members to people unlike ourselves is "a simplistic 'transmission belt' model of civil society, which says that the beneficial formative effects of association spill over from one sphere to another" (Rosenblum, 1998, 48).

Even diverse social ties may not boost trust. Putnam's (2007) argument is the most famous. His focus is mostly on neighorhood trust, which I show in Chapter 3 is not the same as generalized trust. Nevertheless, he does argue that diversity also leads to lower levels of generalized trust. His findings for trust in neighbors are reinforced by similar results by Pennant (2005) for Britain and Leigh (2006) for Australia.

Lancee and Dronkers find in a 1998 survey of Dutch minorities that ethnic diversity reinforces in-group trust and leads to declines in faith in out-groups (2008, 7). They report similar results for native Dutch respondents and argue that "[a]dherents of different religions and persons originating from different cultures can more easily collide about values and norms, thus making it less likely that conditions for optimal contact are met" (Lancee and Dronkers, in press, 19).

Their findings are challenged by other Dutch scholars. Vervoort, Flap, and Dagevos (in press) find that the diversity of neighborhoods leads to less contact between natives and immigrants, but to more contact among members of different ethnic groups. Tolsma, van der Meer, and Gesthuize find that neighborhood ethnic heterogeneity has inconsistent effects on a series of measures of community cohesion: diversity leads to *more* contact with neighbors, greater tolerance of people of different races, and *higher levels of trust* for more educated people, but to lower levels of contact with people of different backgrounds for the highly educated and less volunteering (2009, 300–1; see also Gijsberts, van der Meer, and Dagevos, in press). Far more important than either ethnic or economic heterogeneity of neighborhoods is simple economic status: wealthier neighborhoods are home to people who are more tolerant and trusting and who have more contact with people different from themselves.

Anderson and Paskeviciute (2006) find negative relationships between linguistic and ethnic fractionalization and trust across 44 countries with data from the World Values Survey in a multilevel model. However, Hooghe et al. (2009) found no effect of diversity on trust in a similar model of trust in the European Union using the European Social Survey. Savelkoul, Gesthuizen, and Scheepers (2011), also using the European Social Survey with hierarchical models, find no effect of diversity at the national level for helping or meeting neighbors and a positive effect on intergroup contact; at the regional level, the share of immigrants indirectly promotes helping and meeting others, both of which are spurred by greater diversity. Perceived ethnic threat reduces contact and social cohesion, but diversity does not lead to greater perceptions of threat.

Leigh (2006) finds no connection in Australia between any of several measures of fractionalization and generalized trust. Letki (2008), examining the 2001 United Kingdom Citizenship Survey, reports initial support for a negative relationship between community-level diversity and a composite indicator of social capital, but the result becomes insignificant when she controls for the economic status of the community. Her findings are reinforced by Bécares et al., who report higher levels of in-group trust and social cohesion (respect of ethnic differences and getting along well with others) for whites in areas with greater diversity, but lower levels of in-group trust and cohesion for minorities (2011, 8). However, these effects were dramatically reduced for all groups once they controlled for the economic deprivation of the neighborhood.

Ivarsflaten and Strømsnes (2010) find similar results for Norway and Denmark, respectively: diversity no longer matters when one controls for unemployment (Norway). Dinesen and Sonderskov (2011) find marginally significant but very weak negative effects for Denmark, controlling for income at the community level. Delhey and Newton (2004) also find that diversity drives down trust, but for them it is a measure of good government that suppresses the relationship. Reeskens and Hooghe (2009) find a nonlinear relationship between diversity and trust across Belgium municipalities, but the overall relationship is weak (cf. Dincer, in press), across the American states).

Leigh (2006) reports a negative effect of linguistic diversity on generalized trust for Australian adult immigrants. Dinesen (2011a), however, finds a positive effect of diversity on trust among immigrant students in Denmark (but no effect for native Danes). His findings are consistent with Laurence and Heath, who argue that "far from eroding community cohesion, ethnic diversity is generally a strong positive driver of cohesion.... *It is ... deprivation that undermines cohesion, not diversity*" (2008, 41, emphasis in original). Morales and Echazarra (2010) report positive relations between the level of trust and ethnic heterogeneity across Spanish municipalities. Stolle et al. (2011) also report a positive relationship between diversity and interethnic contact in German municipalities; informal contacts (conversations) rather than bridging friendships with people of different backgrounds leads to greater generalized trust as well as to faith in out-groups.

This brief summary of selected results does not indicate widespread support for the negative arguments on diversity. A more comprehensive analysis of 82 results in 56 studies (Tolsma and van der Meer, 2011) finds even less coherence: An equal share of results either confirm or are inconclusive about the diversity effect (30 percent each), but the largest share is negative (40 percent). Tolsma and van der Meer (2011) present a compelling argument that the research agenda is dominated by a "one size fits all" perspective – so there are few distinctions between what constitutes "social cohesion" (see my argument in Chapter 5), little concern for measurement issues, the presumption that any effects of diversity will be the same for majority and minority groups, and the failure to link diversity with the socioeconomic context in a neighborhood. "The one size fits all model ... faces severe problems with its empirical support," they argue.

The strong negative relationship across many studies between ethnic diversity and various measures of cohesion at the neighborhood level could be real – or it could simply reflect the fact that we tend to have friends very much like ourselves and thus social cohesion may be less likely to occur in more diverse settings. This is especially puzzling since there is little evidence that diversity drives down trust beyond the borders of one's neighborhood. The theoretical confusion Tolsma and van der Meer find is reminiscent of the argument made at a political science conference many years ago by Charles O. Jones about the state of knowledge in comparative state politics in the United States: "Lots of things are related to lots of things, other things being equal."

My goal is to bring greater conceptual and methodological clarification to this debate. I start with a discussion of why diversity is not the cause of low trust.

Across countries, the relationships between trust and a wide range of measures of diversity are minuscule. I examined 11 measures of diversity and a measure of trust covering more countries than in other studies (see Uslaner, in press).[4] The measures include the original Easterly-Levine

[4] My trust measure is based upon aggregate responses to the 1995 survey supplemented with: (1) measures from 1990 when 1995 data are not available; and (2) imputed scores for 13 other countries. Waves from 2000 onward of the World Values Survey have many anomalous results so I do not use them. Here I note briefly the high levels of trust reported in 2000 for Iran and Indonesia and the sharp drop for Canada despite almost identical results to 1995 in three other surveys that year: the Canadian National Election Study, the Quebec referendum survey, and the Ethnic Diversity (ESC) of the University of British Columbia. The variables used to impute trust are gross national product per capital; the value of imports of goods and services; legislative effectiveness; head of state type; tenure of executive (all from the State Failure Data Set); distance from the equator (from Jong-sung You of Harvard University); and openness of the economy (from Sachs and Warner, 1997; data available at http://www.cid.harvard.edu/ciddata/ciddata.html). The $R^2 = .657$, standard error of the estimate = .087, N = 63.

(1997) ethnic fractionalization measure based upon data from an atlas from the former Soviet Union; Alesina's indices of ethnic, linguistic, and religious fractionalization (Alesina et al., 2003); four measures from Fearon (2003), including his own index of fractionalization and measures of cultural diversity, the size of the largest group in a country, and the size of the second largest group; and four measures from Garcia-Montalvo and Reynal-Querol (2005) – their own indices of ethnic and religious fractionalization and their preferred measure of ethnic polarization.

The most common measure of diversity is an index of fractionalization, also called a Herfindahl index (Alesina et al., 2003). Many studies use simpler measures such as the minority share of population, but this is not of major concern since the two measures are largely interchangeable (Alesina, Baqir, and Easterly, 1999, 1270–1). The polarization index is a measure of the relative sizes of different ethnic groups in a country and Garcia-Montalvo and Reynal-Querol argue (2005, 6) that there are "more conflicts in societies where a large ethnic minority faces an ethnic majority." Polarization should thus be more strongly related to trust than is simple fractionalization – especially since the outbreak of civil war is associated with lower trust.

The highest r^2 for the 11 measures are for the Garcia-Montalvo–Reynal-Querol measures. However, they are modest (.118 for polarization and .132 and .110 for the two fractionalization measures). They are higher than the Alesina ethnic fractionalization index (.102) only because they cover fewer countries (66 each compared to 84 for the Alesina measure). The other measures all are modestly related to trust: r^2 = .047 for the Easterly-Levine measure (N = 68), .090 for Fearon's fractionalization measure (N = 82), .086 for the size of the second largest ethnic group (from Fearon, N = 76), and .092 for Fearon's measure of the size of the largest group (sign reversed, N = 82). The other measures all had minuscule r^2 values, less than .01: Alesina's linguistic and religious fractionalization (N = 83, 84) and Fearon's cultural diversity index (N = 82). The scattergrams for each of these measures do not suggest any nonlinearities – diversity seems uncorrelated with trust. In cross-national models of trust similar to those I have estimated earlier (Uslaner, 2002, ch. 8; Uslaner, in press) only four of these measures – the ethnic fractionalization indices from Alesina, Fearon, and Garcia-Montalvo and Reynal-Querol – and Fearon's share of the largest group – achieved statistical significance at the .10 level (one-tailed tests). No measure was significant at the .05 level or greater.[5]

[5] The models included the Gini index of inequality, whether a country had a civil war, the share of Protestants in the population, and a dummy variable for former communist

I also examine the impact of ethnic heterogeneity on trust in another context: across the American states. Richard F. Winters has derived a measure of ethnic heterogeneity across the states in the 1990s using a Herfindahl index. Rodney Hero has estimated the share of each state's minority population for the 1990s. I estimated state-level shares of trusting people from a variety of national surveys conducted from the 1970s through the 1990s;[6] the 1990 data provide trust estimates for 44 states. Ethnic heterogeneity does not predict trust any better in the American states ($r^2 = .007$) than it does cross-nationally – indeed, the coefficient (though insignificant) is slightly positive.

Minority groups are much less trusting than are majorities – especially in the United States where minorities have faced considerable discrimination (Uslaner, 2002, 35–6), so it makes sense to expect that states with large shares of minority residents would, on average, be less trusting, yet even here the relationship is modest ($r^2 = .173$). Ethnic homogeneity and the share of the minority population are, of course, related ($r^2 = .510$), though hardly identical. Yet even the share of the minority population falls to insignificance in predicting trust when economic inequality enters the equation.

There is not significant support for the claims that social ties lead to greater trust, that trust in people you know translates into faith in strangers who may be different from yourself, or that diversity leads to less trust (or to more trust). The many studies on each topic so far lead to a dead end in the quest to understand how these ties and their contexts shape social cohesion.

countries. The Fearon data came from http://www.stanford.edu/group/ethnic/, the Alesina data are available at http://www.anderson.ucla.edu/faculty_pages/romain.wacziarg/papersum.html. I am grateful to Marta Reynal-Querol, Richard Winters, and Rodney Hero for providing me with their data.

[6] I used the following surveys for generating the trust estimates: the General Social Survey (GSS; 1972, 1973, 1975, 1976, 1978, 1980, 1983, 1984, 1986, 1987, 1988, 1989, 1990, 1991, 1993, 1994, 1996, and 1998), American National Election Study (1972, 1974, 1976, 1992, 1996, and 1998), The *Washington Post* Trust in Government survey (1995), the Pew Civic Engagement survey (1997), the *New York Times* Millennium survey (1999), and the 1971 Quality of Life survey of the Survey Research Center. I am grateful to Robert Putnam and John Robinson for making the state codes for the GSS available. The handful of aberrant cases stemmed from easily identifiable outliers, such as a state in which almost all or almost none of the respondents believed that "the government is run by a few big interests." These cases, few in number, were clearly identifiable when looking at the distributions of the data and were the result of small and unrepresentative samples. M. Mitchell Brown and Fengshi Wu helped put the data set together under a grant from the Russell Sage Foundation. For more details, see Uslaner and Brown (2005).

Diverse Ties and Trust

While trust is largely formed early in life, and through your ethnic heritage perhaps well before that, it is not immune to the world you live in. A key reason why social connections don't shape generalized (out-group) trust is that most of us "hunker down" with people like ourselves.

What about people who do have diverse social ties? Are they more trusting? I present data in Table 2.1 from the United States and in Table 2.2 from the United Kingdom, Canada, Sweden, and Australia using the surveys I shall employ throughout the rest of the book.[7] The Social Capital Benchmark Survey asked a variety of trust questions: generalized trust, trust of one's own ethnic group, and trust in various ethnic groups *relative to one's own group*. It also asked about friendship patterns – having friends who are black, Hispanic, Asian, or white, as well as the total number of friendship patterns across groups. Each friendship pattern is based upon out-group friendships only (so having a white friend only includes nonwhite respondents). Correlations are once again very modest – the highest correlation for generalized trust is for nonwhites having a white friend (tau-c = .122), and even this relationship is small. There is no evidence that people who trust their own group highly are less likely to have friends from a different background.

Having a friend of a different group has no effect on how much one trusts African-Americans or whites, and only modest effects on trusting Latinos or Asians. Having a Latino friend makes you slightly more likely to trust Hispanics relative to one's own group (r = .120), and having an Asian friend makes people slightly more likely to trust Asians (r = .133).

[7] The data from the United States come from Putnam's Social Capital Benchmark Survey, a national survey with local add-on samples available for free download at http://www.ropercenter.uconn.edu/data_access/data/datasets/social_capital_community_survey.html. The United Kingdom Citizenship Survey 2007 is a national survey with oversamples of minorities (for a total N of over 14,000) and is available at www.data-archive.ac.uk, registration required. The documentation is available at http://www.communities.gov.uk/publications/communities/citizenshipsurveyaprsep07. The Canadian data come from the two waves of the Equality, Security, Community survey conducted at the University of British Columbia under the direction of Richard Johnston and are available for download at http://www.yorku.ca/isr/download/ESC/esc.html. The Swedish data come from a mail survey conducted by Statistics Sweden for Ersta Sköndal University College. This is a proprietary survey and I am part of the research team under the direction of Lars Svedberg, Lars Tragårdh, and Susanne Lundåsen. The data for Australia are also a proprietary survey from the Scanlon Foundation (the 2007 Mapping Social Cohesion survey; see Chapter 6).

TABLE 2.1. *Trust and social ties in the United States: Social Capital Benchmark Survey*

Dependent Variable	Independent Variable	tau-b / tau-c
Generalized trust	Have black friend	.015
	Have Hispanic friend	.037
	Have Asian friend	.072
	Have white friend	.122
	Number friends different background	.046
Trust own ethnic group	Have black friend	−.022
	Have Hispanic friend	−.017
	Have Asian friend	.045
	Have white friend	.044
	Number friends different background	.008
Trust blacks relative to own group	Have black friend	.094
	Have Hispanic friend	.042
	Have Asian friend	.054
Trust whites relative to own group	Have Hispanic friend	.085
	Have Asian friend	.066
	Have white friend	.073
	Number friends different background	.087
Trust Asians relative to own group	Have black friend	.111
	Have Hispanic friend	.077
	Have Asian friend	.133
	Have white friend	.102
	Number friends different background	.138
Trust Hispanics relative to own group	Have black friend	.112
	Have Hispanic friend	.120
	Have Asian friend	.105
	Have white friend	.044
	Number friends different background	.113

Yet even these relations are modest and there is no evidence that having a friend of an opposite race makes a person more trusting in general.

For the United Kingdom, there are again very small correlations between having friends of different backgrounds and generalized trust. For all respondents, the correlation (tau-b) is a mere .008. For whites and nonwhites separately, the correlations are somewhat higher (.059 and .064, respectively), but still very small. They are not much larger for any

TABLE 2.2. *Trust and social ties: United Kingdom, Canada, Sweden, and Australia*

Independent Variable	Group	tau-b / tau-c
UK Citizenship Survey 2007		
Have friends of different ethnicity	All	.008
	Whites	.059
	Nonwhites	.064
	Black	.051
	African	.050
	South Asian	.074
	Muslim	.037
Canada Equality Security Community Survey 2000 and 2002 (national sample)		
Have friends of different ethnicity	All	.093
	Anglophones	.068
	Quebecois	.103
Sweden Ersta Sköndal Survey 2009		
Friends of different religion	All	.058
	Swedish ethnicity	.081
	Other Nordics	.113
	European/North American ancestry	.023
	Minority	.033
	Identify as Swedish	.073
	Not identify as Swedish	.016
Friends speak different language	All	.047
	Swedish ethnicity	.073
	Other Nordics	.004
	European/North American ancestry	.048
	Minority	.044
	Identify as Swedish	.060
	Not identify as Swedish	−.024
Australia Scanlon Foundation Survey 2007		
Visit friends of different ethnic group	All	.062
	Majority Respondents	.075
	Minorities	.018
Host friends of different ethnic group	All	.062
	Majority Respondents	.072
	Minorities	.032
Visit friends of different religion	All	.077
	Majority Respondents	.082
	Minorities	.035
Host friends of different religion	All	.065
	Majority Respondents	.068
	Minorities	.049

minority group (blacks, people of African or East Indian background, or Muslims).[8] The results are similar for Canada, though the correlations are slightly higher: .093 for all respondents, .068 for Anglophones, and .103 for Quebecois.[9]

The 2009 Ersta Sköndal survey in Sweden does not have a simple question on friendship diversity. It asks about the number of friends of different religions and languages. The correlations are again small – for native Swedes, Nordics born in other countries who have emigrated to Sweden (mostly Finns), people whose ancestry is elsewhere in Europe or North America, and others (minorities). The correlations are somewhat smaller for minorities and people who do not say that their primary identity is Swedish. Since 90 percent of respondents live in neighborhoods comprised of 90 percent or more native Swedes, I restricted the analysis to more diverse neighborhoods (fewer than 90 percent native Swedes). In these more heterogeneous areas, the correlations between friends of different religion actually decrease but they are somewhat greater (around .150) for having friends who speak different languages for all respondents, native Swedes, and people who do not identify as Swedes. For most other groups, the sample sizes are too small to make many claims one way or the other. For language, there does seem to be a positive spillover in more diverse areas from friends of different backgrounds to trust – but even here it is rather small.

The Australian survey asks people whether they visit friends of other ethnicities and religions at their homes or host people of other ethnicities and religions in their own homes, which may come closer to the deeper sorts of ties essential for Allport's optimal conditions. As elsewhere, there are at best modest correlations between trust and any of these measures of contact. The correlations are somewhat higher for majority respondents than for minorities – presaging the results for Australia in Chapter 6.

Diverse social contacts might lead to increased trust if they were more common, especially if they are more intense. Volunteering to help people different from yourself rests upon a foundation of trust but also leads to more trust in turn (Andreoni, 1989; Uslaner, 2002, 133–41). And the very committed civil rights volunteers in the United States in the 1960s had

[8] These categories are not mutually exclusive, of course. African background is defined as being born in Africa, having either one's father or mother born in Africa, or speaking an African language as the primary language at home. South Asian background is similarly defined.

[9] There are too few Francophone respondents outside Quebec to analyze and it is hazardous to treat Francophones outside Quebec with Quebecois.

much higher levels of trust than other Americans and their trust increased over time (Uslaner, 2002, 161). Volunteering for civil rights engaged people with people unlike themselves in pursuit of a common goal – fulfilling Allport's optimal conditions.

Diverse contacts *do* make a difference in settings where they are most likely to be both intense and of equal status – as youngsters in school. High school students who had a friend of a different race were more likely to become trusting adults (Uslaner, 2002, 169). Higher education also leads to greater trust: at university, we meet people of different backgrounds and become exposed to courses on different culture. Education, Smith argues, "may cultivate a more benign view of the world and of humanity" (1997, 191). Students in integrated grade schools are more trusting of out-groups (Rotenberg and Cerda, 1994). A college education broadens our horizons by teaching us about people different from ourselves and bringing us into contact with them (Sniderman and Piazza 1993). Education, one might think, simply represents higher status, but if this were the case, income would be a significant predictor of trust as well and it is not (Uslaner, 2002, 35).

This leads to the question of how and where we can find the optimal conditions for contact to boost trust.

Segregation and Trust

The problem is not diversity, but residential segregation. Living in segregated neighborhoods reinforces in-group trust at the expense of out-group (generalized) trust.

Concentrated minorities are more likely to develop a strong identity that supercedes a national sense of identification (trust in people who are different from oneself) and to build local institutions and political bodies that enhance this sense of separateness. Segregation may also lead to greater political organization by minority groups, which can establish their own power bases in opposition to the political organizations dominated by the majority group as their share of the citizenry grows (cf. Alesina and Zhuravskaya, in press). Massey and Denton write about twentieth-century America:

> Segregation increases the susceptibility of neighborhoods to ... spirals of decline.... In the face of persistent neighborhood disorder, residents come to distrust their neighbors and to look upon them as threats rather than as sources of support or assistance ... they ... limit their contacts outside of close friends and family.... The historical confinement of blacks to the ghetto ... meant that blacks

shared few political interests with whites..... The existence of solid black electoral districts ... did create the potential for bloc voting along racial lines ... an alternative status system has evolved within America's ghettos that is defined *in opposition* to basic ideals and values of American society. (1993, 13, 138, 155–6, 167, emphasis in original)

Blalock argues similarly: "It is difficult ... to imagine how groups can socialize their members to prefer insulation without, at the same time, instilling in them a basic fear and distrust of outsiders, including other minorities. This is all the more true if there has been a previous history of mutually hostile contact" (1982, 111).

Wirth made a similar argument about the impact of residential segregation on Jews in big cities in the 1920s:

Through the instrumentality of the ghetto there gradually developed that social distance which effectively isolated the Jew from the remainder of the population. These barriers did not completely inhibit contact, but they reduced it to the type of relationships which were of a secondary and formal nature. As these barriers crystallized and his life was lived more and more removed from the rest of the world, the solidarity of his own little community was enhanced until it became strictly divorced from the larger world without. (1927, 61–2)

When residential choice is determined by race, language, income, or social status rather than by choice, "the task of holding organizations together and maintaining and promoting intimate and lasting acquaintanceship between the members is difficult" (Wirth, 1938, 17).

Isolation has been far more pervasive and destructive of social ties for African-Americans. Anderson argues forcefully that segregation builds in-group trust at the expense of generalized trust for African-Americans: "Many working-class and poor blacks are ethnocentric because they have limited exposure to white people who are not agents of the dominant society in the ghetto. The social isolation they experience encourages them to feel that the wider society is profoundly unreceptive to them and to all black people" (2011, 214).

For some, segregation is a way station toward integration with the larger society. Immigrant groups arrive in a new nation with few assets and fewer social connections. People from their home countries are a key support base for social relations, religion, food, and, critically, jobs and economic security. Chinatowns in America have served to ease the transition into the larger communities. Yet, for all of the positive contributions ethnic enclaves can bring, they can also entrap people in their insulated worlds and make it more difficult for them to advance both socially and economically (Portes and Landolt, 1996; Zhou, 1997, 2003).

While most immigrant and minority groups succeed economically and move out of segregated areas (Massey and Denton, 1993, 27, 33, 87; Peach, 2005, 18), some – most notably African-Americans in the United States – remain segregated. One-third of blacks are "hypersegregated": not only are they clustered together in small areas of central cities, they also live closer to other segregated minorities and farther away from the majority white population (Massey and Denton, 1993, 74). Other American minorities, such as Hispanics, are rarely hypersegregated while neither Asian-Americans nor Native Americans are so isolated. Even as the incomes of African-Americans has risen, their isolation from white society has persisted. Middle-class blacks find it difficult to escape the ghetto as upwardly mobile members of other minorities have done. White ethnic groups were never as isolated in enclaves as African-Americans are today. (Massey and Denton, 1993, 32, 74, 85, 87, 144; Wilkes and Iceland, 2004, 29, 34).

Segregation, and especially hypersegregation, leads to an unwelcome harvest of bad outcomes: low incomes, lack of jobs, drug use, teenage pregnancies, unmarried parents, low birth weight babies, higher levels of AIDS infections, low rates of education fostered by less government spending on schools, lower levels of entrepreneurship, more crime, and deteriorating public housing (Carter, Schill, and Wachter, 1998, 1906; Cutler and Glaeser, 1997; Cutler, Glaeser, and Vigdor, 2008; de Souza Briggs, 2005; Fischer and Massey, 2000; LaFerrara and Mele, 2005; Massey and Denton, 1993, 13).

Hypersegregation is primarily an American phenomenon and segregation rates are higher in the United States than elsewhere. The ghetto is distinctly American, but other Western nations (including the United Kingdom, Canada, and Sweden, the focus here) have enclaves where members of many minority groups live together and away from the majority white populations. What is distinctive about the United States is not only the extent of segregation, but also the worsening of conditions for African-Americans in the central cities. As black incomes have risen, middle-class African-Americans have deserted the inner cities – often to segregated suburbs rather than to mixed neighborhoods. This exodus has wrecked havoc with the quality of life in the cities. The absence of a middle class has led to spiraling rates of joblessness and low rates of graduation from high schools that has created a "sense of social isolation" (Wilson, 1987, 56–7).

Segregation breeds mistrust because it isolates groups from each other. Its effects are even more pernicious because of *how segregation shapes the lives of those with less voice in where they live.* Just as we socialize with people very much like ourselves, we often choose to live among people from our own background. Economically mobile people are likely to find people of similar interests and economic status from different backgrounds. Living in neighborhoods primarily or exclusively made up of people from your own background is often not a matter of choice. Sometimes it is a matter of discrimination, of not being able to find a place to buy or rent in a more diverse neighborhood. Sometimes it reflects entrapment in a ghetto without the means to get out. Either – or both – destroys trust in outsiders. If we look around our neighborhood and *only* see people very much like ourselves, we are likely to develop a much stronger sense of in-group identity that leaves little room for trust in strangers. In highly segregated Philadelphia, African-Americans reported few friends other than blacks (Massey and Denton, 1993, 161).

Segregation also leads to mistrust because it leads to despair and especially to inequality. Since trust depends upon a foundation of optimism and control – the belief that the world is a good place, it is going to get better, and I am the master of my own fate (Uslaner, 2002, 23, 112) – residents of the ghetto have little reason to believe that their lives will get better, that they are the masters of their fates, or that "most people can be trusted."

Anderson writes: "Segregation of social groups is a principal cause of group inequality" (2010, 2). Bowles, Loury, and Sethi argue that "when segregation is sufficiently great, group equality cannot be attained even asymptotically, no matter what the initial conditions may be" (2009, 11; cf. Massey and Denton, 1993, 127–8). There is a close connection between segregation and inequality, both cross-nationally and across communities in the United States. The ties between racial and economic segregation have become stronger in recent years. Ironically, the overall level of residential segregation has declined modestly for African-Americans (Iceland and Weinberg with Steinmetz, 2002, 110), leaving the poor behind in the inner cities.

Racially isolated neighborhoods are far more likely to be poor than in the past, as middle-class minorities move out and the ghetto increasingly becomes the home of the "truly disadvantaged" (Wilson, 1987). With better transportation and the rise of suburbs, middle-class people no longer need to live in the city to find work, leaving only the poor – and minorities – living in the central cities (Massey, 1996, 397–8). The poor – notably poor African-Americans – lag behind wealthier whites on such measures as the black-white achievement gap in schools (Card and Rothstein, 2007, 2189). Minorities in segregated communities are isolated from jobs and receive less police protection than wealthier neighborhoods – exacerbating the pathology of disorder in the ghetto (Anderson, 2010, 2, 41).

The migration of the middle class to the suburbs led to a tighter connection between racial and economic segregation in the United States from the 1970s to 2000 (Fischer, 2003; Jargowsky, 1996, 990; Soss and Jacobs, 2009, 123; Watson, 2009, 15). While most whites have upward economic mobility across generations, 78 percent of African-Americans move down the economic ladder (Sharkey, 2009, 11).

The concentration of lower-income blacks in the central cities exacerbates despair. Once vibrant, if economically depressed, communities are now dysfunctional. Massey and Denton argue:

> Residents modify their routines and increasingly stay indoors; they minimize their time on the streets and limit their contacts outside of close friends and family. This withdrawal only promotes further disorder by lowering the number of watchful neighbors in public places and by undermining the community's capacity for collective action.... If disorder is allowed to increase, it ultimately creates conditions that promote not only additional disorder, but also crime.... Perceptions of crime and danger gleaned from friends and neighbors who have been victimized, or who have heard of victimizations, cause residents to increase their mistrust of neighbors and to withdraw from public participation in the community. (1996, 138)

Blacks in segregated neighborhoods have lower rates of civic efficacy (Anant and Washington, 2009).[10]

This syndrome of discouragement and inequality depresses trust among a minority that never had much reason to express faith in "most people" (Campbell, Converse, and Rodgers, 1976, 456).

Segregation seems inimical to trust. It isolates us from people different from ourselves and it leads to despair and perceptions of unfairness among those who live apart from those better off. However, living in an integrated neighborhood is not sufficient to boost trust since we can live among people of different backgrounds and stay away from them (Allport, 1958, 260). Knowing people of different backgrounds doesn't imply that the relationships will be close: Only a minuscule share of the Jews in the Elmira study who knew blacks had close ties and about

[10] As noted earlier, Oliver finds that African-American turnout and participation in organizational meetings falls as the share of whites in the city increases and that white participation in both forms of political action falls as the share of blacks increases (2001, 120).

half did not call their acquaintances by their first names (Williams et al., 1964, 210). Students across 144 schools in 80 American communities in 1994–5 largely formed friendship networks within their own race and ethnic group, even among third-generation immigrants (Quillian and Campbell, 2003). Young people are especially likely to seek friends of their own ethnic group (across 13 countries) if their neighborhoods are segregated or if their parents came from lower status groups (Phinney et al., 2006, 94).

Bradburn, Sudman, and Gockel report few cross-racial friendships in the most comprehensive survey of race relations in integrated and segregated neighborhoods across 100 segregated and 100 integrated neighborhoods in 35 cities in 1967:

> Eighty-one per cent of whites in integrated neighborhoods report that neither they nor any member of their family has even stopped and talked with a Negro neighbor in the past few months, and 95 per cent also report no equal-status interracial contact in the home or at parties, movies, or neighboring meetings. These figures are particularly striking since they refer to interracial contact in integrated neighborhoods. But the great bulk of Americans live in segregated neighborhoods. Thus, the absence of equal-status interracial contacts is underplayed by our data. (1970, 394–6)

Much may have changed since 1967, but there is little reason to believe that the overall pattern is markedly different. Equal contact and friendships across race and ethnicity seem to be the exception rather than the rule.

Might inequality lead to segregation rather than the other way around? The logic seems to be more compelling about segregation being the prime mover. The initial choice of residence for minority groups seems less predicated upon income than upon a desire to live among people from their own group (Koopmans, 2010, 15). Most immigrant groups move out of segregated areas after acculturating themselves to their new home country – as I show for Hispanics and Asians in the United States and immigrants of most backgrounds in Canada, the United Kingdom, Sweden, and Australia in the chapters that follow. Escape to integrated neighborhoods does not necessarily lead to greater economic equality. Economic and residential segregation have become increasingly intertwined, even as the latter has generally fallen (Iceland, 2009, 113). Those minorities left behind in segregated communities – notably African-Americans in the United States – fall deeper into poverty, suggesting that segregation is the moving force behind inequality. Segregation may have economic foundations, but they are considerably less important than are people's

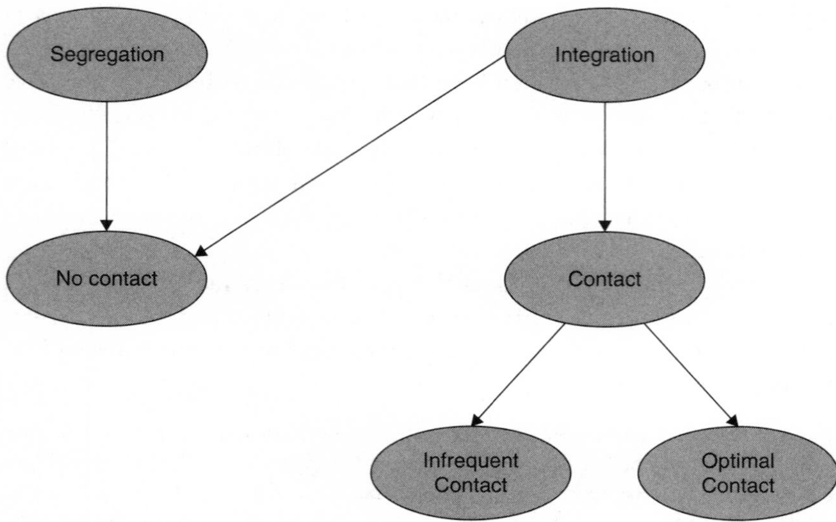

FIGURE 2.1. Segregation, integration, and contact

preferences for where they want to live, as I show in Chapter 8. The connection between persisting segregation and inequality is more direct.

The effects of segregation on trust (or other beliefs) are not straightforward. Segregation by itself may be sufficient to drive down trust, but integration does not automatically lead to greater trust (see Figure 2.1). Segregation will lead, with very high probability, to little contact across racial or ethnic lines. It isolates groups from each other. Integration may also lead to social isolation if you don't make friends with your neighbors. Even if, as seems likely, integrated neighborhoods are more likely to lead to contact across group lines, these interactions may be infrequent or superficial. Deeper ties, as Allport envisioned them, are only one possible outcome in an integrated community – and not necessarily the most likely pattern.

In the United States (Detroit, Michigan) and Canada, Stolle and her colleagues have found that living in a diverse neighborhood and having friends of different backgrounds makes a person more trusting (Marschall and Stolle, 2004; Stolle, Soroka, and Johnston, 2008). Hooghe refines this thesis when he argues that *both* diverse and segregated neighborhoods must occur to lead to a decline in trust (2007, 719). Rothwell (2010) finds that segregation alone is correlated with distrust but for whites, trust rises if they live in integrated *and* diverse neighborhoods.

The issue here is that diversity and segregation *are not the same thing*. I elaborate on this below, but for now I offer the central hypothesis of my argument: *Living in a diverse and integrated neighborhood with close friends of different backgrounds leads to a greater likelihood of trust. Living in a segregated and less diverse neighborhood without friends of different backgrounds makes someone less trusting.*

I find support for this claim in the United States, where segregation is strongest, as well as for the United Kingdom, Canada, and Sweden (and in results not reported here, for Australia). Outside the United States, segregation is not as widespread, so there is less need to interact segregation with diversity. Only in Canada and Australia can I obtain distinct measures of segregation and diversity, but the relationship between the two indices is stronger in Canada than in the United States, making estimation of distinct effects especially with interaction terms more problematic. In Australia (see Chapter 6), the relationship is curiously negative, owing to a small number of outliers. But this means that creating an interaction term is problematic.

Outside the United States, having friends of different backgrounds in integrated neighborhoods leads to greater trust. Except in Sweden, the impact of living in an integrated (and diverse) neighborhood and having friends of different background matters more for majority (white) populations than for minorities. (In Australia, the optimal conditions matter *only* for minorities.) Whites are less likely to have friends of different backgrounds than are minorities (cf. Dinesen, 2011b for similar findings on Denmark). So when they do come closer to meeting Allport's optimal conditions, the impact is greater on majorities. Rothwell finds that "[s]egregation is associated with significantly more racist views on Black intelligence and more psychological distance from Blacks" and that "[i]ntegration ... is strongly and robustly correlated with higher levels of trust, voter turnout, and more favorable views of Whites towards Blacks" (2010, 18–19; cf. Anant and Washington, 2009, 814).[11] Whites who moved from segregated to integrated neighborhoods viewed minorities more positively (Hamilton, Carpenter, and Bishop, 1984, 105; Hunt, 1959–60, 207–8).

Minorities are less trusting for good reasons – they face discrimination and inequality, so there is only so much that we can expect living conditions and social relations to do in building trust. Minorities are most

[11] Rothwell uses the 2000 General Social Survey and has access to the municipal codes (not generally available) to merge the Iceland segregation data I employ here.

likely to become more trusting under Allport's conditions where segregation and inequality are most profound: the United States (see Chapter 3). Yet, even here, the effects are tempered by the profound segregation shaping the lives of African-Americans.

It is important to issue a caveat to the results ahead. The cross-national results are based upon analyses of surveys conducted independently in each country. There is no common set of questions, so the models of trust depend upon the available variables that might influence faith in others. Thus, inferences across countries must be taken with some caution. Just as critical, most of the surveys do *not* permit a direct test of Allport's optimal conditions. Most surveys ask simple questions about having friends of different backgrounds, not questions about the depth and quality of such friendships. So I cannot fully test Allport's optimal conditions. *Nevertheless, despite these reservations, the findings for all five countries support my arguments that segregation matters – and that context matters as well: simply having friends of different backgrounds is not sufficient to build trust, but having diverse networks in an integrated (and diverse) community does seem to build trust.*

Segregation and Diversity

Is my distinction between segregation and diversity merely a semantic distinction, what the British would call "not much of a muchness"? Is segregation really different from diversity? The simple answer is "yes."

Diversity is usually measured as a Herfindahl or fractionalization index, although sometimes it is more crudely estimated as the share of minorities or immigrants in a neighborhood. To compute the fractionalization (Herfindahl) index, you sum the squared proportions of each group in the population. The resulting measure is an estimate of the probability that two randomly selected individuals in the population come from different groups (Alesina et al., 2003).

Fractionalization measures such as those used by Putnam and others cannot distinguish between simple population diversity and residential segregation. A city/state/nation /neighborhood with a highly diverse population – and thus a high fractionalization index – may be marked by either high or low residential segregation. Figure 2.2 presents alternative scenarios on residential segregation. They represent hypothetical neighborhoods of blue and red ethnicities. Each neighborhood has equal

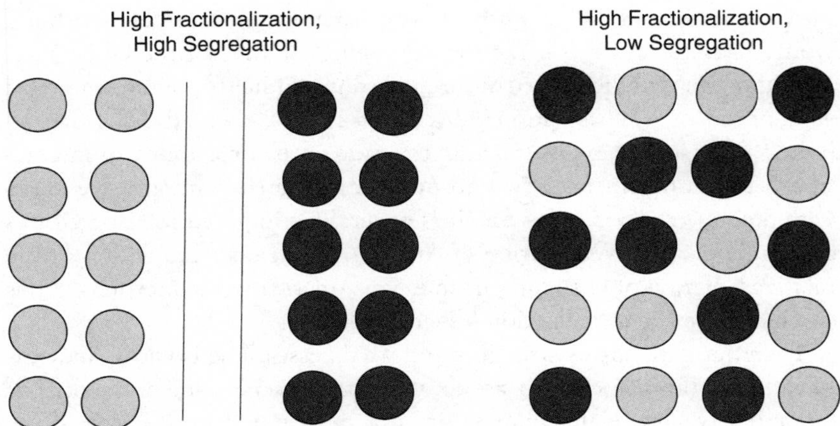

FIGURE 2.2. Diversity and segregation

shares of blue and red residents. In the community on the left, the two ethnic groups live apart from each other, divided by a highway or railroad tracks, so there is less of an opportunity to interact. In the community on the right, the neighborhood is mixed. Each blue (red) resident has at least one red (blue) neighbor. Yet the fractionalization indices are identical.

There are multiple measures of segregation, with five dimensions identified in the literature (Iceland and Weinberg with Steinmetz, 2002, 8, 119–22):

- *Evenness* measures how people are distributed across neighborhoods and cities.
- *Exposure* measures the probability of contact between members of different groups.
- *Concentration* is a measure of how tightly each group is packed into an area.
- *Centralization* is a measure of concentration in the center of an urban area.
- *Clustering* is a measure of how closely minority groups live to each other.

When a group is disadvantaged on most (generally at least four) of the dimensions, it is said to be hypersegregated.

The most widely used measure is based upon evenness. It is the *index of dissimilarity*, which measures how evenly groups are spread out across metropolitan areas. What proportion of each group in a neighborhood would have to move to make the area representative of the larger metropolitan area (in the United States, the standard metropolitan statistical area, or SMSA)? The isolation index (P*) is less widely used. The isolation index, a measure of exposure, is an estimate of the probability of interaction between members of two groups in an area (Iceland and Weinberg with Steinmetz, 2002, 119–22). It is generally computed for two groups at a time: the relative isolation of African-Americans from whites or the relative isolation of Hispanics from Asian-Americans. Its interpretation is similar to the fractionalization (diversity) indices.

Each measure has its strengths and weaknesses. The isolation index is sensitive to the size of each group, while the diversity index is not. The dissimilarity and related indices are not determined by the size of the group but are affected by the size of the units measured. The share of each group that would have to move to make the neighborhood resemble the larger area depends upon how large both the neighborhood and the metropolitan area are (Racial Residential Segregation Measurement Project, n.d.).

Echenique and Fryer (2007) developed an alternative measure based upon large-scale surveys of high school students' interactions with members of different ethnic and racial groups and have argued that their Spectral index is only moderately correlated with any of the other indices. However, the Spectral index is not available over time or across countries so I do not use it.

The dissimilarity index has three key strengths. First, its meaning is intuitive and it seems to fit what we think segregation means. Second, it seems reasonable that a measure of segregation should not depend upon the size of different groups in a population. This is a weakness of the fractionalization measures (and of P*). Third, since it is widely used, it is available at different levels and across countries. The Alesina and Zhuravskaya (in press) cross-national measure is based upon the dissimilarity index and measures in other countries are usually based upon this same formula. These are compelling reasons to use the dissimilarity index.

For the United States, I use a variation on the dissimilarity measure, the entropy index. This construct is "the (weighted) average deviation of each areal unit from the metropolitan area's 'entropy' or racial and ethnic diversity, which is greatest when each group is equally represented in the metropolitan area (Iceland and Weinberg with Steinmetz, 2002, 119). It is based upon the same logic as the dissimilarity index and is the measure employed by the United States Bureau of the Census (Iceland,

2004).[12] The entropy index, like the traditional dissimilarity measure, is an index of "the percentage of a group's population that would have to change residence for each neighborhood to have the same percentage of that group as the metropolitan area overall" (Iceland and Scopilliti, 2008, 83). It is weighted by the diversity of each census tract so that "the diversity score is influenced by the relative size of the various groups in a metropolitan area, the entropy index, being a measure of evenness, is not. Rather, it measures how evenly groups are distributed across metropolitan area neighborhoods, regardless of the size of each of the groups" (Iceland, 2004, 8). Dissimilarity measures – as with indices of isolation – only reflect the level of segregation between two groups. Iceland estimates Theil's measure of "multigroup entropy," providing a single indicator for segregation across all ethnic and racial groups.

The segregation measure "varies between 0, when all areas have the same composition as the entire metropolitan area (i.e., maximum integration), to a high of 1, when all areas contain one group only (maximum segregation)" (Iceland, 2004, 3, 8). Iceland also reports a traditional diversity measure based on census tract data providing a direct comparison between indices of segregation and diversity.

Diversity and segregation are not the same thing. Across 325 communities, the simple correlation for the two measures in 2000 is just .297 (and .231 for 1990 and .270 for 1980).[13]

[12] The segregation/diversity data are available at http://www.census.gov/hhes/www/housing/housing_patterns/housing_patterns.html, accessed October 28, 2008. The Social Capital Community Benchmark Survey was conducted in 40 jurisdictions, but eight were either states or areas (such as "Rural Southeast South Dakota") that could not easily be linked to any city. Of the remaining 32 cities, only 20 had matching data from the residential segregation data. The ethnic groups used in the indices are non-Hispanic whites, non-Hispanic African Americans, non-Hispanic Asians and Pacific Islanders, Non-Hispanic American Indians and Alaska Natives, non-Hispanics of other races, and Hispanics (Iceland, 2004, 3).

[13] The P* indices for Asian-American and Hispanic isolation from whites, as well as white isolation from minorities, are all highly correlated with Iceland's diversity (Herfindahl) index (between -.73 and -.76). The correlations of the P* indices for Asian-Americans, Hispanics, and whites are only modestly correlated with segregation (-.22 and -.23) and the P* index for Asian-Americans is barely correlated with segregation (-.04). The index for African-American isolation from whites is strongly correlated with both diversity and the entropy index of Iceland (-.66 and -.70, respectively), which is hardly surprising since African-Americans are hypersegregated (segregated on multiple dimensions). The N is 239 for all correlations (P* is available for fewer SMSAs than are the segregation and diversity measures). In Chapter 6 I show that diversity and segregation are not the same thing across Australian neighborhoods either, although the correlation is somewhat higher (r = .405).

The diversity measure is actually a surrogate for the percentage of nonwhites in a community (r = -.793) while the segregation measure is only modestly correlated with the nonwhite share (r = -.279) for the 2000 data (see also Vervoort, Flap, and Dagevos, in press, and Tolsma, van der Meer, and Gesthuizen, 2009, 302, for similar findings for the Netherlands). Alesina, Baqir, and Easterly admit that their measure of ethnic diversity is strongly correlated with the percentage of African-Americans in a community (r = .80) and worry that their diversity measure "could just be proxying for black majorities versus white majorities" (1999, 1271). They show that ethnic diversity matters even in majority white communities, but this does not resolve the issue of whether diversity is another name for the share of the minority population.

Segregation is *not* as strongly correlated with the share of African-Americans in a community (r = .542) or the share of minorities – African-Americans, Hispanics, and Asians – more generally (r = .150, both N = 237). The Social Capital Benchmark Survey in the United States includes city-level and other subnational samples in addition to the national survey. I aggregated data to the community level (as they are called in the data set) and there is a strong negative correlation between trust and diversity (r = -.662, N = 41). When I add the shares of population in a community who are African-American and Hispanic to a regression, diversity is no longer significant (t = -.032), while the African-American and Hispanic population shares are significant at $p < .001$ and $p < .10$, respectively (t = -3.41 and -1.62, one-tailed tests). We know that minorities have less generalized trust than whites (Uslaner, 2002, 35–6, 98–107).

The measure of diversity, like the similarly constructed P* index, is sensitive to the size of the minority population in an area. Does diversity drive down trust or does it merely reflect the lower trust levels of groups that have long faced discrimination? If the latter, we might expect segregation to be more important in shaping faith in others than the mere fact of population diversity. I turn to how segregation shapes trust and other outcomes that in turn may lead to greater faith in others.

Segregation, Inequality, and Trust

Segregation is a major factor leading to inequality in the United States and across nations. And inequality leads to lower levels of trust. Alesina and Zhuravskaya (in press) find strong effects of ethnic and linguistic (but not religious) segregation on reducing trust[14] in both simple models and more complex ones using instrumental variables and controlling for the quality of government. Using two different measures of segregation, I find strong support for the argument that segregation leads to lower levels of trust across countries. First, I employ a crude measure of segregation from the Minorities at Risk (MAR) project of the Center for International Development and Conflict Management at the University of Maryland, I estimated the geographical isolation of major minority groups within a wide range of countries.[15] The MAR project created a trichotomous index for each major minority group in a country, and I aggregated the scores across countries. This is an approximation, to be sure, but it is the best available measure of geographical separation. Countries where minorities are most geographically isolated have the lowest levels of generalized trust, a relationship that is considerably strengthened when I eliminate countries with a legacy of communism (Figure 2.3).[16] The r^2 values are .182 and .342, respectively, substantially higher than for any of the measures of diversity.

Second, I examine the Alesina-Zhuravskaya measures of segregation. They computed indices of ethnic, linguistic, and religious segregation for 97 countries, 62 of which also have trust estimates in my cross-national data set. Neither linguistic nor religious segregation is even modestly correlated with trust, but segregation by ethnicity is ($r = -.377$), and the results are even stronger when countries with a communist legacy are excluded ($r = -.489$), again higher than one finds for diversity.[17] I present a plot of trust and segregation across 47 countries in Figure 2.3. At the very lowest levels of segregation, the relationship with trust seems rather muted, becoming stronger as ethnic groups become more likely to live apart from each other.

The direct impact of ethnic segregation on trust is rather modest in a multivariate model, whether I exclude countries with a legacy of

[14] They also find that segregation leads to a lower level of quality of government on multiple indicators.

[15] The data are available for download at http://www.cidcm.umd.edu/inscr/mar/data.htm, accessed May 10, 2004. I am grateful to Alberto Alesina and Ekatarina Zhuravskaya for sharing their cross-national segregation data.

[16] See Uslaner (2002, 226–31) for a discussion of why countries with a legacy of communism are excluded. Inequality is artificially low and the survey measures of trust may not be reliable.

[17] The correlation between trust and ethnic fractionalization in the Alesina data set is -.320 for all cases ($N = 84$) and -.370 excluding countries with a legacy of communism ($N = 63$).

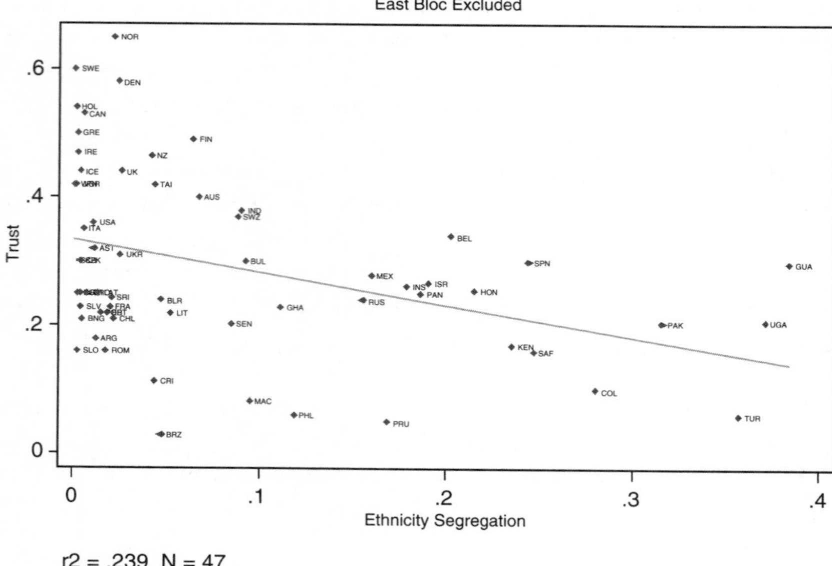

FIGURE 2.3. Trust by ethnic segregation

communism or include a dummy variable for these countries. When I estimate a model similar to my previous work (Uslaner (2002, 233–40), ethnic segregation does drive down trust, but the coefficient is significant only at $p < .10$.[18]

A more compelling story is how segregation leads to lower levels of trust because of its effects on inequality. I estimated a model for trust instrumenting inequality with ethnic segregation and two other measures: the extent of ethnic tensions as measured by the International Control Risk Group in 2005 and an index of the size of the informal sector from the 2004 Executive Opinion Survey of the World Economic Forum.[19] The logic of the instruments is straightforward: segregation and inequality are strongly linked (as I argued above). Ethnic tensions should lead to discrimination against the minority by the majority, hence

[18] The other variables in the model are the share of Protestants in a country and the level of economic inequality (the Gini index from the United Nations Development Programme for 2003, available at http://hdr.undp.org/statistics/data/).

[19] Is the size of the informal sector exogenous to inequality? Being constrained to work in the informal sector may increase inequality, but the very existence of a large informal sector seems (at least theoretically) to have a greater effect on inequality than any reverse causality.

TABLE 2.3. *Cross-national model of trust: segregation as an instrument for inequality*

Model for Trust (Second Stage)			
Variable	**Coefficient**	**Std. Error**	**t Ratio**
Gini Index UNDP 2003 (instrumented)	−.009****	.002	−4.70
Proportion Protestant in population	.002****	.001	3.93
(Former) communist dummy	−.123***	.037	−3.30
Constant	.627****	.084	7.44
Model for Gini Index (Instrumental Variable Estimation)			
Ethnic segregation	30.759**	13.254	2.32
Ethnic tensions (ICRG)	3.045**	.991	3.07
Informal sector (World Economic Forum)	3.165**	1.068	2.96
Nordic dummy	−20.393****	5.984	−3.41
Proportion Protestant in Population	.132**	.069	1.93
(Former) communist dummy	−6.525***	2.654	−2.46
Constant	12.317**	6.099	2.02

* p < .10 ** p < .05 *** p < .01 **** p < .0001 (all tests one tailed except for constants)
N = 51

Equation	R^2	S.E.E.	F Statistic
Trust	.601	.089	20.00
Gini Index (instrument)	.571	7.227	9.77

Sargan test for overidentification of instruments: 4.582, p = .205

to greater inequality. A larger informal sector means that some workers are marginalized, without protection from exploitive employers, leading to greater inequality.

Segregation leads to greater economic inequality across 51 nations and inequality leads to lower trust (see Table 2.3).[20] Alternatively, an argument that inequality might lead to greater segregation – a possible if not as plausible alternative causal mechanism – also receives strong support. Inequality in this model (not shown) is a powerful determinant of segregation and the instrument also has a powerful impact on trust.

Both across nations and American standard metropolitan statistical areas (SMSAs), segregation, not diversity, leads to greater inequality. I estimated a simple model for inequality across 65 nations with only Alesina's ethnic segregation and fractionalization measures as predictors

[20] The instruments are all insignificant predictors in a single-equation estimation of trust. The Nordic dummy is not significant when inequality is entered as a predictor.

TABLE 2.4. *Effects of segregation and diversity on inequality for United States SMSAs*

Model for Minority/White Income Level

Variable	Coefficient	Standard Error	t ratio
Segregation	−.436****	.041	−10.78
Diversity	−.004	.015	−.24
Percent minority high school degree	.001**	.0005	2.17
Percent minority homeowners	.002****	.0004	4.36
Percent suburban SMSA	.001***	.0002	2.72
Percent minority English speakers	.001***	.001	2.63
Constant	.553****	.049	11.09

RMSE = .061 R^2 = .473 N = 323
* p < .10 ** p < .05 *** p < .01 **** p < .0001 (all tests one tailed except for constants)

Model for LaFerrara Gini Index+

Variable	Coefficient	Standard Error	t ratio
Segregation	.0868****	.014	6.22
Diversity	.006	.005	1.03
Percent minority homeowners	−.0004	.0002	−.32
Percent suburban SMSA	−.001****	.0001	−7.02
Percent minority English speakers	−.0004**	.0002	−1.73
Constant	.447****	.019	23.01

RMSE = .061 R^2 = .473 N = 323
* p < .10 ** p < .05 *** p < .01 **** p < .0001 (all tests one tailed except for constants)
+ Percent minority high school degree dropped because of collinearity in this subsample.

together with a dummy variable for (former) communist nations. The coefficient for segregation (significant at p < .005) is almost six times as great as that for diversity (not significant). I also estimated models for two measures of inequality for American SMSAs using a measure developed by Iceland (2004), the ratio of minority income to majority (white) income in each jurisdiction and a Gini index for each SMSA estimated by Elena LaFerrara.[21] The income ratio is available for 323 SMSAs, but the LaFerrara Gini only covers 227.

The story in the two models is essentially the same (see Table 2.4): Segregation is a major determinant of inequality – in the first model, *the* major influence on inequitable distributions of resources. Diversity

[21] I am grateful to Elena LaFerrara for providing the Gini index data.

doesn't matter. Other factors also shape the income ratio – how many minority group members are high school graduates, own their own homes, and speak English as well as the percent suburban. The suburban ratio is especially important for the Gini index while the share of English speakers is also significant. *The story for trust is all about the relative impacts of segregation and diversity, and it is segregation, not diversity, that creates economic divisions across nations and within American communities.*

Segregation leads to many bad outcomes and I focus on two that are central to trust and inequality: crime and well-being. The publisher CQ Press developed a database on crime across American communities and standard metropolitan statistical areas for 2003, 2006, and 2007. The Gallup organization developed an indicator of community well-being for 113 metropolitan areas in 2010. Clearly many other negative outcomes stem from segregation. I focus on crime and well-being since they are widely discussed consequences of segregation and metropolitan-area data are available.

Crime is high where trust is low (Uslaner, 2002, 209–10, 244–5) and where people are poor. High rates of crime are also associated with large minority populations, since minorities are poor and the ghetto is associated with so many negative outcomes associated with high crime: high unemployment, low rates of graduation, single-parent families, and an atmosphere of despair (Liska, Chamlin, and Reed, 1985, 128; Massey, 2007, 195; Massey and Denton, 1993, 138; Wilson, 1987, 38). The effects of segregation on crime are disputed. There is evidence that segregation leads to substantially higher rates of crime, largely because segregation and poverty are so tightly connected. Yet even segregated white neighborhoods also have higher rates of crime (Krivo, Peterson, and Kuhl, 2009, 1786–91). Desegregation has resulted in lower rates of crime (Weiner, Lutz, and Ludwig, 2009, 35). Yet others hold that integration brings more minorities into predominantly white (and presumably safer) communities, increasing the rates of arrest for homicide, rape, assault, robbery, burglary, larceny, and auto theft (Liska, Chamlin, and Reed, 1985, 128).

I cannot resolve this issue here, but I want to distinguish between the effects of segregation and diversity (minority population) on crime rates in American SMSAs. Using the CQ data for 2007 (Morgan and Morgan with Boba, 2009), I estimated a series of regressions for crime rates in American communities. The dependent variables are first the simple rates of robbery, murder, violent crime, assault, burglary, larceny, property crime, motor vehicle theft, rape, and overall crime for 2007 using the

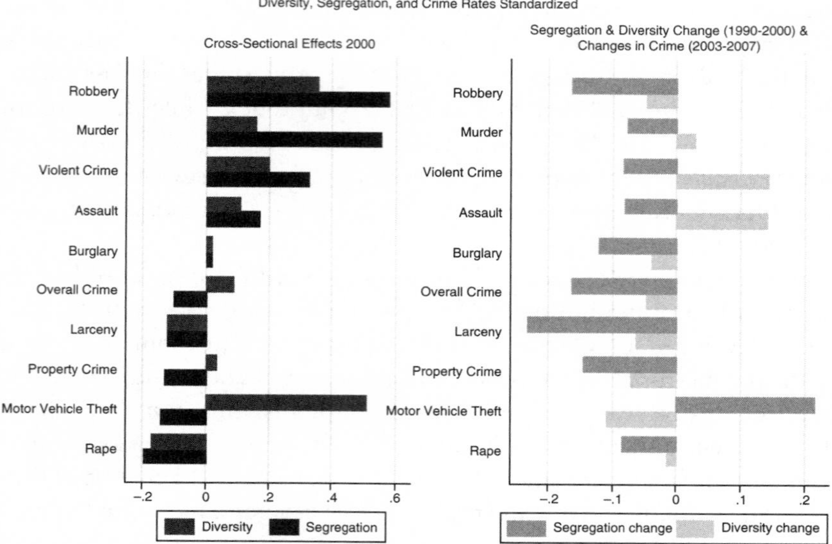

FIGURE 2.4. Effects of segregation and diversity on crime in US SMSAs

2000 measures of segregation and diversity from Iceland (2004) as well as other measures from his database: that might lead to high levels of crime: the percentage of vacant housing in a community, the share of minority homeowners, and the share of minorities with a high school degree. I expect that higher rates of minority home ownership and education should lead to less crime, while greater vacant housing rates should lead to more crime. The key variables are segregation and diversity. Next, I examine whether changes in segregation from 1990 to 2000 lead to changes in crime rates. The crime change data (2003–7) are not aligned with increases or decreases in segregation. They are the closest I can get to any estimates of change. I present graphical depictions of the regression coefficients for both sets of models based upon 210 to 220 communities) in Figure 2.4.

The results in Figure 2.4 for the cross-sectional models do not tell a simple story about segregation. Overall crime and rates of larceny, motor vehicle theft, property crime, and rape are higher in *integrated areas*. But robbery, murder, violent crime, assault, and burglary rates increase as segregation becomes more pronounced. Every crime rate except those for rape and larceny are greater when there is more diversity (greater minority populations). Whether the impact is positive or negative, the impact of segregation is almost always substantially greater than it is for diversity. Generally property crime is greater in integrated neighborhoods, which are likely to be wealthier with more to steal. The one area where the effect of diversity is greater – indeed substantially greater – than segregation is motor vehicle theft. Violent crimes, with the exception of rape, are higher in segregated communities. This fits in with the general notion of the ghetto as a place of despair.

The story is different for change in segregation. Communities that became more integrated (negative coefficient on change in segregation) from 1990 to 2000 had substantial reductions in crime on most measures – most notably overall crime, larceny, property crime, and robbery. But more violent crime rates, for violent crime overall, assault, murder, and rape fell in communities that became more integrated. The only exception is for motor vehicle theft. While violent crime, assault, and murder increased as communities became more diverse, they fell as neighborhoods became more integrated. Again, the effects for segregation change dwarf those of diversity change.

Segregation *is* associated with greater rates of crime – notably most violent crime – and more integration leads to greater adherence to the law.

With lower crime should come better well-being in general. As part of a broader effort to measure well-being across nations, the Gallup organization in 2010 measured well-being on five dimensions across over 100 American communities. The well-being index consists of indicators of life evaluation, access to basic services, and physical, emotional, and personal health based upon samples of 353,000 respondents.[22] Are diversity or segregation factors in shaping well-being in American communities?

[22] I copied the data by hand from the website since the data are not downloadable. The well-being site is http://www.gallup.com/poll/116497/rankings-reveal-state-strengths-weaknesses.aspx#1; the indicators are life evaluation at present and in five years, physical well-being (sick days in the past month, disease burden, health problems that get in the way of normal activities, obesity, feeling well rested, daily energy, daily colds, daily flu, and daily headaches), emotional health (smiling or laughter, learning or doing something interesting, being treated with respect, enjoyment, happiness, worry, sadness, anger, stress, and diagnosis of depression); personal health (smoking, eating healthy food, weekly consumption of fruits and vegetables, and weekly exercise frequency); work environment (job satisfaction, ability to use one's strengths at work, supervisor's treatment, an open and trusting work environment), and basic access (access to clean water, medicine, a safe place to exercise, affordable fruits and vegetables; enough money for food, shelter, healthcare; having health insurance, having a doctor, having visited a dentist recently; satisfaction with the community, the community getting better as a place to live, and feeling safe walking alone at night). Wording is taken directly from the Gallup site. For the municipality data, see Page (2010).

TABLE 2.5. *The effects of segregation and diversity on well-being in American communities model for segregation*

Variable	Coefficient	Standard Error	t ratio
Segregation	−2.270**	1.188	−1.91
Percent minority high school degree	.092****	.017	5.51
Percent incomes 150 percent and above poverty level	4.505***	1.807	2.49
Average hourly wage	.002**	.001	2.03
Constant	44.658****	7.951	5.62

RMSE = 1.103 R^2 = .460 N = 113
* p < .10 ** p < .05 *** p < .01 **** p < .0001 (all tests one tailed except for constants)
Model for Diversity

Variable	Coefficient	Standard Error	t ratio
Diversity	.495	.494	1.00
Percent minority high school degree	.105****	.015	6.92
Percent incomes 150 percent and above poverty level	4.322**	1.871	2.31
Average hourly wage	.001	.001	1.21
Constant	48.651****	8.2890	5.87

RMSE = 1.116 R^2 = .447 N = 113
* p < .10 ** p < .05 *** p < .01 **** p < .0001 (all tests one tailed except for constants)

I estimated regressions for segregation and diversity and present the results in Table 2.5. The models also include the share of minorities with a high school degree, the percent in a community living at 150 percent of the poverty level or higher, and the average hourly wage (all from Iceland, 2004). In both models, the share living above the poverty rate and especially the level of education predict well-being. So does segregation – moving from the most to the least segregated of the 113 communities leads to an 11 percent increase in well-being.[23] But diversity has no impact on well-being. Its coefficient is less than a quarter as large as that for segregation and it fails to reach statistical significance. *For both crime and well-being, segregation leads to worse outcomes (most of the time). Diversity matters either to a lesser extent or not at all.*

[23] I calculated this effect by multiplying the difference in segregation (.44) by the regression coefficient for segregation and dividing by the range of the well-being index (from the minimum of 63.5 to the maximum of 72.5).

The Weakness of Strong Ties

Economic inequality lowers trust by creating a world of "us against them." When you believe that others have advantages over you, you will not see any common bonds with them. This lowers generalized trust and increases faith in your own in-group (Uslaner, 2002, ch. 2). Segregation may be strongly linked to inequality in the United States and across nations. This link is not universal. It is much weaker in Canada (Fong, 1996, 205; Phan, 2008, 37–8; Reitz and Banerjee, 2007, 520), Sweden (Andersson, 2008, 20; Harsman, 2006, 1350), the United Kingdom (Finney and Simpson, 2009, 128), and Australia (see Chapter 6), largely because the overall level of segregation is lower in these countries. Residential choices play a role as do housing policies (as I discuss throughout the book).

However, another government policy in Canada, the United Kingdom, and (in the past) Sweden and Australia may reinforce the low trust that immigrants "carry over" from the home country. Multiculturalism is designed to ease the transition to a new home as people "make new friends but keep the old, one is silver and the other gold."[24] Marx argued that you can be a farmer in the morning, a laborer in the afternoon, and a philosopher in the evening. Multiculturalists argue that you can be a Brit in the morning and a Bangladeshi in the evening, a Chinese in the morning and a Canadian in the afternoon, (to a lesser extent) a Swede in the afternoon and an Eritrean in the evening, a Vietnamese at breakfast and an Australian at dinner.

Multiculturalism encourages dual identities. Kymlicka argues: "immigrants do best, both in terms of psychological well-being and sociocultural outcomes, when they are able to combine their ethnic identity with a new national identity" (2010b, 10). Cultures, Lord Parekh (n.d.) argues, must be fluid, adapting to what a country's population looks like now, not in the past. Modood argues that "assimilation into an undifferentiated national identity … is unrealistic and oppressive as a policy. An inclusive national identity is respectful of and builds on the identities people value and doesn't trample upon them … multiculturalism is the need to give respect to stigmatized or marginalized identities that are important to people and cannot be disregarded in the name of the individual, or … social cohesion, integration, or citizenship" (2007, 150, 121). Such identities can peacefully coexist with a commitment to a broader national

[24] From an American children's song, author unknown, lyrics at https://kids.niehs.nih.gov/lyrics.makenew.htm.

identity, even if the ethnic/racial/religious identity is the dominant one (Modood, 2007, 115).

Multiculturalism is connected to segregation in two ways. First, encouraging immigrants to adopt a dual identity, especially through government policies that promote identification with the "old country," is likely to lead to social segregation – to a friendship network centered around people very much like oneself. This is social segregation and it works against the unitary temperament that I argue is central to generalized trust. Second, fostering in-group identity may lead people to remain in communities composed of people of their own kind.

Koopmans finds that Northern European countries with strong multiculturalism policies have more residential segregation than those placing a greater emphasis on assimilation (2010, 15–18). Multiculturalism may thus promote both residential and social segregation.

The American model of the "melting pot" or *E pluribus unum* ("one out of many") is an alternative to multiculturalism. The focus on integration into a common identity includes an expectation that immigrants will assimilate into a "superordinate" (or dominant) American identity. While people have a variety of identities – I am a professor, a husband and a father, a Chicago White Sox (baseball) fan, a native of New Jersey but now a resident of Maryland – the assimilationist model is based upon the idea that my *primary* identity is as an American. Multiculturalism emphasizes at least dual identities – from the old country and the new. Governments adopt policies that help groups sustain their identity, such as the multilingual broadcasting network in Australia and newspapers in the language of the home country in Sweden. Such government support has the potential to maintain strong in-group identity.

Every country I examine here other than the United States has adopted multiculturalism. It originated in Canada but has spread widely across Western countries as they try to adapt to increased immigration into cultures that have traditionally not had to contend with increasing diversity. The debate over diversity and who is an American has a long and tortured history in the United States. It was always discussed in terms of integration and assimilation – since almost everyone in America (save for American Indians) came from somewhere else and the national motto of the country extolled diversity. Ironically, the country with the greatest commitment to an assimilationist (rather than multiculturalist) model of identity has the most residential segregation (in contrast to Koopmans's findings for Europe) – and this will shape how social ties with diverse groups in integrated neighborhoods shapes trust (see Chapter 3).

Supporters of multiculturalism argue that this policy, which Canadians call the "mosaic," makes immigrants feel less alienated from the majority (white) culture. Trevor Phillips (2005), chair of the Equality and Human Rights Commission in the United Kingdom, argued in support of multiculturalism in a speech to the Manchester Council for Community Relations: "We need to be a nation of many colours that combine to create a single rainbow. Yes, that does mean recognising diversity and rejecting assimilation." Lord Parekh (2002, 18) argues: "The danger is … compounded in the case of an imperial or post-imperial nation like Britain, where the differences between 'us' and 'them' are imagined to be racial, rooted in unalterable nature." Under multiculturalism, there is no single primary identity.

By promoting dual or multiple identities, multiculturalism may inadvertently lead to lower levels of trust. Generalized trust is based upon the notion of a common identity. As I argued :

> Generalized trusters have a distinctive view of civil society: They see it as *one* society united by a set of common values.… Trusters want to empower minorities and other groups that have faced discrimination. Yet they worry that disadvantaged groups might be wary of forming broad coalitions. Empowerment might easily lead to fractionalization. This would go against the very lesson that trusting people put highest on their agenda: working to include rather than exclude folks who are different from yourself. So trusters are especially likely to say that ethnic politicians should *not* primarily serve their own communities. And, reflecting their view that there *is* a common culture, trusters are wary of the claim that high school and college students spend too much time reading classic literature. (Uslaner, 2002, 191, 197)

It is easier for minorities to assimilate into a culture that does not have a dominant race or ethnicity, where virtually everyone has come from somewhere else and there are national symbols and holidays that are not based upon race, ethnicity, or religion. It is more difficult for people to become part of a culture that has a dominant race, ethnicity, or culture. But the alternative – remaining true to the culture you left behind – leads to lower levels of trust for the minorities seeking to establish bonds with their new home.

Reitz et al. (2009, 40) find (italics in original): "*ethnic attachments seem to have a clearly negative relation to the emergence of a 'Canadian' identity, and for immigrants to the acquisition of Canadian citizenship*." Turkish immigrants with the strongest senses of national and religious (Muslim) identity are least likely to identify with their new home countries and have friendships across different ethnic groups in three

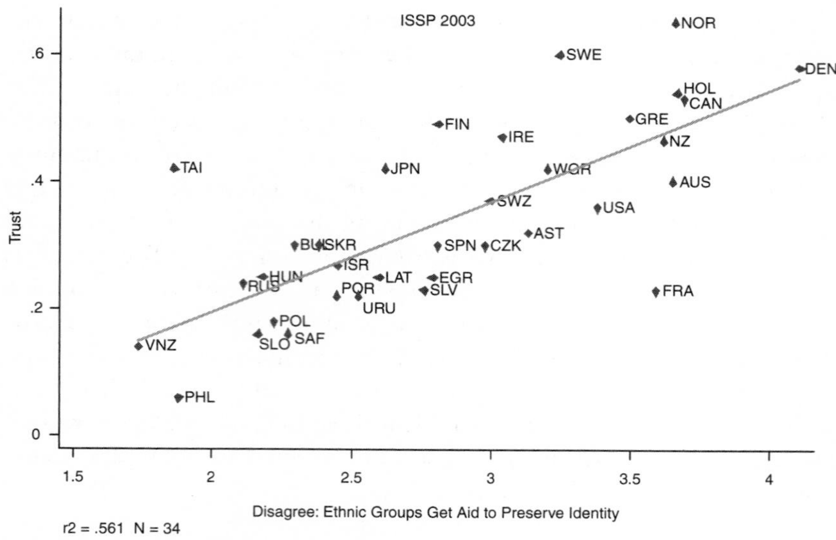

FIGURE 2.5. Trust by no aid to preserve identity

European countries (Germany, France, and the Netherlands). In-group ethnic and religious identification are strongest in the Netherlands, with a long-standing multiculturalism policy, and weakest in assimilationist France (Ersanilli and Koopmans, 2009).

Data across countries and in the United States, Canada, and the United Kingdom support this argument. The International Social Survey Program (ISSP) asked respondents in 2003 whether they opposed government aid to minorities to preserve their culture (an unusual negatively worded question). Kymlicka (2007b, 260) identifies this as a key government policy designed to promote multiculturalism. Since generalized trust is based upon an inclusive sense of your community, I would expect a negative relationship between support for this policy and generalized trust. And this is what I find: in Figure 2.5 I show a strong negative relationship (r^2 = .561) between the level of generalized trust in 36 countries and the extent of opposition to government support for this multiculturalism policy. Perhaps ironically, Canadians are among the most supportive of multiculturalism in general[25] but are among the strongest opponents

[25] Kymlicka reports that 89 percent of Canadians regarded multiculturalism as central to their national identity in a 2003 survey (2010, 7). See also Harrell (2009) for a compendium of survey findings on Canadian support for multiculturalism.

of government aid to ethnic groups in maintaining their identity. The governments of Sweden and Australia are committed publicly to multiculturalism, though more recently mixed with overtures back to assimilation – and their publics show high levels of both trust and opposition to government aid to ethnic groups to maintain their home identities.

There is a modest relationship between trust and whether people think that their ethnic identity is very important from the 2003 ISSP (r^2 = .223). When we consider the strength of ethnic identity across different groups, the picture changes. For both the United States and Canada, the more strongly members of a group feel that their ethnicity is important, the lower their levels of trust. For the United States, I aggregated responses to ethnic identity strength and trust by group from the General Social Survey. For Canada, Jantzen (2005) reports levels of trust and the strength of ethnic identity by ethnic group. Her figures encompass responses to the 2002 Ethnic Diversity Survey for all respondents and second-generation immigrants. When we focus on how identity shapes trust by group rather than for entire populations, we see much stronger relationships between the strength of identity and trust. Across 16 groups in the United States (Figure 2.6), there is an almost perfect linear relationship between the aggregate scores on the strength of identity and trust (r^2 = .824). Minorities – African-Americans, Puerto Ricans, Latin Americans, and Mexicans – are strongly attached to their ethnicity and have lower levels of trust. People of European background are generally far less attached to their ethnicity and also are more trusting.

The same pattern holds for Canada – notably there is a strong relationship between the aggregate level of trust and the strength of ethnic identity *for second-generation immigrants* (Figure 2.7, r^2 = .767 across 19 groups). The strength of ethnic identity for the children of immigrants remains strong for "visible minorities" (as they are called in Canada): Caribbeans, Africans, East Indians, Filipinos, Arabs, Latin Americans, and Chinese – as well as Southern Europeans (Portuguese and Italians). Chinese immigrants are less bound to their ethnic identity and have higher levels of trust, but this may reflect the higher socioeconomic status of Chinese immigrants to Canada (as it does among Asian-Americans more generally). Northern Europeans have both the highest levels of trust and the least identification with their homelands.

One group notably missing from this figure is Quebecois – no data are reported for second-generation immigrants, and this makes sense since Quebecois are not a new or visible minority. Quebecois are

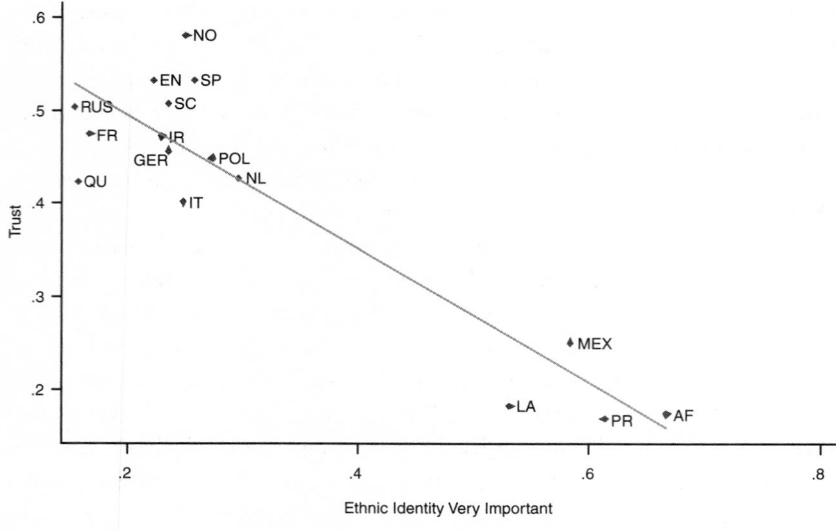

FIGURE 2.6. Trust and ethnic identity in the United States. By Ethnic Background U.S. General Social Survey
Legend: AF (African) EN (English) FR (French) GER (German) IR (Irish) IT (Italian) LA (Latin American) MEX (Mexican) NL (Dutch) NO (Norwegian) PHL (Filipino) POL (Polish) PR (Puerto Rican) QU (Quebecois) RUS (Russian) SC (Scottish) SP (Spanish)

included in the data for the "current" generation, where we see similar results (Figure 2.8, r^2 = .742 across 19 groups).[26]. Quebecois have a strong sense of ethnic identity and a level of trust even lower than one would expect from their in-group ties. Otherwise, the picture for the current generation looks remarkably like that for second-generation immigrants.

For both the United States and Canada, there is a strong relationship between a group's levels of ethnic identity and trust. Multiculturalism cannot be the culprit in this story, since Americans favor assimilation rather than a mosaic. Yet, even in a high-trusting country such as Canada, multiculturalism is not a rising tide that lifts all boats. Visible minorities remain low trusting. Africans, and especially Caribbeans, in Canada are barely more trusting than are African-Americans. And visible minorities

[26] Chinese and Portugese were strong outliers, so I excluded them from this graph.

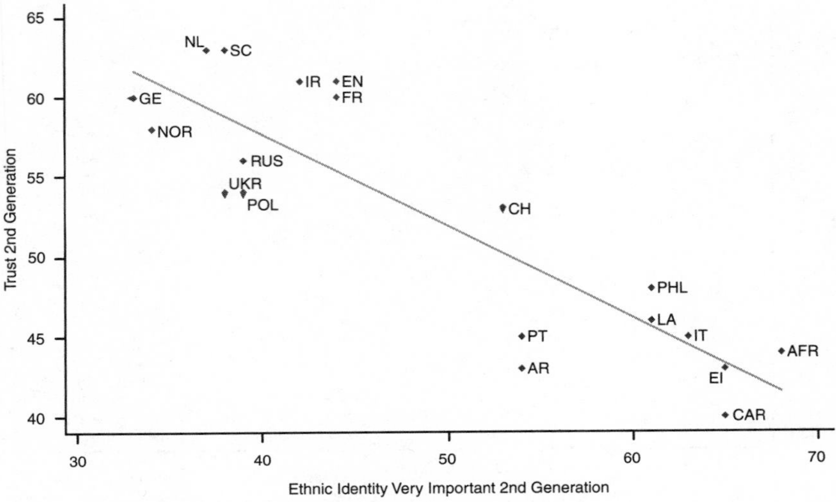

r2 = .767 N = 19

FIGURE 2.7. Trust and ethnic identity in Canada: second generation. By Ethnic Background Ethnic Diversity Survey Canada 2002
Legend: AF (African) AR (Arab) CAR (Caribbean) CH (Chinese) EI (East Indian) EN (English) FR (French) GE (German) IR (Irish) IT (Italian) LA (Latin American) NL (Dutch) NO (Norwegian) PHL (Filipino) POL (Polish) QU (Quebecois) RUS (Russian) SC (Scottish) UKR (Ukrainian)

remain tied to their ethnic identities even after a generation has passed. Every visible minority except Chinese and Filipinos has a *stronger* ethnic identity after a generation has passed while the in-group ties of most Northern European minorities remains constant (and low). Most visible minorities have either unchanged or lower levels of trust after a generation.

By encouraging minorities to maintain a strong affinity for the home country, multiculturalism may lead to social segregation. Strong bonding with one's own ethnic group may inhibit trust, especially if immigrants bring with them a low level of faith in others from the home country (Uslaner, 2008b) and if the mores and values of the host country seem strange or threatening.

Multiculturalism is not without its critics among minorities in countries that place a high value on this ideal. Kenan Malik (2011), a British writer, argued in the *New York Times* that multiculturalism has led to

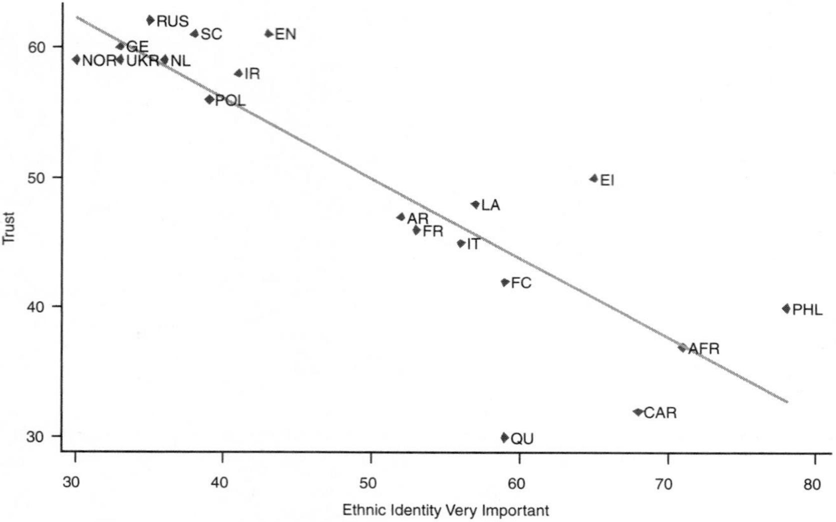

FIGURE 2.8. Trust and ethnic identity in Canada: current generation. By Ethnic Background Ethnic Diversity Survey Canada 2002
Legend: AF (African) AR (Arab) CAR (Caribbean) EI (East Indian) EN (English) FC (French Canadian) FR (French) GE (German) IR (Irish) IT (Italian) LA (Latin American) NL (Dutch) NO (Norwegian) PHL (Filipino) POL (Polish) QU (Quebecois) RUS (Russian) SC (Scottish) UKR (Ukrainian)

a radicalization of immigrants, most notably European Muslims: "In place of citizenship and a genuine status in society, the state 'allowed' immigrants to keep their own culture, language and lifestyles. One consequence was the creation of parallel communities ... this has resulted in the scapegoating of immigrants and the rise of both populist and Islamist rhetoric." Neil Bissoondath (1998), a Canadian novelist, argues that many immigrants "recognize that multiculturalism ... has exoticized, and so marginalized, them.... Multiculturalism, which asked that I bring to Canada the life I had in Trinidad, was a shock to me. I was seeking a new start in a land that afforded me that possibility. I was *not* [emphasis in original] to live in Toronto as if I were still in Trinidad." Such claims may exaggerate the level of alienation among minorities (see Chapter 9). The larger point is that multiculturalism does encourage a continuing identification with a culture that is distinct from that of the host country and thus is inimical to forming bonds of trust across groups.

Hanging with the Homeboys: The Route to Low Trust[27]

Are strong connections to your in-group necessarily destructive of generalized trust? Clark, Putnam, and Fieldhouse suggest otherwise:

> [S]tronger intra-racial bonds and stronger interracial bridges can be positively, rather than negatively, correlated ... the same American or Brit who has more ties to others of their *own* racial and ethnic group is actually *more* likely, not less likely, to have more social bridges to other racial or ethnic groups.... American whites who trust whites more tend also to trust Latinos more, not less than whites who distrust whites ... our research tends to support public policies which foster the building of strong bonds within ethnic groups ... because that could be an important prelude to the broader social bridging we seek.... A social salad bowl is thus a better ideal than a homogenizing melting pot. (2010, 142–3)

Not quite. This argument pays little heed to how trust is developed and expands. If I trust people who are very different from myself, I will surely trust my wife, my son, and my close friends. But if I trust my wife, this says nothing about trust in people who are different from myself (Uslaner, 2002, 145–8).

Clark, Putnam, and Fieldhouse focus primarily on trust in one's neighbors rather than generalized trust. In Putnam's Social Capital Benchmark Survey, I examined the interrelationship among generalized trust and dichotomized measures of trusting one's neighbors and trusting your own race. For whites, the modal category is trusting other whites and your neighbors but not "most people" (43.7 percent). Only 3 percent have faith in "most people" but not in their neighbors. The simple correlation between the two measures is modest (tau-b = .225), at least in part because so many people trust their neighbors (85 percent). About two-thirds of whites trust other whites, but less than half (46 percent) of those who trust people of their own race believe that "most people can be trusted." Eighty-nine percent of whites have faith in others of their race and 86 percent of them also trust their neighbors.

Forty-six percent of African-Americans trust their neighbors but not people in general, while 30 percent do not trust either their neighbors or "most people." Two-thirds of African-Americans trust blacks but not "most people," while almost 60 percent trust blacks *and* trust their neighbors. *For whites and especially for blacks, the modal pattern is to trust their neighbors and their own racial group but not people in general.*

[27] *Homeboys* is a term used by some African-Americans to refer to their close-knit group, especially in ghettos.

The same pattern holds for the United Kingdom. In the 2007 Citizenship Survey, the modal pattern (56 percent) for all respondents is to trust their neighbors (a dichotomized measure) but *not* people in general. The pattern again is particularly strong for minorities, with approximately two-thirds of blacks, Africans, South Asians, and Muslims giving particularistic trust responses. Almost twice as many minorities trust only their own kind as have faith in their in-group and in people in general. Fifty-two percent of whites, who are far more trusting overall, have faith in their neighbors but not people in general.

Trusting people like yourself is not part of a "transmission belt" to faith in people unlike yourself. Faith in in-groups is primordial, trusting out-groups is not. Strong in-group trust often, indeed usually, crowds out faith in strangers, especially for minorities who are more likely to have faced discrimination.

In-group ties go hand in hand with attachment to place. High levels of in-group trust are most common among groups who do not live intermingled with the majority. And attachment to place also leads to weaker ties with the larger community.

The 2007 UK Citizenship Survey asked respondents to rate on a four-point scale how important various factors are to "a sense of who you are." The possible answers are interests, occupation, education, income, gender, age, your family, where you live, religion, ancestry, your ethnicity/race, and national identification. Then people were asked which factor was the most important in self-identification. I present the results in Figure 2.9 for all respondents, whites, nonwhites, Africans, South Asians, and Muslims (the first bar is for the share of trusting respondents for each group).

For all respondents and for each group, people who identify themselves by their interests are the most trusting. People who say that their identity is shaped primarily by their level of education and their occupation are more likely to trust most people. The lowest trusting respondents cite ancestry, ethnicity and race, religion, and especially *where they live* as the basis for their identity. The sole exception for religion is for whites. Whites in the United Kingdom are largely members of the Church of England, a mainline Protestant denomination religion with a strong ecumenical outreach (see Chapter 4 and Schoenfeld, 1978, 64).

Where you live shapes your identity more if your neighborhood is more segregated, especially for minorities. Thirty-eight percent of whites say where they live shapes their identity if almost everyone living within 15 or 20 minutes walking distance of their home are like themselves.

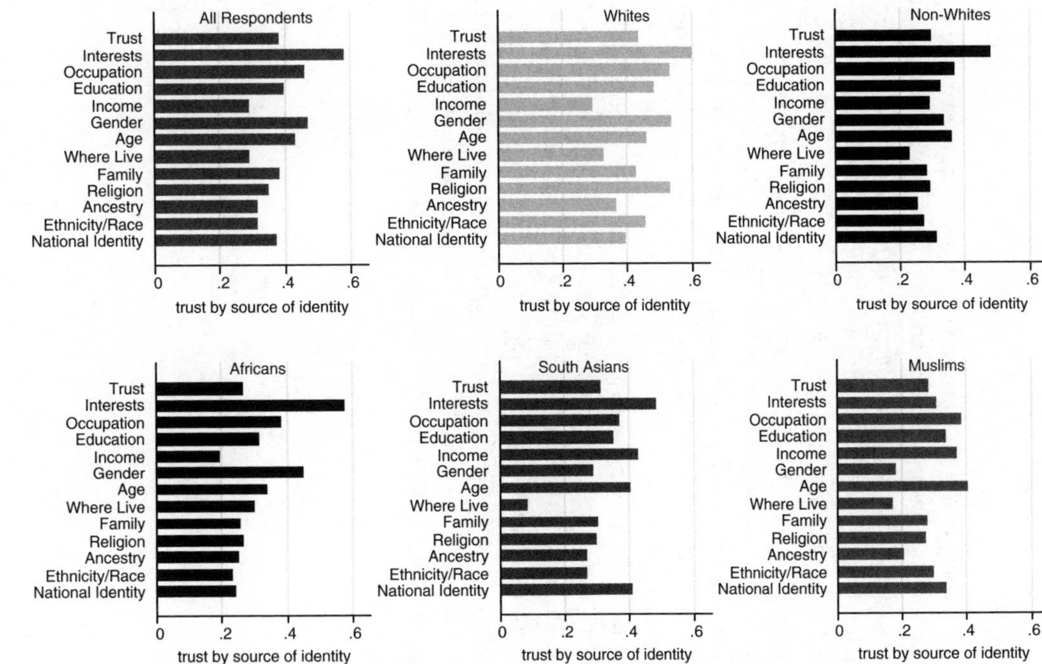

FIGURE 2.9. Trust by source of identity. UK Citizenship Survey 2007 Ethnicity

Only 27 percent give this source of identity if less than half are of their same background. For nonwhites the comparable figures are 49 and 31 percent. Segregation reinforces in-group identity, which in turn leads to lower out-group trust.

The Path Ahead

I move now to a consideration of how living in an integrated and diverse neighborhood and having a diverse friendship network can boost trust. The evidence suggests that such connections can lead people to be more trusting – at least until we realize that residential choice itself depends upon trust (Chapter 8). My argument in this chapter sets the stage for various threads in the rest of the book: why inequality depresses trust for minorities, why it also mostly depresses the effects of Allport's conditions for contact for minorities, why one country (Sweden) stands out as distinctive, and why in the end we need to place segregation in the context of economic inequality.

We cannot understand why segregation's effects are so pernicious and why they are so difficult to overcome if we don't make the connection of isolation with inequality. Even in countries with much lower levels of inequality than the United States and without the pronounced hypersegregation faced by African-Americans, the combination of ethnic enclaves, inequality, and discrimination cannot be easily overcome by rearranging housing patterns as if we were playing a game of Monopoly.

3

Building Trust in a Segregated Society: The United States

> It is very appropriate then that from this Cradle of the Confederacy, this very Heart of the Great Anglo-Saxon Southland, that today we sound the drum for freedom as have our generations of forebears before us done, time and time again through history. Let us rise to the call of freedom-loving blood that is in us and send our answer to the tyranny that clanks its chains upon the South. In the name of the greatest people that have ever trod this earth, I draw the line in the dust and toss the gauntlet before the feet of tyranny ... and I say ... segregation today ... segregation tomorrow ... segregation forever.
>
> Inaugural address of Governor George C. Wallace of Alabama, January 14, 1963

> Ain't gonna let segregation turn me around
> Turn me around, turn me around
> Ain't gonna let segregation turn me around
> I'm gonna keep on a-walkin', keep on a-talkin'
> Marchin' up to freedom's land
>
> Children's song from the civil rights movement in the United States

> All persons shall be entitled to be free, at any establishment or place, from discrimination or segregation of any kind on the ground of race, color, religion, or national origin, if such discrimination or segregation is or purports to be required by any law, statute, ordinance, regulation, rule, or order of a State or any agency or political subdivision thereof.
>
> Title II, Section 202, Civil Rights Act of 1964[1]

[1] Text of Wallace's inaugural address is available at http://www.archives.state.al.us/govs_list/inauguralspeech.html. "Ain't Gonna Let Nobody Turn Me Around" lyrics at http://www.songsforteaching.com/folk/aintgonnaletnobodyturnmearound.php; text of the Civil Rights Act of 1964 available at http://coursesa.matrix.msu.edu/~hst306/documents/civil64.html, all accessed January 11, 2011.

Americans once were a trusting people. In 1960, almost 60 percent of Americans believed that "most people can be trusted." Throughout the 1960s over half of Americans were trusters, but the 1970s brought a precipitous decline and by the 1990s only 38 percent of Americans gave trusting responses (Uslaner, 2002, 6–7). By 2006 and 2008, barely more than a third did.[2]

The United States *should be* a high-trusting country. It was America, after all, where Tocqueville (1945, 122–3) uncovered "self-interest rightly understood," the idea that people base their actions on core values (religious for Tocqueville) that lead them to think beyond gains for themselves. "Self-interest rightly understood" is now widely acknowledged to be the root of generalized trust.

America was destined to be a trusting society. Trust rests upon a sense of optimism and economic equality. Optimistic people are willing to take the risks involved in trusting people they don't know and who may be different from themselves. Their belief that the world is a good place and that it is going to get better is a (psychological) insurance policy that makes people feel more secure. Optimists are also more likely to have a sense of control – to believe that *they can make the world better through their own actions*. Herbert Croly, the progressive theorist, expressed what became known as the American Dream well:

> Our country is ... figured in the imagination of its citizens as the Land of Promise. [Americans] believe that somehow and sometime something better will happen to good Americans than has happened to men in any other country ... the future will have something better in store for them individually and collectively than has the past or the present. (1965, 3)

Henry Steele Commager argued, "Nothing in all history had succeeded like America, and every American knew it" (1950, 5). In public opinion polls taken from the late 1930s to the 1960s, Americans believed that their children would have a better life than they did (Uslaner, 1993, 76). This creed is essential to American culture; it was the promise that guided immigrants to come to a land where streets were paved with gold. David Potter (1954) called Americans a "people of plenty."

Control over our environment is also central to American values. The *Economist* (1987, 12) expressed this ideal well and linked it to the more general belief that tomorrow will be better than today: "Optimism, not necessity, has always been the mother of invention in America. To every

[2] The 2006 and 2008 data come from the General Social Survey. Other data cited come from this source unless otherwise noted.

problem – whether racial bigotry or putting a man on the moon – there has always been a solution, if only ingenuity and money were committed to it."

America was also an egalitarian society – if not yet economically, then at least socially. Lord Bryce, like Tocqueville a nineteenth-century European visitor to the United States, saw social equality as the key to understanding why Americans were more trusting and generous than Europeans:

> People meet on a simple and natural footing, with more frankness and ease than is possible in countries where every one is either looking up or looking down.... This naturalness ... enlarges the circle of possible friendships.... It expands the range of a man's sympathies, and makes it easier for him to enter into the sentiments of other classes than his own. It gives a sense of solidarity to the whole nation, cutting away the ground for the jealousies and grudges which distract people. (1916, 873–4)

Americans were both optimistic and trusting in the 1960s, a period of great prosperity that historian William O'Neill (1986) called the "American high." American income was more equitably distributed in the post-World War II period through the 1970s than it was in other periods of American history (Pikkety and Saez, 2004, esp. table 2).

Economic and social equality solidified the idea of America as a melting pot, with the national motto *E pluribus unum* (one out of many). This overarching national identity breaks down barriers among groups and leads to generalized, rather than particularized, trust.

Trust began to drop as inequality began to rise in the mid-1970s. To be sure, inequality initially rose more slowly than trust fell. Factors in American life such as urban discontent and the war in Vietnam may have started the downward slide in trust, and trust and inequality moved strongly in opposite directions (Uslaner, 2002, 183–7). As inequality increased, Americans no longer felt so sure that life would be better for the next generation or for the average person today. As Americans became less confident in the future, they had less faith in each other (Uslaner, 2002, 166).

In this chapter I examine levels of trust in American society and how living in a diverse integrated neighborhood with heterogeneous friendship networks can lead to greater faith in others. The effects are considerable, in part due to the high levels of segregation and inequality in the United States compared to other Western countries. Segregation and especially inequality lead to low levels of trust, especially among minorities. African-Americans and Hispanics have markedly lower levels of trust than do whites – but whites have become less trusting over time. The evidence I present in this chapter suggests that having friends of different backgrounds in diverse and integrated neighborhoods can boost faith in others among whites, African-Americans, and Hispanics. The effects are somewhat greater for whites than for blacks, but the effects for both are substantial, especially in comparative perspective. I also show that diversity *does* drive down trust, but that Allport's optimal conditions build trust more than diversity leads to lower faith in people.

Cracks in the Melting Pot

The Liberty Bell (in Independence Hall in downtown Philadelphia) is a classic symbol of American freedom. The bell rang on July 8, 1776 to call citizens to the first public reading of the Declaration of Independence. However, the bell is cracked. The fissure ultimately made the bill unable to be rung.[3]

The crack also highlights the fissions in the melting pot. While Bryce and others (including Tocqueville) were duly impressed with the equality and sociability of Americans, the descendants of early settlers did not always treat new immigrants as equals. During boom times Americans could be welcoming and inclusive, but when the economy was struggling, the dominant white Protestants could be hostile to people who did not look like themselves (Fetzer, 2001). From the mid-nineteenth century through the 1930s, Catholic and Jewish immigrants were widely viewed as "so much slag in the melting pot" (cited in Higham 1951, 277) by the Protestant majority. The Know-Nothing Party in the 1850s sought to restrict the voting rights of Catholics, while other associations sought to end immigration by members of ethnic and religious minorities because they were seen as genetically inferior (McCloskey and Zaller, 1984, 68–9). Over time Catholics and Jews entered the mainstream and "became white" (Goldstein, 2006). By 2008, white Americans rated Jews and Catholics at 65 and 66 on a "feeling thermometer" scale (in the American National Election Study) ranging from 0 to 100, with whites at 73 and Christians at 76. Catholics became undistinguishable from other Americans on generalized trust (in the 2006 and 2008 General Social Survey), while Jews are substantially more trusting (by 11 percent), though this may reflect their higher level of education.

[3] See http://www.ushistory.org/libertybell/.

Some groups, however, have a much higher hurdle to overcome to become accepted as fully American (much less white): Asian-Americans, Hispanics, and especially African-Americans. Whites proclaim that they view each of these groups positively, with average thermometer ratings of 64, 63, and 66, respectively. Asian-Americans are the most integrated of these minorities, often called a "model minority."[4] Asian-Americans have more education than do whites and live among whites in integrated neighborhoods. Asian-Americans are, unsurprisingly, as trusting as whites, even as they have higher levels of education.[5]

The two largest minorities – African-Americans and Hispanics – are less well integrated into white society. For African-Americans, the history of racial discrimination, from slavery to Jim Crow (discriminatory laws primarily in the South),[6] needs no elaboration. Race is – and continues to be – the major divide in American society. Myrdal argued that race was the defining issue challenging the idea that the United States could become "one out of many":

> *The "American Dilemma" ... is the ever-raging conflict between ... the "American Creed," where the American thinks, talks, and acts under the influence of high national ... precepts, and, on the other hand, the valuations on specific planes of individual and group living, where ... group prejudice against particular persons or types of people... dominate his outlook.* (1964, lxxi, italics in original)

Myrdal wrote, "Discrimination against the Negro ... is so great that it becomes qualitative ... the fettering of the Negro spirit is not accomplished so much by simple discrimination as by the prejudice inherent even in the most friendly but restrictive expectancy." Three decades after the original publication of Myrdal's *An American Dilemma*, Campbell, Converse, and Rodgers restated the same thesis: "The history of the black experience in America is not one which would naturally inspire confidence in the benign intentions of one's fellow man" (1976, 456). It is not surprising that minorities in the United States and elsewhere are less trusting of their fellow citizens.

The Social Capital Benchmark Survey (SCBS), which has both national and subnational samples, has higher estimates of trust than those in other

4 See http://www.asian-nation.org/headlines/2009/06/model-minority-image-balancing-praise-caution/.

5 In the combined 2006 and 2008 General Social Survey, 41 percent of Asian-American respondents believed that "most people can be trusted," compared to 40 percent of whites, an insignificant difference. Asian-American respondents had on average 15 years of education, compared to 13.7 for whites.

6 See http://www.jimcrowhistory.org/history/creating2.htm.

surveys, but for this and other surveys whites are considerably more trusting than minorities. For the SCBS, 54 percent of respondents – and 61 percent of whites in the subnational sample – give trusting responses; 31 percent of Hispanics and 28 percent of African-Americans are trusters. For the General Social Survey – which has the longest and most complete time series on trust of any American survey – in 2006 and 2008, 34 percent of all respondents, 39 percent of whites, but just 16 percent of Hispanics and 15 percent of African-Americans have faith in others.[7] The estimate for Hispanics is identical to that for the 1989–90 Latino survey I shall employ below (de la Garza, Garcia, and Garcia, 1998).[8]

Whites have become less trusting over time, closely tracking increases in inequality. In 1960 and 1964, almost 60 percent of whites were trusters; as late as 1972–3, 53 percent of whites believed that "most people can be trusted."[9] Trust levels among African-Americans are less precisely estimated because of smaller samples of blacks in national surveys. In 1964, 22 percent of African-Americans were trusters. In the General Social Survey, 19 percent of African-Americans were trusting from 1972–80 and 15 percent thereafter. The 1996 National Black Election Study, with almost 1,200 African-American respondents, had 18 percent trusting respondents.

The larger story is twofold. First, trust among the majority whites was high in the United States at well over 50 percent until the mid-1970s. Only a handful of other countries – the Nordic nations, the Netherlands, Canada, and Australia – now have a majority of their respondents as trusters. Whites in the United States have become less trusting and America now ranks below other industrialized nations on trust and above them on inequality.[10] Second, minorities – notably African-Americans and Hispanics – have much lower levels of trust than do whites. At least for African-Americans, there is far less evidence of a downward trend in trust

[7] The *New York Times* Millennium Survey (1999) reports 39 percent of respondents as trusting. The 2001 World Values Survey – which I find problematic for many countries – reports 36 percent of Americans as trusting, far closer to the --- GSS than to the SCBS.

[8] For a description of this national survey, see http://www.icpsr.umich.edu/icpsrweb/ICPSR/studies/6841/detail.

[9] The 1960 estimates are from the Civic Culture survey, the first time the trust question was asked in a national survey in the United States. The 1964 estimates are from the American National Election Study. The 1972–3 and later surveys are from the General Social Survey.

[10] On inequality, see Deininger and Squire (1996) and the WIDER World Economic Inequality Database (available at http://www.wider.unu.edu/research/Database/en_GB/database/).

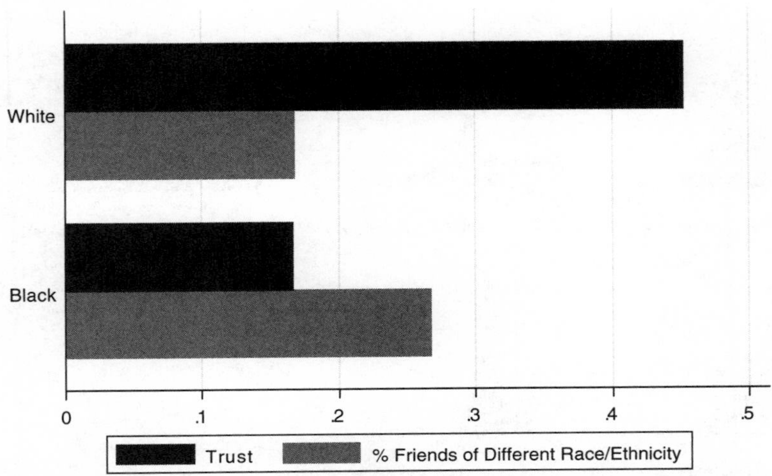

FIGURE 3.1. Trust and friendship mix by race. US General Social Survey

as we see for whites with a weaker tie to inequality.[11] Trust was low and remains low.

African-Americans are not mistrusting because they don't know whites or have white friends. Twenty-seven percent of African-Americans have a friend of a different race, compared to only 17 percent of whites, even as they are less considerably trusting (see Figure 3.1).[12] As 11 percent of the population, blacks are simply more likely to have friends of a different race than are whites (70 percent). African-Americans are more likely to live in racially isolated neighborhoods than are whites (see Figure 3.2). While Asian-Americans and Hispanics largely live in integrated neighborhoods, whites and African-Americans are more likely to live among people like themselves.

Residential Isolation in the United States

Segregation among minority groups is ubiquitous. New immigrants seek out people like themselves to ease their transition into a new country (de

[11] I estimated trust for African-Americans from a variety of national surveys over time (though with perilously small samples for some years). The simple correlation between trust for all respondents and annual Gini indices is -.77, compared to -.36 for African-Americans' trust.

[12] These results come from creating a dummy variable for having friends of a different race using the entire General Social Survey data set from 1972 to 2008.

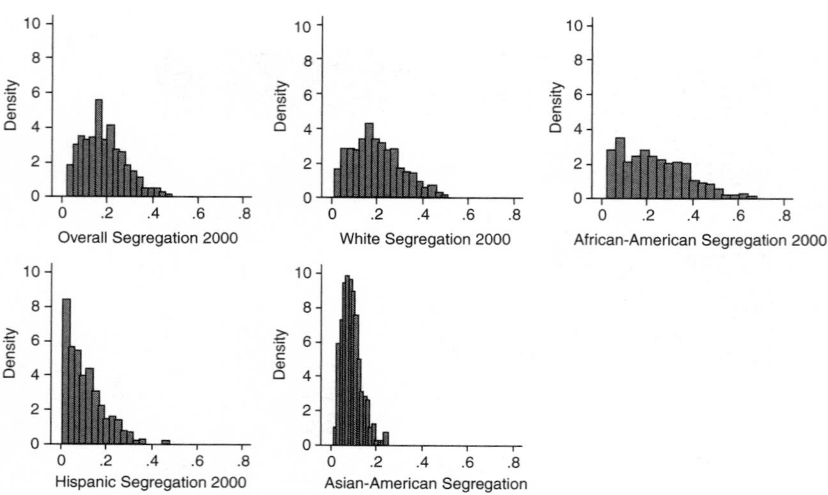

FIGURE 3.2. Segregation in American SMSAs. Iceland Data for 325 Areas

Souza Briggs, 2005, 72). Ethnic enclaves provide havens of familiar food, religious institutions, and conversation and periodicals in one's native language. Wirth (1927, 1938) wrote of how the ethnic ghetto isolated Jewish immigrants at the turn of the century (see Chapter 2), but Massey and Denton disputed the notion of a self-contained ghetto (1993, 32–3). Enclaves at the turn of the twentieth century in the United States, much like those found in many Western countries today, were a mish-mash of ethnic groups (but see Lieberson, 1961, 55): "even at the height of their segregation early in this century, European ethnic groups did not experience a particularly high degree of isolation ... ethnic enclaves proved to be a fleeting, transitory stage in the process of immigrant isolation." For most ethnic groups, including Hispanics and Asians, as succeeding generations achieve economic success, they move into majority white neighborhoods (Cutler, Glaeser, and Vigdor, 2005, 206; Massey and Denton, 1993, 87).

In the nineteenth century, segregation was not pronounced in the United States. From the end of the nineteenth century through 1940, segregation became commonplace as African-Americans moved from the South to the North. White immigrant groups lived in enclaves that were moderately segregated but in close proximity to each other. African-Americans, though not so numerous, and whites also lived near each other in both the North and the South (Massey and Denton, 1993, 17).

By 1910, the index of racial segregation in Northern cities increased by almost 30 percent from its 1860 level, and by 1940, whites and blacks in Northern cities largely lived in different worlds. Segregation was on a consistent upward march: by 1940, 70 percent of African-Americans would have to move for neighborhoods to resemble overall demographic patterns of the city; by 1970, the share had increased to 80 percent. Most African-Americans lived in census tracts that were more than two-thirds black (Cutler, Glaeser, and Vigdor, 1997, 471; Massey and Denton, 1993, 30–1).

The large-scale influx of blacks to the North created the modern American ghetto. Wilkes and Iceland argue that "black segregation is unique" (2004, 33). No other group has experienced such hypersegregation: African-Americans live apart from other groups, concentrated in small areas and centralized in the center of an urban area. There were no hypersegregated American Indian or Asian-American cities in 2000 and just two Hispanic hypersegregated metropolitan areas, but 29 communities with black–white hypersegregation (Massey and Denton, 1993, 74; Wilkes and Iceland, 2004, 29–32). Fewer than 15 percent of African-Americans live in areas where blacks constitute less than 10 percent of the population and a third live in census tracts that are two-thirds or more African-American (Clark, Putnam, and Fieldhouse, 2010, 29). Because of this isolation of African-Americans, the United States has far more pronounced segregation than other English-speaking countries (Johnston, Poulsen, and Forrest, 2007).[13]

Industrialization in the early twentieth century created a need for blue-collar workers in the North. As blacks moved north for better jobs, whites took action to ensure that their neighborhoods remained white. Real estate agents were the central actors enforcing segregation. Their professional association's code stated: "a realtor should never be instrumental in introducing into a neighborhood a character of property or occupancy, members of any race or nationality, or any individuals whose presence will clearly be detrimental to property values in that neighborhood" (Morrill, 1975, 155). Insurance companies would direct whites and blacks to different neighborhoods, make mortgage requirements and down payments more onerous for African-Americans, and refuse to

[13] The Alesina data give different results: The United States ranks 20th of 97 countries, ahead of the United Kingdom (39th), New Zealand (46th), and Australia (56th); and industrialized non-English-speaking countries such as Finland (55th), Switzerland (61st), and Belgium (80th).

make some loans at all. Many communities had restrictive covenants, sometimes implicit but often explicit – as in Baltimore's 1910 ordinance establishing distinct areas in the city for whites and African-Americans. Strong demand from the large number of new migrants to large cities led to price spikes for housing, so rents and house prices were much greater than those in white areas (Johnston, 1991, 252; Massey and Denton, 1993, 36, 41–2).

The federal government did little to block segregation. The Supreme Court in 1917 ruled that a residential segregation law in Louisville, Kentucky was unconstitutional. However, neither the courts nor any other agency of the government took strong action to block segregation. Franklin D. Roosevelt's New Deal included an experimental public housing program that grew rapidly during and after World War II. These projects were overwhelmingly segregated and remained so through the 1970s. In 1962 President John F. Kennedy signed an executive order banning discrimination in federal properties. Yet despite his actions, two civil rights laws outlawing discrimination in both public and private housing, and a stronger code by realtors in the 1970s, segregation persisted. The Department of Housing and Urban Development did not receive any resources to begin investigations of discrimination and to take action against violators until 1988 (Coulibaly, Green, and Jones, 1998, 69–71, 82, 93, 118; Johnston, 1991, 252–3; Massey and Denton, 1993, 36, 41–2, 195–6, 210–11).

In recent decades, segregation between whites and African-Americans has slowly decreased (Iceland and Weinberg with Steinmetz, 2002, 110), although it has increased for Hispanics and Asians as many new immigrants have come to the United States (Iceland and Scopilliti, 2008, 85). Cities have become more diverse (less white) and overall segregation levels have fallen (Iceland, 2009, 113).

Decreasing segregation for African-Americans is *not* strongly linked to upward mobility for blacks as it is for other groups. Even wealthy blacks are largely isolated from whites (Massey and Denton, 1993, 85; Watson, 2009, 23). For most groups, segregation reinforces economic inequality. Of course, it does so for African-Americans as well, but it also leads to social isolation even for blacks who have succeeded economically. The departure of middle- and upper-income blacks from the ghetto has led to even greater inequality for those left behind (Wilson, 1987). While racial segregation may have declined, *income segregation* has dramatically increased since 1970, especially isolating poor African-Americans. They are less likely to live among people who are not poor, and this mixing of economic and racial segregation has occurred in almost every metropolitan area (Jargowsky, 1996, 990; Massey, 1996, 397; Soss and Jacobs, 2009, 123). Two-thirds of African-Americans now live in neighborhoods with at least 20 percent in poverty compared to six percent of whites – this leads to a sharp drop in income for most blacks from one generation to the next (Sharkey, 2009, 9–11).

The most diverse communities in the United States are New York City, Oakland (California), Jersey City (New Jersey), and Los Angeles.[14] The most segregated communities are Detroit, Cleveland, Gary (Indiana), and Monroe (Louisiana). There is no overlap in these "top" ranked areas. The least diverse areas – three cities in Pennsylvania (Altoona, Scranton, and Johnstown), one in West Virginia (Parkersburg), and one in Iowa (Dubuque) – do not show up in the most integrated communities.

African-Americans are more segregated than any other group, with a mean multigroup entropy score of .23, followed by whites at .19, Hispanics at .11, and Asian-Americans at .09. (The medians are virtually identical to the means.) The most segregated cities are not necessarily the largest: the correlations between the entropy measures and population size range from .30 for African-Americans to .39 for Hispanics). Nor are segregation patterns similar across different groups. The correlations range from .30 to .40 except for two groups that are segregated in the same communities: African-Americans and Hispanics. The entropy correlation for the two groups correlate at .85. Blacks and Hispanics are most segregated in two smaller cities (Lawrence, Massachusetts and Reading, Pennsylvania) and one big city (Chicago). Whites, as the largest population group, are most isolated where overall segregation is greatest (Detroit; Monroe, Louisiana; and Cleveland). Asians are most segregated in smaller communities (Lafayette, Louisiana; Amarillo, Texas; Ann Arbor, Michigan) and one big city (New York).

Can "Optimal Contact" Build Trust?

In the face of such high levels of segregation between blacks and whites and of declining trust, can "optimal contact" build trust? I test this argument with data from the SCBS (see Chapter 2), which has the advantage of including local subsamples for 40 communities, and I match data on diversity and segregation for the 20 communities that correspond to

[14] All of these results come from Iceland's (2009) database of 325 Standard Metropolitan Statistical Areas.

standard metropolitan statistical areas.[15] I merge the aggregate data on diversity and segregation with survey data on trust. I then estimate models of trust for all respondents, whites, and African-Americans. There are not sufficient numbers of respondents to estimate models for Hispanics or Asian-Americans. For Hispanics, I use the 1989–90 Latino National Political Survey that includes questions on trust, friendship networks, and the perceived diversity of their neighborhoods. There are no city codes to merge demographic data with the survey data, so I will have to make do with perceptions of community diversity/segregation.

I estimate the models for trust by probit analysis, with standard errors clustered by community,[16] and assess the impacts of each variable by the change in the probability of trusting obtained by setting each variable first at its minimum and then at its maximum while leaving all of the other variables at their "natural" values – what Rosenstone and Hansen (1993) call the "effects" of a variable. Positive effects indicate that trust increases as one moves from the minimum to the maximum value of the predictor in question (other things being equal). I present these effects in Figure 3.3. For these models and others I present the effects for the core variables of interest in figures, which provide a more vivid presentation of results than do tables.[17]

For the SCBS I can test the effects of segregation and diversity on trust to see which matters more. However, using the simple measure of segregation does not work well for American communities. Segregation is measured as the share of people in a neighborhood who would have to move to make the area resemble the larger community. If both a neighborhood and a community are overwhelmingly white – as we see in the least segregated city in the data set, Yakima, Washington – the area can be segregated but not diverse.

15 Some communities were either too large (states such as Indiana, Montana, and New Hampshire) or too poorly defined ("rural Southeast South Dakota," "Central Oregon," and "East Tennessee") to merge survey and aggregate data. I cannot use the General Social Survey (which has a more reliable estimate of trust), since codes for residence are not readily available. The larger number of cases for the local subsamples in the SCBS) make the results of merging data more reliable overall. The average sample size for the 20 communities is 509, with the minimum being 449 (Houston-Baytown-Sugarland, Texas) and the maximum being 1,409 (Charlotte-Gastonia-Concord, North Carolina-South Carolina). Nine had samples with fewer than 500 respondents.

16 Clustering the standard errors corrects for variations in the individual-level coefficients that may be due to variations across communities.

17 More detailed results are available upon request.

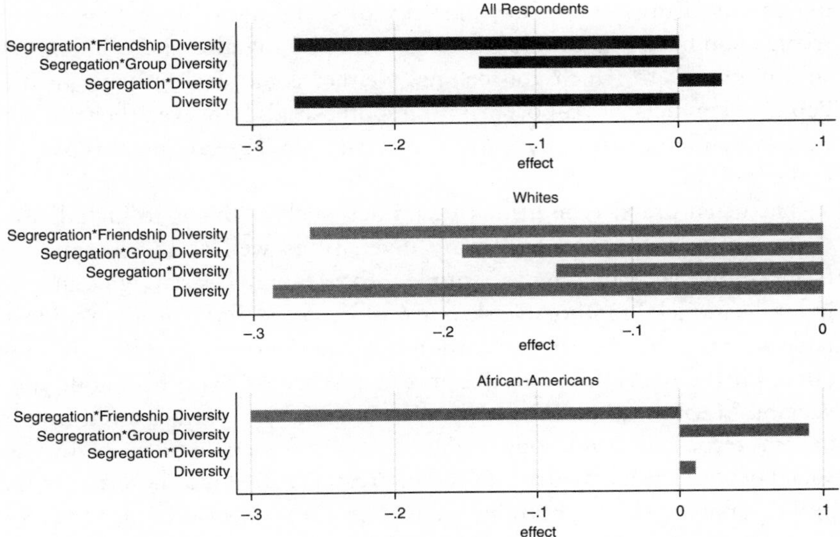

FIGURE 3.3. Probit effects for segregation, diversity, and social networks in the United States. Social Capital Benchmark Survey

While diversity is more of a surrogate for the minority share of the population and segregation is not, there is at least a moderate relationship between residential segregation and the nonwhite share of a city's population. The two most integrated communities (Lewiston, Maine and Bismark, North Dakota) are almost all white. The segregation measure has the interpretation of the share of members of each neighborhood that would have to move in order to make that area representative of the larger community. For a very homogenous community, few would have to move but we would not consider that area integrated in our normal discourse. So I create an interaction term between the measures of diversity and segregation that captures the idea of an integrated *and* diverse community. A simple multiplication of the segregation and diversity indices would yield maximum values for highly segregated and diverse communities and minimum values for integrated but less diverse communities. So my interaction term has lower values for *integrated and diverse communities* and higher values for segregated communities, leading to the expectations of *negative* signs for this interaction (and the composite measures discussed below) to indicate greater trust.

For the models I estimate for the United States, I include the diversity measure and the interaction between diversity and segregation. I also use two measures of the heterogeneity of social networks – how many friends you have of a different background and the diversity of membership in groups to which you belong. Neither is an ideal measure of the depth of contacts, as Allport (1958) hypothesized. However, they are the best available measures and group diversity may approximate the optimal condition.

The usual practice in estimating models such as this is to include the measures of group and friendship diversity as well as the interaction terms. However, including the simple measures induces strong collinearity in the model. Brambor, Clark, and Golder argue that "the analyst must have a strong theoretical expectation that the omitted variable ... has no effect on the dependent variable in the absence of the other modifying variable" (2006, 68) and the ... modifying variable ... is measured with a natural zero. Both conditions hold here. I have argued that a more diverse social network is insufficient to lead to greater trust – and the segregation and diversity measures both have natural zero points (Iceland, 2004, 8). Including the simple measures of friendship and group diversity does not gain us anything theoretically since I expect that their coefficients should be insignificant – and doing so induces substantial collinearity, driving all coefficients to insignificance.

I use the interaction term by itself and to create two more complex interactions reflecting my theoretical framework. Diversity and segregation should not matter as much as *living in an integrated and diverse neighborhood and having diverse social networks*. I thus interact the segregation/diversity measure with the breadth of friendship networks and groups people join. The interactions give us measures of whether people have diverse social networks (friendships and group memberships) *in diverse and integrated neighborhoods*.

These interaction terms lead to complications in interpretations. The usual tests of significance are not applicable to interaction terms in probit models. Nor can one estimate changes in probabilities for each term independently (Ai and Norton, 2003). Instead, I derive probabilities for each of the four terms (diversity, segregation/diversity interaction, and the three-way interactions) by setting the other three measures at their median values and the variable of interest at its minimum value (with the remaining variables at their "natural" values). I then "reset" the variable of interest to its maximum and estimate another set of probabilities. The difference in these probabilities are the effects.

I estimate the models (with standard errors clustered by municipality) for all respondents and then separately for whites and African-Americans and present the effects for core variables in Figure 3.3.[18] We know that African-Americans are less trusting and that the determinants of trust are different for blacks and whites (Uslaner, 2002, 35–6). Since African-Americans are likely to live in segregated communities, the effects of segregation might be different for blacks and whites. Since segregation is so pervasive, segregation or diversity might not directly effect the levels of trust of African-Americans, but where blacks do live among whites and have close white friends, I would expect such ties to shape trust for African-Americans and whites.

There is also evidence that older and especially more highly educated people are more trusting (Uslaner, 2002, ch. 4). I include race, age, education, and the share of African-Americans and the mean level of education in a city. I also include a measure of whether people treat you as dishonest, since negative treatment may lead to distrust.[19] I wanted to estimate a model for trust based upon my previous work (Uslaner, 2002, ch. 4, esp. 99), however, the SCBS did not have measures of optimism or control, so the model here is a truncated one.

For all respondents and whites, diversity *does* seem to drive down trust substantially. For all respondents, living in the most diverse city (Houston)

[18] The most highly educated respondents are 34 percent more likely to trust others than the least educated. Negative effects indicate less trust for the higher values of the predictor. African-Americans (coded 1) are 21 percent less trusting than nonblacks (coded zero). Race, age, and especially education (both at the individual and city level) have powerful effects. If people treat you as if you were dishonest, you will be less likely to trust them. Predictors – education, age, the average level of education in a city, and the percent of African-American in a city – matter more for whites than for African-Americans. Even being treated as dishonest leads to a sharper drop in trust for whites (15 percent) than for blacks (11 percent), which seems remarkable since 42 percent of African-Americans compared to half as many whites believe that people treat them as if they were dishonest. The answer to this puzzle may rest in a more general account of why African-Americans are less trusting: even if a black person has not experienced discrimination, he or she will certainly know someone who has faced such bias, and such knowledge can readily translate into distrust. Personal experiences play a lesser role in explaining the level of trust for African-Americans than for whites (Uslaner, 2002, 35–6). Such an explanation may also account for the weaker, indeed insignificant, effects of joining a group with diverse membership on blacks. People who have long faced discrimination might well demand more than group diversity to prove that people of different backgrounds are trustworthy. Closer personal ties through friendship in integrated settings seemingly reduces the trust gap for blacks.

[19] Putnam treats honesty as simply a measure of trust (2000, 135–6). My previous work (Uslaner, 2002, 72, n. 18) shows that the two are related but not the same thing: the 1972 American National Election Study included both the generalized trust question and whether "most people are honest." The correlation (tau-c) between the two measures is modest (.345) and barely more than half of respondents who said that "most people are honest" agreed that "most people can be trusted."

will reduce the probability of trusting others by 27 percent compared to residing in the least diverse city. The effect for whites is 29 percent, but diversity is insignificant for African-Americans (with a minuscule effect). The interaction of segregation and diversity seems to have a perverse positive effect: living in the most integrated diverse city (Seattle) is predicted to lead to a 22 percent decline in trust for all respondents in the most diverse integrated city (Seattle) compared to the most segregated diverse city (Detroit). This result is anomalous since trust is far higher in Seattle (70 percent) compared to Detroit (49 percent). This result vanishes in the estimations for both whites and African-Americans and is likely due to the collinearity between the interaction term and diversity and the two three-way interactions (all with correlations above .6).

Integration is not simply an alternative to diversity. The diversity measure is a surrogate measure for the share of a city's population that is white. For the 20 SCBS communities in this analysis, the correlation between the diversity index and the percentage of a city's population that is white is -.917 for the 20 SCBS cities with comparable measures from Iceland (2004), compared to just -.305 for the segregation measure.[20] The diversity index may simply show low levels of trust in communities with large nonwhite populations rather than a reluctance of people to interact with people of different backgrounds.

Friendship networks matter in integrated and diverse areas *for blacks and whites equally*. Having friends of different backgrounds in communities with lower segregation boosts trust by 27 percent for all respondents and for whites and by 30 percent for African-Americans. This effect offsets the "loss" for diversity for all respondents and whites and is the only measure of segregation or diversity that matters for African-Americans. All respondents and whites get an additional boost if they join a group with diverse membership in an integrated community – by 13 percent and 19 percent. It is ironic that African-Americans do *not* become more trusting from membership in diverse group memberships, because they are considerably more likely than whites to be members of groups with

[20] The SCBS has a Herfindahl measure for each community. The zero-order correlation for the 41 communities between fractionalization and percent white for the aggregated data is -.959. The aggregate data show a strong negative correlation between trust and diversity ($r = -.662$, $N = 41$). When I add the shares of population in a community who are African-American and Hispanic to a regression, diversity is no longer significant ($t = -.032$), while the African-American and Hispanic population shares are significant at $p < .001$ and $p < .10$, respectively ($t = -3.41$ and -1.62, one-tailed tests). See also the discussion in Chapter 2.

diverse memberships. *The central result is that diverse friendship networks in integrated diverse communities build trust for both whites and African-Americans.*

Membership in diverse groups only seems to matter for whites. It may be that group ties may be more optimal or close for whites than for blacks. This suggests that the optimal conditions are not as easily met for minority groups as they are for the majority (which we shall encounter elsewhere). Nevertheless, social ties in an integrated and diverse setting do seem to matter for both whites and African-Americans more than diversity (however conceived) leads to lower levels of faith in others.

I also estimate a model for particularized trust, using the racial trust measures in the SCBS. Particularized trust is having faith *only* in your own group. I measure such in-group favoritism as having a very high level of trust for one's own race (white, African-American, or Asian) but *not* trusting other races.[21] Particularized trust is negatively related to generalized trust (tau-c = -.280). So I expect that the results for particularized trust, which I present in Figure 3.4, to mirror those for generalized trust – similar effects but reversed signs. Since particularized trust is a categorical variable, I estimate the models by ordered probit, but this means that there is no simple overall effect for each variable. I present results for the probability of strong particularized trusters (only trusting their own race), which are a distinct minority (three percent of respondents), and for the cutpoint between generalized and particularized trusters (a zero value for the index). This "middle category" is by far the most prevalent, comprising almost 70 percent of respondents.

For all respondents, living in a segregated area without diverse friendships leads to a predicted sharp rise in the probability of particularized trust – by nine percent overall and 14 percent for whites, outside the bounds of the share of particularized trusters. The effects are even greater for the cutpoint: 13 and 14.4 percent, respectively. *Residential and social isolation leads to strong in-group trust at the expense of a generalized faith in others, at least for whites.* For African-Americans, the effects seem to be either small or perhaps perversely negative. I am tempted to dismiss these results since the SCBS yields very high levels of trust in racial out-groups for blacks, who have low levels of generalized trust.

21 The index runs from -2 (high trust in one's own race and both other races) to +1 (high trust in your race but little trust in either of the other races). The overall racial trust measures are highly skewed in the SCBS (with about 60 percent trusting people of different races), so this is a very conservative measure.

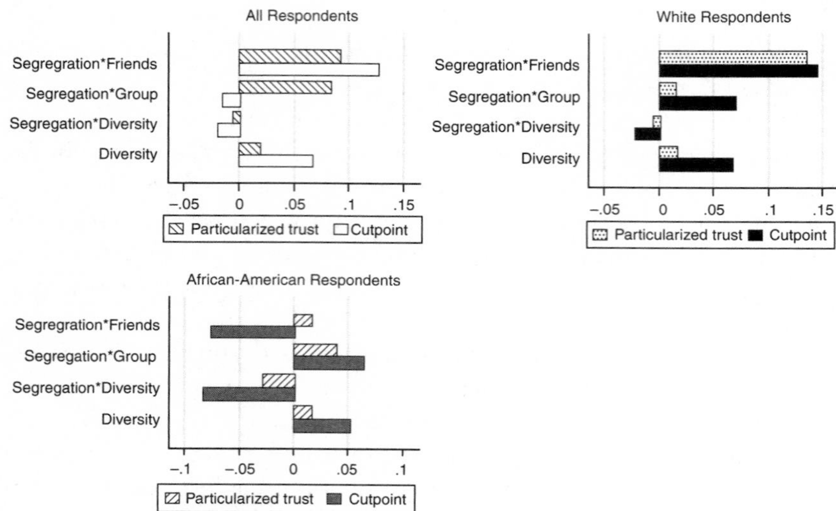

FIGURE 3.4. Probit effects on particularized trust. Social Capital Benchmark Survey

Living in a segregated neighborhood and belonging to groups consisting only of members of your own race seems to increase in-group favoritism overall and for African-Americans in particular. Living in a segregated and diverse area seems to have little effect by itself on whites, but for African-Americans seems to reduce in-group bias. For everyone, diversity leads to more in-group trust. The effects are small for particularized trust, but greater for the cutpoint. The evidence for particularized trust is not as powerful as it is for generalized trust, most likely because of the skewed distributions of this measure of in-group trust. The clearest pattern is for segregation and homogenous social networks for whites, which strongly predicts in-group favoritism.[22]

Trust, Context, and Social Ties for Hispanics

Hispanics are less segregated from whites than are African-Americans. However, they still fare badly on many socioeconomic indicators. On home ownership, education, and income, Hispanics are considerably below whites and similar to African-Americans (Rodriguez, 2006). And

[22] Education, age, and being treated dishonestly are all highly significant in each model. The mean level of education is not significant in any of the estimations.

there is evidence that segregation is increasing (Martin, 2007, 43) and that Hispanics face considerable discrimination (Charles, 2006, 60, 149). Segregation has increased as more immigrants from Latin America have entered the United States and seek out others from their home country. Hispanics are hardly monolithic and form their identity based upon their country of origin – trust across Latino groups (Porter and Washington, 1993, 141) and a strong sense of identification with the mother country is likely to lead to strong in-group trust. Perceptions of discrimination reinforce this identity and are associated with low out-group trust as found in multiple surveys. While only 27 percent of Hispanics report personal experiences of discrimination in the 1989–90 survey, more than a third say that different Latino groups – Mexican-Americans, Cuban-Americans, and Puerto Ricans – face discrimination, about the same share who see bias against African-Americans.

The level of segregation for Hispanics is far lower than it is for African-Americans. A third of Hispanics say that their friends are a 50–50 mix of Anglos and Hispanics and an additional seven percent say that they are mostly Anglos. The results are almost identical when people are asked with whom they socialize. Perhaps the closest indicator of Allport's optimal conditions are the people you relax with and respondents clearly have diverse networks: 55 percent say that these networks are half or more with Anglos. There are thus many opportunities for interactions with people of different backgrounds. The survey also asked about the Hispanic density of one's neighborhood. So I interact each measure of the heterogeneity of one's networks with the level of diversity of one's neighborhood. Since the three indicators are closely related, I estimate a separate model for each. I use instrumental variable probit since I cannot assume that the heterogeneity of networks is exogenous – that is, it is unrelated to other social factors. The instrumental variable technique derives predicted values for each measure of social ties in segregated/integrated neighborhoods and these estimates are used as predictors of trust in turn.[23]

[23] For the first estimation of the interaction of friendship heterogeneity and the diversity of one's neighborhood, speaking Spanish, being born in Cuba, being a member of a Hispanic organization, and living in a neighborhood that is mostly nonresidential lead to less diverse ties in a segregated neighborhood. More highly educated and higher-income people have more diverse networks in integrated neighborhoods. There were no effects for being born in the United States, having a parent born in the United States, age, expectations of future financial status, being black, having faced discrimination, or perceiving that Hispanics face more discrimination than other groups. These results indicate that

The model for trust includes these instrumental variable estimates for heterogenous ties in diverse neighborhoods. Hispanics who live in more integrated neighborhoods (with smaller percentages of Hispanics) and who have diverse friendships or social networks are 31 percent more likely to trust others. If they "go to relax" with people of different backgrounds and live in integrated neighborhoods, they are 35 percent more trusting.

The model also includes other variables related to trust (Uslaner, 2002, ch. 4): race, perceptions of discrimination, perceptions that Hispanics face more discrimination than other groups, income, education, age, type of neighborhood (what share is residential), and beliefs that one's financial future will be bright. Other than neighborhood type (people living in residential neighborhoods are more trusting), education, and income, no other variable is significant.

For Hispanics, the usual suspects in models of trust – age, perceptions of fairness, optimism for the future – are not significant. This mirrors results for African-Americans (Uslaner, 2002, 35–6). Personal experiences of discrimination do not lead to less trust, likely because Hispanics may know others who have faced discrimination even if they have been free from bias themselves. The insignificant result for perceptions of group discrimination are more puzzling until we realize that all three interaction terms have moderate correlations (about .20) with the belief that Hispanic groups face considerable discrimination.[24] Hispanics who live in segregated neighborhoods and who do not socialize with Anglos may shun such contacts (or neighborhoods) because they feel unwelcome. We shall see this pattern again for African-Americans in Chapter 7.

Reprise

For whites, African-Americans, and Hispanics, living in an integrated and diverse neighborhood and having friends of different backgrounds leads to greater trust. For whites and blacks, diversity – or living in a largely minority neighborhood – does reduce trust. But the gain from approximating Allport's optimal conditions is greater than any loss from diversity. Living in a more diverse neighborhood might lead to an aversion to differences (Putnam's view). It might also reflect a "selection effect."

strong in-group ties lead people to have fewer friends of different backgrounds (in more segregated areas).

[24] Thus there might be moderate collinearity driving the coefficients to insignificance.

Neighborhoods that are overwhelmingly black are likely to be poor. Whites living in such diverse (but not integrated) areas might reside there by financial necessity rather than by choice – and they will have little contact with African-Americans (Bradburn, Sudman, and Gockel with Noel, 1970, 247–9).

So far there *is* evidence that contact matters when the context is right – and it matters for whites, African-Americans, and Hispanics. It matters mightily – the impacts are strong, about 30 percent for each group, and at least as large as we find for other predictors. The effects are telling in a society with a relatively high degree of segregation, a segregation based upon unequal status and resources. Contact under the right conditions can be a great equalizer.

Or can it? Trust is lowest in the communities with the highest level of segregation (Houston, Los Angeles, and Atlanta) and highest in the least segregated areas (Boulder, Colorado and St. Paul, Minnesota). Whites are more likely to live in integrated and diverse communities than African-Americans: 58 percent of whites live in communities that are less segregated and more diverse than the median area (in the merged survey and aggregate data for 20 communities), while 57 percent of African-Americans reside in more segregated communities. Whites also are more likely to have mixed friendship groups in such communities: 57 percent rank above the median, compared to 63 percent of African-Americans falling below the median. African-Americans may gain from diverse contacts in a multiracial setting, but most of them don't live in communities where the optimal conditions hold.

Segregation thus creates an unequal world for blacks and whites – not only economically, but also socially. The choice of where people live also reflects their values (Chapter 7), so the task of building trust in an integrated and diverse community is even more complex than this analysis reveals.

4

Canada: Trust, Integration, and the Search for Identity

[T]here cannot be one cultural policy for Canadians of British and French origin, another for the original peoples and yet a third for all others. For although there are two official languages, there is no official culture, nor does any ethnic group take precedence over any other. No citizen or group of citizens is other than Canadian, and all should be treated fairly.

Prime Minister Pierre Elliot Trudeau (1971) in the Commons, October 8, 1971, announcing Canada's multiculturalism policy.

Canadians are far from sanguine about the country's increasing diversity.... While visitors often marvel at the multicultural mix evident on our city streets, there is growing evidence that Canada's fabled mosaic is fracturing and that ethnic groups are self-segregating.... Despite good efforts and well-intentioned policies, poverty and disenfranchisement in Canada are becoming increasingly race-based.... Over the coming years, Canada's ability to accommodate diversity is sure to become a central issue. As is the case in England, France, and other advanced liberal democracies, national unity in Canada is threatened by the growing atomization of our society along ethnic lines.

Allan Gregg, "Identity Crisis" (2006)

[T]he hyphenation of Canadian identity prevents people from full citizenship in Canada, but at the same time allows them to retain their heritage. I, like many of my peers, have found it difficult to accept that we are not viewed to be "full Canadians." In many ways people of colour are contained within Canadian society, but they're never quite a part of it, they are seen as the "other," as harsh as it may seem.

Auvniet K. Tehara (2010), an Indian-Canadian

[Renee] St. Germain [seventeen years old, of Ojibwa and British parents], who identifies herself as Canadian, says it is already impossible to define a

> single Canadian identity. "But I like that we're not all the same," she says. "I would hate to be somewhere where everyone is the same."
>
> Quoted in Bhattacharya, Kassam, and Siad (2007)

> We feel cultural and ethnic art, music and traditions should be celebrated as in Winnipeg's Folklorama. However, we must remain Canadian first and reinforce that fact through education and cultural events. We must have a strong core to avoid being distracted from who we are.
>
> Focus group report, Richmond, British Columbia, Uniting Canada (UNI), 1991

If trust rests upon a common culture among citizens and optimism for the future, Canadians should have little faith in each other. Canadians debate what, if anything, binds them together and fret that this search may not lead to a happy ending.

Canada is the home of multiculturalism, where it was first proclaimed in 1971 as a solution to the perennial problem of national unity. Unlike the United States, Canada never had an independence movement, much less a revolution. The colonial power, Great Britain, walked away in 1856, leaving the new country without a shared vision of its foundation. Was this new country a federation of ten provinces or two founding peoples (the English and the French)? Where did the native inhabitants (now called the "First Nation") fit in?[1] "There is no sense ... of a differentiated national nationality," Resnick argues. Nor is there a "Canadian culture" (2005, 25).

While Americans brag about their commonality in the "melting pot" and the national motto, *E pluribus unum*, Canadians extol their country as a "mosaic" (Gibbons, 1938), or what former Prime Minister Joe Clark called "a community of communities," with each community maintaining its own identity and customs. Yet it is not always a happy family.

Quebecois (French residents of Quebec) have never reconciled themselves to being part of a country where "to be Canadian implied a sense of racial identification with the British Isles, with its people, its customs, and its traditions" (Resnick, 2005, 25). The two "founding peoples" live together in what novelist Hugh MacClennan (1945) called the "two solitudes." Southerners in the United States have reconciled themselves to a common identity with Northerners. They no longer hold dear their Civil

[1] As with native minorities in the United States, Australia, and Sweden, there is simply not enough data to consider attitudes of the First Nation. See my discussion in Chapter 1.

War anthem, "Dixie" – where "Old times there are not forgotten."[2] But residents of Quebec, the overwhelmingly French province, are reminded daily of the long-standing grievances against English Canada: their car license plates have the message "Je me souviens" ("I remember") from an 1883 carving by architect Eugene-Etienne Tache, which the Quebec government says reflects "a declaration of the French Canadian nation remembering its past: the glories, the misfortunes, and the lessons."[3] Another interpretation is recalling the grievances of the military victory by British forces over the French in the Plains of Abraham in Quebec City in 1759, a century before Canada became independent.[4] Even as independence referenda in Quebec went down to defeat in 1980 and 1995, Canadians constantly bicker over who really is part of their moral community.

If optimism is the foundation of trust, Canadians should not display much faith in their fellow citizens. Scholars of Canadian politics have pondered the nation's future in such volumes as *Must Canada Fail?* (Simeon, 1977), *Canada in Question* (Smiley, 1980), and *Canada's Unity Crisis* (Fry, 1992). Forbes (1993, 82) worries that Canadians are "searching for its universally valid truths where perhaps none are to be found." The satirical troupe, the Royal Canadian Air Farce,[5] opined in 1982 about their country: "Things are going to get a lot worse before they turn bad."

Canada's population is becoming more diverse, but its population is far less heterogenous than that of its southern neighbor, the United States. Canada was the 34th *most* diverse nation among 190 on Alesina's ethnic fractionalization index, with a score of .712. The United States, at .490, ranked 89th. Canada also ranks 61st of 201 countries on linguistic fractionalization, with a score of .577. The United States ranks 118th, with a score less than half of that of Canada (.251). Half of Canadians now have heritages that are neither British, French, or First Nation (Kymlicka, 2010a, 303). Nonwhites are called "visible minorities" in Canada, and in 2000 they constituted 12 percent of the country's population, less than half that of the United States (Peach, 2005, 5–6).

Canada regularly ranks as one of the most trusting countries in the world – fifth out of 94 in Uslaner's (2002, ch. 8) data set (Uslaner, 2002, ch. 8), one of a handful of countries where more than half of the people

[2] The history of the song and the lyrics are at http://kids.niehs.nih.gov/lyrics/dixie.htm.

[3] See http://www.provincequebec.com/info_quebec/motto-license-plate/.

[4] See http://ca.answers.yahoo.com/question/index?qid=20091024091321AATTqrX.

[5] Their home page is http://royalcanadianairfarce.ca/index2.html. I have no source for this line from the Farce other than my own memory.

believe that "most people can be trusted." The 53 percent of Canadians who trusted others in 1995 remained remarkably consistent across three different surveys in 2000. While trust seems to have fallen somewhat – to 48 percent in 2008 – Canada still outranks all but a handful of countries in the faith its citizens have in others.[6]

Why are Canadians so trusting? First, Canada is relatively equal. Its Gini index for 2003 from the United Nations Human Development Index is .315, ranking 22nd of 122 countries. Four years later, the index rose slightly to .331.[7] Second, Canada has relatively low segregation. On the Alesina-Zhuravskaya index of ethnic segregation, it ranks 16th of 97 countries (with a score of .0056) – very close to Italy, which is far less diverse. Canada has low levels of segregation in part because minorities are concentrated in the three largest cities – Toronto and Vancouver, where visible minorities constitute more than a third of the population, and Montreal, where minorities comprise 14 percent of residents (Hou, 2006, 1196). Winnipeg has a somewhat smaller share (Walks and Bourne, 2006), and other large cities such as Calgary and Edmonton have few minorities. Third, not all Canadians are high trusters. English Canadians are far more trusting than French Canadians and visible minorities from Asia have substantially higher levels of faith in others than do black immigrants (see Stolle and Uslaner, 2003 and the data presented below).

[6] The three surveys showing trust at 54 percent in 2000 are the Canadian National Election Study (http://prod.library.utoronto.ca:8090/datalib/codebooks/utm/elections/2000/ces_td_001.pdf), the Economy, Security, Community Survey at the University of British Columbia (see ch. 2, n. 6, and the Quebec Referendum Panel Survey (http://prod.library.utoronto.ca:8090/datalib/codebooks/utm/elections/1980/can.elec.80.cdbk). The links are to the codebooks. The 2008 survey is the one I use in this chapter, the General Social Survey (http://www.statcan.gc.ca/dli-ild/data-donnees/ftp/gss-esg/gssc-esgc2008-eng.htm). The GSS is only available to Canadian residents and with geocodes it is only available at sites affiliated with Statistics Canada. I used the offices of the Quebec Inter-University Center for Social Statistics (QICSS) at the Universite de Montreal after receiving academic and security clearances. I am grateful to Franck Larouche of QICSS (http://www.ciqss.umontreal.ca/) for his great help in preparing and merging the data sets, Feng Hou of Statistics Canada for generating the diversity and segregation data, Jean Poirer and Isabel Cadieux of QICSS, Carmen Charette and Matthieu Ravignat of the Social Sciences and Humanities Research Council of Canada, and Denis Gonthier of Statistics Canada for logistical help.

[7] The 2007 index is from the CIA Fact Book and it placed Canada 35th of 123 countries (though many countries with lower Ginis were former communist countries, which historically have lower reported rates of inequality). These data are available at http://www.photius.com/rankings/economy/distribution_of_family_income_gini_index_2007_0.html.

Who Lives Where in Canada?

Canada, the United States, and Australia (see Chapter 6) are the three "settler" societies in this study – lands where immigrants from Europe displaced the native populations. The United States is distinctive in two ways: alone among these three nations, it brought large numbers of blacks from Africa to the New World to serve as slaves, and alone among these three nations, the United States shares a border with Mexico. The influx of immigrants, both legal and illegal, from and through Mexico has brought greater diversity to the United States compared to Canada and Australia.

Canada and Australia have long had restrictive immigration policies. As with Australia, immigrants to Canada came almost exclusively from Europe. As recently as 1980 only 5 percent of Canadians had non-European (and non-indigenous) backgrounds (Trovato and Wu, 2005). Prior to 1967, Canadian immigration policy changed to a system Australia would adopt about 20 years later: country (and effectively racial and ethnic) quotas were replaced by a point system based upon educational and occupational qualifications. Canada was on its way to becoming a far more diverse country. By the 1970s, more than half of all immigrants were visible minorities, compared to just over 10 percent a decade earlier; by the 1990s, visible minorities comprised three-quarters of all immigrants and 13 percent of the population, compared to less than 1 percent in 1971 (Reitz and Banerjee, 2007, 489). From the 1960s to the 1970s the share of immigrants from Europe dropped from two-thirds to one-third and by 1996 almost two-thirds of all migrants came from Asia (Peach, 2005, 6–7).

The 1967 law established three major categories of immigrants: economic migrants, family reunions, and refugees. By 2010 economic refugees constituted two-thirds of all immigrants, with family unifications constituting another fifth (Citizenship and Immigration Canada, n.d. [b]). The points system is based upon language proficiency (in English and French), level of education, professional qualifications, previous work experience in one's profession, and a certified offer of work in Canada (Citizenship and Immigration Canada, n.d. [a]).[8] By 2001, more than half of all immigrants were skilled workers, and 45 percent had university degrees. Immigrants are better educated than the average Canadian,

[8] The points system is based upon a total of 100 points. Potential immigrants must score at least 67 on this scale based upon education (25 points), language proficiency (24 points),

23 percent of whom have college degrees (Adams with Langstaff, 2007, 61–2).

The new immigrants from Asia, especially China and India, were highly educated and came with strong professional credentials (as in Australia, see Chapter 6; Murdie and Ghosh, 2010, 302). Their levels of trust and segregation are comparable to Canadians of English background. However, black Canadians are far less educated, less trusting, and more segregated. Overall, Canada is substantially less segregated than is the United States – one estimate leads to segregation levels 1.5 times as great below the 49th parallel (border) as above it (Peach, 2005, 14). Johnston, Poulsen, and Forrest (2007) place Canada – with the United Kingdom – between Australia and the United States in levels of segregation, though Peach (2005, 22) sees Canada closer to the United States if one excludes the extreme case of African-Americans.

There is substantial segregation within some white communities – the English and French live apart from each other and Jews are the most highly segregated ethnic/racial group in the country (Fong and Wilkes, 2003, 590; Hou, 2004, 24; Peach, 2005, 15; 21). The overall segregation (and diversity) indices do not include measures of isolation for groups within the white population, which nevertheless are considerably lower than black-white segregation in the United States (Peach, 2005, 21).

Asian immigrants have very high levels of education and professional skills and, compared to blacks in the United States, they are not isolated from the majority community. Nevertheless, segregation levels are relatively high for Asians in Canadian communities, especially in Vancouver, where they are most numerous (Balakrishnan and Gyimah, 2003, 121). Even where most Asians live in mixed neighborhoods, such as in Toronto, the level of segregation tripled from 1981 to 2001 – and segregation has increased for all visible minorities (Hou, 2006, 1196–1202). The increase in segregation is largely traceable to the growth of the minority population in major cities; new immigrants choose to live in neighborhoods with people from their own background (Hou and Picot, 2004, 12). Yet succeeding generations of visible minorities are not less segregated (Balakrishnan and Gyimah, 2003, 123). As in the United Kingdom (see Chapter 5), while minorities are not hypersegregated, they tend to live in

experience (21 points), age (10 points), arranged employment (10 points), and "adaptability" (10 points). See http://www.cic.gc.ca/english/immigrate/skilled/apply-factors.asp and http://www.cic.gc.ca/english/immigrate/skilled/factor-adaptability.asp for the measure of adaptability.

neighborhoods where most of their neighbors come from their own or other visible minority groups (Hou, 2006, 1207).

Racial segregation is greatest for blacks, who constitute 1 percent of Canada's population, and lower-income Asians, notably the Vietnamese and Bangladeshis (Fong and Shibuya, 2000, 454; Fong and Wilkes, 2003, 591–2; Murdie and Ghosh, 2010, 306; Peach, 2005, 14). While segregation is not as strongly linked to inequality as in the United States (Fong and Wilkes, 2003, 597), groups with fewer resources live in more segregated neighborhoods and in communities with clusters of different visible minorities.

Diversity and Multiculturalism

Prime Minister Pierre Elliot Trudeau announced Canada's multiculturalism policy in a speech to Parliament on October 8, 1971. Multiculturalism was a response to the growing diversity of Canadian society – as in the United Kingdom (Chapter 5) and Sweden and Australia (Chapter 6), recognizing the heritage of different minority groups was an attempt to make new immigrants feel at home without forcing them to adapt to a majority culture that was not their own (Kymlicka, 2010a, 303). Under the "older" assimilationist policy, "[i]mmigrants were encouraged to assimilate to the preexisting British mainstream culture, with the hope that over time they would become indistinguishable from native-born British Canadians in their speech, dress, recreation, and way of life in general" (Kymlicka, 2010a, 303). Multiculturalist policies, Kymlicka (2007a, 158) argues, "can positively assist in reducing the cultural, political, and economic inequalities facing immigrant ethnic groups."

Multiculturalism fit more naturally into the Canadian mosaic than it would do in the United Kingdom, Sweden, or Australia. Canadian identity has always been contested. British heritage was only part of Canadian history, a legacy resented by a considerable share of the country's population. Moreover, Canada has not simply been divided between Anglophones and Francophones. A third group, Allophones (speakers of languages other than English or French), is a significant force in Canadian society. There are portions of Montreal where people speak neither English nor French, but Italian. In the prairie provinces, immigrants long held to the languages of their homelands.[9] Retaining your

[9] In the 2001 census there were 469,000 native Italian speakers, 423,000 German speakers, 208,000 Polish speakers, 148,000 Ukrainian speakers, and 129,000 Dutch

home country's language in a community that is linguistically (or ethnically) segregated has long been acceptable in Canada's "community of communities." Multiculturalism came naturally to Canada. To some extent, it has always been in place.

Kymlicka argues that assimilationist policies elsewhere in the West "were intended to ensure that all citizens, wherever they live, would have certain identical experiences and expectations of national citizenship, and that these would be the source of solidarity, trust, democratic responsibility and community of fate. This strategy was never possible in Canada, given our bilingual and federal structure. We cannot have a single monolingual public sphere ... and we cannot have a unitary national education system ... even pan-Canadian institutions like the CBC and the army are divided along linguistic lines" (2007a, 72). Soroka, Johnston, and Banting argue in a similar vein: "seeking to build a single, overarching sense of identity may well be counterproductive; in the case of the relationship between Canada and Francophones Quebec, the most feasible strategy is probably to try to strengthen the sense of attachment to a Canada that incorporates distinctive identities ... this thinner sense of a Canadian culture among the historic communities may actually have benefits in a multicultural era, making it easier for new immigrants to feel comfortable here" (2007, 585).

Trudeau's 1971 announcement was not simply a response to growing immigration. As the quote at the beginning of the chapter indicates, it was part of his larger agenda to patriate the constitution (make it independent of the Crown in London), to enact a Charter of Rights for all Canadians (patterned after the American Bill of Rights), and to "create" a sense of national identity. Multiculturalism was at the heart of this new Canadian identity and especially to blunt the demands of Quebecois for equality with English (and Allophone) Canada. Canada would no longer be a country of two founding peoples. It would be a land where *all* cultures would be equal and treated as such. Canada had no single overarching culture, but Trudeau sought to create a "coat of many colors" (as in the biblical story of Joseph) from the red and white maple leaf flag (adopted as a neutral symbol in 1964) of Canada and the blue and white fleur de lis flag of Quebec. Multiculturalism was not popular among Quebecois, who quickly realized Trudeau's agenda. The prime minister's policy faced a strong backlash in

speakers in Canada (see http://www12.statcan.ca/english/census01/products/standard/themes/RetrieveProductTable.cfm?Temporal=2001&PID=55534&APATH=3&METH=1&PTYPE=55440&THEME=41&FOCUS=0&AID=0&PLACENAME=0&PROVINCE=0&SEARCH=0&GC=99&GK=NA&VID=0&VNAMEE=&VNAMEF=&FL=0&RL=0&FREE=0&GID=431515).

Quebec, leading to demands for independence or at least autonomy so that Francophones could protect their language and culture:

> [T]he pluralistic and formally egalitarian bent of the multiculturalist logic propounded by the Canadian state puts French Canadians and Quebec francophones on the same footing as any other ethnocultural minority group, thus neutralizing their historical status as one of Canada's founding nations and delegitimizing the nationalist aspirations of Francophones Quebecers..... The Quebec state ... has moved toward a thick definition of Quebec citizenship, which subordinates nonfrancophone forms of ethnic identification to a national community and a common culture primarily defined by the French-speaking majority. (Salée, 2007, 114, 115–16)

Multiculturalism further divided English and French Canada. Did it bridge the gap between English Canada and the new visible minorities?

Canadians say that they favor multiculturalism: 85 percent replied that it is important to Canadian identity in a 2003 survey, up from 74 percent six years earlier. Immigrants express pride in Canada, especially its multiculturalism. Immigrants are well integrated into politics, with high levels of political participation (Kymlicka, 2010b, 7–8; cf. Reitz et al., 2009, 11). Focus groups in 1991 nevertheless revealed wariness about government support for programs that reinforced home country culture at the expense of a common set of values (UNI, 1991).

Integrating into a Multicultural Canada

Minorities may participate in the political process in Canada, but they are less integrated into Canadian society on measures such as belonging and trust. Discrimination against minorities persists, and this is a barrier to generalized trust.

Visible minorities are substantially less likely to identify as Canadians – they are 30 percent less likely to say that they feel like Canadians compared to whites (Jiminez, 2007; Reitz and Banerjee, 2009, 134). Reitz et al. report that visible minorities as a whole are no less trusting than whites. Yet some groups – notably blacks – are substantially less likely to have faith in others (Reitz et al., 2009, 34–6; Reitz and Banerjee, 2009, 141, 150; cf. Phan, 2008, 37; but see Soroka, Helliwell, and Johnston, 2007, 106). I report similar results with a different data set, the 2008 General Social Survey, below.[10] Reitz and his colleagues find that minorities have

[10] Reitz and his co-authors use the 2002 Ethnic Diversity Survey (http://www.statcan.gc.ca/cgi-bin/imdb/p2SV.pl?Function=getSurvey&SDDS=4508&lang=en&db=imdb&adm=

lower levels of life satisfaction and a sense of belonging to Canada, both of which I show lead to greater trust.

Inequality by itself does *not* explain variations in trust or belonging to Canada. However, perceived discrimination is a strong predictor of lower trust. Visible minorities have much lower incomes and higher rates of poverty compared to other immigrants (Reitz and Banerjee, 2007, 491, 520–1). Forty-four percent of the least trusting visible minority – blacks – speak of recent discrimination–but even 35 percent of the most trusting minority – the Chinese – report racial bias. One's sense of identity has a strong effect on trust. Immigrants who identify only with their home country are substantially less likely to trust others than are minorities who define themselves as primarily Canadian or as both Canadian and their nationality of origin. When you perceive discrimination, you are more likely to define your identity in terms of your group and thus are less likely to trust others. This effect is much stronger in Quebec than in the rest of Canada, most likely because the sense of ethnic identity among Quebecois is stronger than it is in the rest of Canada (see Chapter 2; Phan and Breton, 2009, 107).

Living in a diverse neighborhood leads to a withdrawal of political participation for majority whites, but has no effect on minorities (Gidengil, Roy, and Lawlor, 2009). Phan reports similar null findings between neighborhood diversity and trust (2008, 41–2). Yet whites who live in diverse neighborhoods have weaker in-group ties and greater attachment to Canada (Wu, Schimmele, and Hou, 2009, 28–9). Hou and Wu (2009, 706) report positive effects of neighborhood diversity on trust for the majority: "in the White population, exposure to racial minorities has a positive effect on trust in neighborhoods where the White population remains dominant and the minority neighbors are relatively evenly distributed across multiple racial categories rather than concentrated in only one or two groups." For whites, living in a homogenous neighborhood leads to stronger in-group ties (Wu, Schimmele, and Hou, 2009, 28). Soroka, Johnston, and Banting report that majority respondents in a neighborhood are more trusting when surrounded by members of their own group – although they use a different measure of trust than I employ (2007, 286).[11] However, minorities do *not* become more trusting if they

8&dis=2#b3), while I use the 2008 General Social Survey. I chose the GSS because it included better questions for estimating a model of trust and is more recent.

[11] Their measure is how likely a person is to return a wallet found on the street to a stranger, a neighbor, or the police.

have lived in Canada for a long time (Soroka, Johnston, and Banting, 2007, 584).

Stolle, Soroka, and Johnston use a framework more consistent with mine, and they report positive results for the effect of contact in diverse neighborhoods (using a different data set):

> Respondents who have diverse neighbors and talk to them on a regular basis are significantly more trusting than those who have diverse neighbors and do not talk to them. In short, diversity is a challenge to trust only when it is not accompanied by enough social interactions ... virtually all of the negative effect of diversity occurs among those who do not talk to their neighbors. (2008, 68–9)

Canadians like multiculturalism in theory. But they are less enamored of it as policy granting special favors to minorities. Visible minorities still face discrimination – and those who have had the least economic success (blacks, some Asians) are substantially less likely to trust others. Some visible minorities have prospered, live in high-income integrated neighborhoods, and trust their fellow citizens as much as other Canadians. Is this socialization – or, as we shall see for Australian minorities, the result of Canada's immigration policy that "selects" well-off and educated migrants who might already have high levels of trust?

Trust, Friendships, and Segregation in Canada

Does contact in integrated neighborhoods lead to more trust in Canada? And, if so, for whom? The 2008 General Social Survey was a telephone poll of 20,401 respondents throughout Canada except for the Northwest Territories and Nunavut. The survey focused on social connections and norms and the large sample size makes it possible to focus on a wide range of ethnic and racial groups within the country (see n. 5). These groups have different levels of trust, contacts with people of *visibly* different ethnicities and who speak different languages, and live in communities with different levels of segregation. The GSS question on "visibly different" ethnicities taps bridging ties that are more in the spirit of "optimal contact" than simply having friends of different ethnicity.

In addition to the sample of all respondents, I focus on whites, Anglophones, Francophones, immigrants from Northern Europe, Southern Europeans, visible minorities (nonwhites), Asians, and blacks. These categories are *not* mutually exclusive.

The Anglophones and Francophones are the most numerous groups in Canada and generally regarded as the two "founding peoples." Anglophones come from historically high-trusting cultures and Francophones, in Canada and elsewhere, are considerably less trusting (Uslaner, 2008b; Soroka, Helliwell, and Johnston, 2007, 106; Stolle and Uslaner, 2003). Francophones are concentrated in Quebec and are more segregated, especially from minorities (Balakrishnan and Gyimah, 2003, 121). Over the past half century, Quebec has become more diverse, but the growth has come exclusively from speakers of languages other than English and French. The Anglophone population of Quebec has dropped from 13.8 percent in 1951 to 8.2 percent in 2006.[12] European immigrants are highly trusting – they come from countries with high levels of trust (Uslaner, 2008b), but they also live apart from visible minorities and live in more segregated communities (Balakrishnan and Gyimah, 2003, 125). The Europeans are the immigrants with the longest history in Canada – and they are likely to live among the two charter groups (Anglophones and Francophones) more than more recent immigrant groups.

Southern and Central Europeans come from countries lower in trust, reflected in somewhat depressed levels of faith in others and higher segregation. Visible minorities may not be as starkly segregated as minorities in the United States (Fong, 1996), but they are largely isolated from whites. Asian immigrants, especially Vietnamese, live in more segregated neighborhoods than do minorities in Britain or Australia (Walks and Bourne, 2006). Blacks are the most segregated minority. Since they constitute such a small share of the Canadian population, they are much more likely to have contact with whites than are African-Americans (Fong, 1996, 205). Isolation does *not* fade over time – succeeding generations of visible minorities are as segregated as their immigrant parents (Balakrishnan and Gyimah, 2003, 123) – nor do immigrants become more trusting over time (Soroka, Johnston, and Banting, 2007, 584).

Anglophones and immigrants from (Northern) Europe have the highest levels of trust. Anglophones live in the least diverse neighborhoods, followed by Francophones and European immigrants. Visible minorities live in more diverse *and* highly segregated neighborhoods, but some minorities (Asians) have high levels of trust and others (blacks) have less faith in others. The trust levels of different groups largely follow the historical trust of their ancestry (Uslaner, 2008b). However, Asian immigrants stand out as far more trusting than their countries of origin would

[12] See table 2.1.1 at http://www.statcan.gc.ca/pub/89–642-x/2010002/tbl/tbl211-eng.htm. The relative weight of Anglophones has fallen by half over the same period (table 2.1.3) at http://www.statcan.gc.ca/pub/89–642-x/2010002/tbl/tbl213-eng.htm.

lead us to expect. (There is a more modest boost in trust for Southern Europeans).

I present levels of trust and intergroup contact in Figures 4.1 (trust and friends of different ethnicity) and 4.2 (the share of members of different ethnicity and language in groups to which you belong). Where linguistic diversity will serve as a proxy for ethnic diversity elsewhere (see the discussion of Sweden in Chapter 6), in Canada both matter. Language may be even more salient a dividing line in a country with two official languages as ethnicity, although the rise of multiculturalism as official policy has brought ethnic heritage to the fore as well. Language and ethnicity are often intertwined, as new immigrants may be more comfortable with their native language even if they are required to be proficient in English to enter Canada.

As in the American data, the group membership measure may be a stronger measure of "optimal contact" since interactions in groups *might* be more intense. The three measures of contact are all five-point scales ranging from all members/friends from the same background to all members of different background.[13] To make comparisons with trust simpler (as in other chapters), I "normed" the friendship and group contacts to a 0–1 scale.

The Anglophones and Europeans are the most trusting. Aside from the French, however, they are *the least likely to have friends and fellow group members from diverse backgrounds*. The French are both less trusting and more isolated in their social networks. About 30 percent of Francophones believe that "most people can be trusted," almost half as many as Anglophones and European immigrants. And their social networks are the least diverse: Francophones have friendship and group ethnic diversity scores of between .10 and .15 (on a range of 0–1) and a linguistic group diversity score not much greater. All white groups have relatively low levels of interaction with people of different backgrounds. Europeans are the "exception" in having a more moderate score (.25) for belonging to groups with people speaking different languages. Francophones stand out as the least trusting and the most isolated. Visible minority groups have more friends and group members of different ethnic and linguistic backgrounds – which is at least partially a matter of simple mathematics. Minorities with many friends are simply more likely to have white acquaintances. This is clearly the case for both Asians and

[13] The variable "friends who speak the same language" was recoded to "friends who speak different languages" for consistency with other measures.

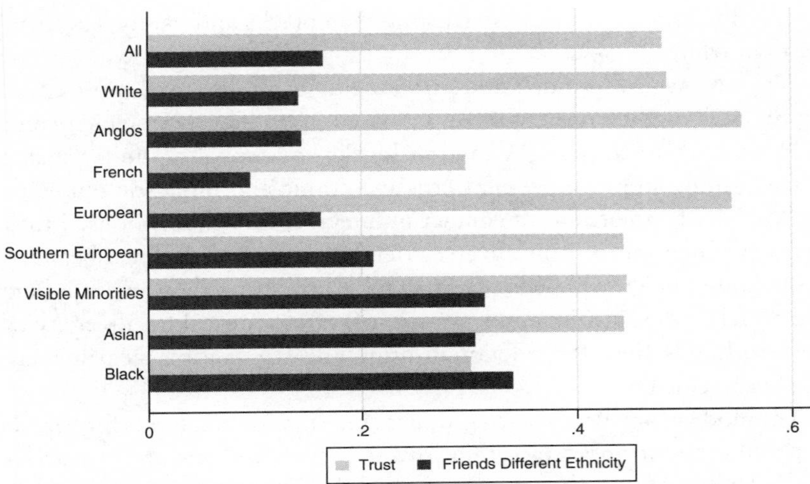

FIGURE 4.1. Trust and friendship mix by race and ethnicity. General Social Survey Canada 2008

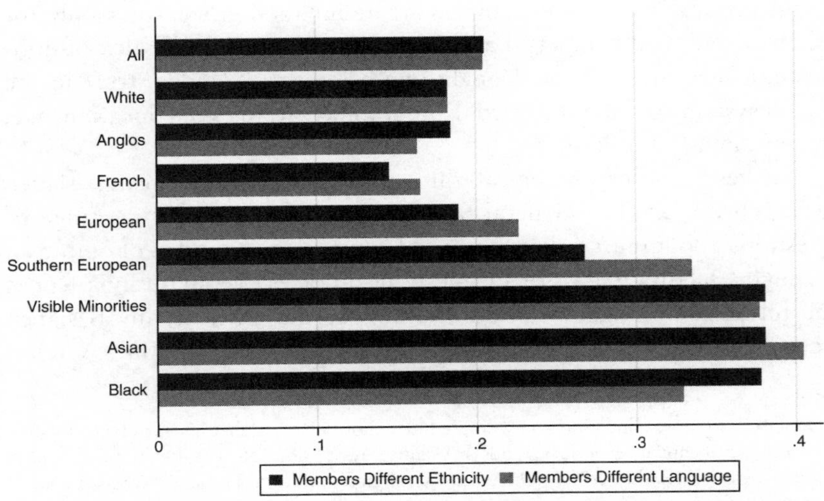

FIGURE 4.2. Organizational membership mix by race and ethnicity. General Social Survey Canada 2008

blacks. But Asians are far more trusting than blacks and barely less trusting than whites.

Why are Asians so much more trusting than blacks – and more trusting than we might expect them to be based upon their heritage? It can't be levels of contact, since Asians and blacks have roughly similar shares of friendships and memberships crossing ethnic and linguistic boundaries. Might it be the result of contact in integrated neighborhoods? I turn to an examination of how diverse friendships and group memberships in integrated neighborhoods might shape trust across the various ethnic and racial groups in Canada. I cannot separately control for diversity of neighborhoods since the fractionalization and segregation measures are highly correlated.

The models for trust for each group include interaction terms for friendship and group membership ethnic diversity with multigroup entropy. As in the United States, the construction of the interaction terms leads to an expected *negative* coefficient on the interaction term if the optimal conditions lead to greater trust. I also include a simple measure of group members who speak a different language and I also expect a negative coefficient. The segregation measure is based upon different racial and ethnic groups, so it makes sense to create interaction measures only for ethnic diversity in contacts. I also include in the model an index of optimism, a measure of how strongly one belongs to Canada, trust in the health system, and the standard demographic variables of education, age, income, and Catholicism.[14]

The key social-psychological foundation of trust is optimism (Uslaner, 2002, chs. 2, 4). The General Social Survey included a wide range of questions about one's worldview and I constructed an index of optimism through a factor analysis of 11 questions on one's overall outlook – does the future look bright and can you shape your own destiny (Uslaner, 2002, 31) – as well as the beneficence of people around you.[15] While I

[14] People with more education and who are older should have higher levels of trust. Income is not significant in American models (Uslaner, 2002, 99, 108–10), but these are more sparse models. Catholicism is a hierarchical religion and should be associated with lower trust (Putnam, 1993, 107; Stolle and Uslaner, 2003 on Canada).

[15] The questions and their loadings on the single optimism factor (with the largest loadings in bold) are: I experience a general sense of emptiness (.49); there are plenty of people I can rely on when I have problems (-.40); there are many people I can trust completely (-.34, -.48 on a second factor); I often feel rejected (.44); you have little control over the things that happen to you (.55); there is really no way you can solve some of the problems you have (.57); there is little you can do to change many of the important things in your life (.61); you often feel helpless in dealing with problems of life (.66); sometimes

argued above that pessimism is central to Canadian culture, this negative outlook seems limited to the polity and to group relations. In their personal lives, Canadians tend to have a sunny disposition. Across the 11 measures I used to construct the optimism scale, only one had fewer than 70 percent positive responses, six had 85 percent or greater agreement, and the remaining four had agreement greater than 75 percent.[16] Across white ethnic groups, there is little variation in levels of optimism. Visible minorities are less optimistic, with blacks notably less sanguine than Asians.

Trust rests upon the perception of a common fate and identity (see Chapter 2) – in contrast to a strong sense of in-group identity (Jantzen, 2005, 115). Belonging to Canada, rather than identifying mostly with your home province, should promote generalized trust. Federal versus provincial power has long been central to Canadian politics. Prime Minister Pierre Eliot Trudeau's attempt to forge a distinctive national identity in the 1980s focused on centralizing power in Ottawa rather than in the provinces. Provincial identity in Canada is thus a rejection of the idea of common bonds among all Canadians. Visible minorities whose ethnic identity is strong have a substantially weaker sense of Canadian identity (Reitz et al., 2009, 40). A key exception are Chinese immigrants, who feel as strongly Canadian as migrants from Europe (Reitz and Banerjee, 2007, 507–9). Given the weak sense of what constitutes Canadian identity, a sense of belonging should promote generalized trust.

Kumlin and Rothstein argue that a social welfare regime based upon universal coverage can build trust by treating all people fairly and leading to greater equality (2008, 2010). Their argument focuses on Sweden, and I shall show in Chapter 6 that confidence in the universal welfare state does indeed boost trust, especially for minorities. In Canada, the universal health care system is often portrayed as the defining characteristic of national identity:

you feel that you are being pushed around in life (.49); what happens to you in the future mostly depends on you (-.33); and you can do just about anything you really set your mind to (-.43). The low loading of the "trust completely" measure on the optimism factor and the strong relationships of optimism for trust I report supports my overall argument that generalized trust does not stem from trust in specific people, especially people you are close to (Uslaner, 2002, chs. 2, 3, 5).

16 Levels of agreement are: feel rejected (4 percent); feel emptiness (7 percent); feel helpless (14 percent); little you can do (15 percent); pushed around (19 percent); little one can do to change (20 percent); no way to solve problems (22 percent); little control (26 percent); have friends to rely on (80 percent); future depends upon you (89 percent).

> [F]or many English-speaking Canadians "medicare" has become part of the very definition of the country. The nationwide reach of the system has been celebrated as part of the social glue that holds together a society otherwise divided by language and region; and its universal coverage is widely seen as one of the defining features distinguishing Canada from its powerful neighbour to the south. (Johnston et al., 2010, 368–9)

They show that support for the health care system leads to a stronger sense of national identity. Can such a program also create trust? If so, does its reach go beyond the majority population (as it does in Sweden)?

I focus on the segregation interaction terms as well as the linguistic diversity of group membership, the sense of belonging to Canada, and trust in the public health system. The other variables perform mostly as expected.[17] I report the main results in Figures 4.3 (all respondents, whites, and Anglophones), 4.4 (Francophones, Europeans, and Southern Europeans), and 4.5 (all visible minorities, Asians, and blacks).

The key results are that contact with people of different ethnicities, both as friends and in organizations, builds trust if you live in integrated neighborhoods and if you are a member of a dominant group (white, Anglophone, Francophone, or to a lesser extent a European immigrant). Optimal contact works for the majority. It has limited effects for visible minorities – such contact is only effective for blacks. The effects are smaller for whites and Anglophones (as well as for all respondents) than those for the United States – but about the same as I shall report for majorities and minorities in the United Kingdom (Chapter 5) and for whites in Australia (Chapter 6). Having diverse friends in integrated neighborhoods matters slightly more for all whites than for Anglophones and the effect of diverse group membership in integrated communities has a tiny effect for Anglophones. Having friends who speak a different language does not boost trust for all respondents or whites by an appreciable amount and seems to have a small negative effect for Anglophones.

The big effects seem to occur for Francophones, among whom having many friends of different ethnicities and living in an integrated neighborhood boosts trust by 47 percent, and joining groups with diverse

[17] Variables that do not attain significance and the models for whites are: education (Europeans and Southern Europeans); age (Francophones, Southern Europeans); income (Francophones); and Catholicism (Anglophones, Europeans, Southern Europeans). For visible minorities, income and Catholicism are insignificant. For Asians, only Catholicism and optimism are significant, the latter barely at $p < .10$. For blacks, only age, optimism, and belonging are significant, the latter at $p < .10$.

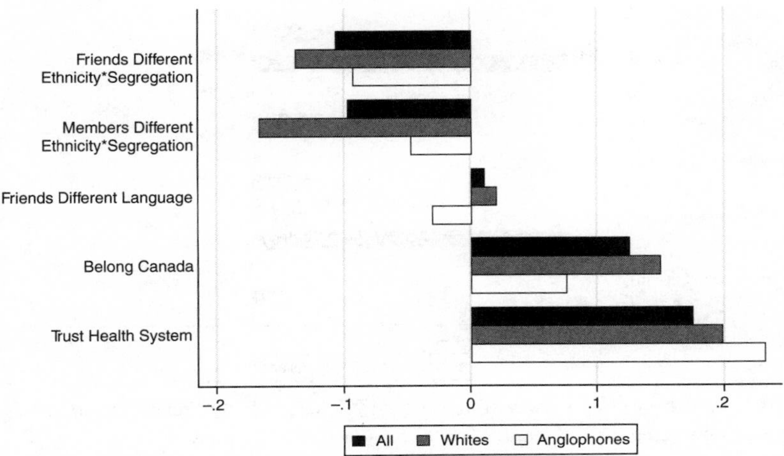

FIGURE 4.3. Probit effects for all, whites, and Anglo respondents for trust and segregation. General Social Survey 2008 Canada

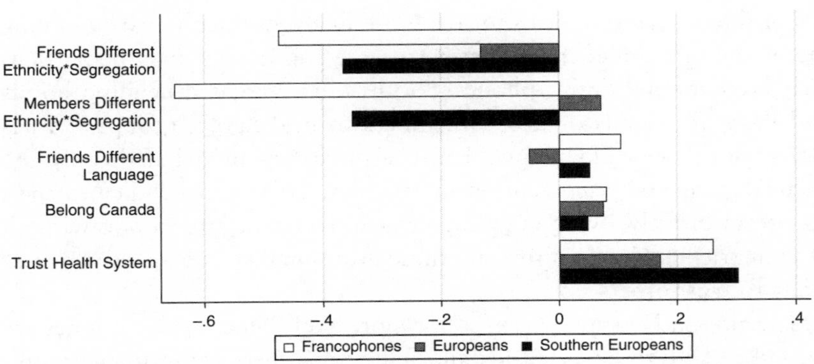

FIGURE 4.4. Probit effects for Francophone, European, and Southern European respondents for trust and segregation. General Social Survey 2008 Canada

members in a similar context leads to a 65 percent increase in faith in others. Having many friends who speak a different language further boosts trust by 10 percent. If all of this seems too good to be true, it probably is. Francophone respondents are the least likely to have friends of a different ethnicity or to join groups made up largely of members from a different ethnic or linguistic group. Francophones are also unlikely to live in areas with visible minorities.

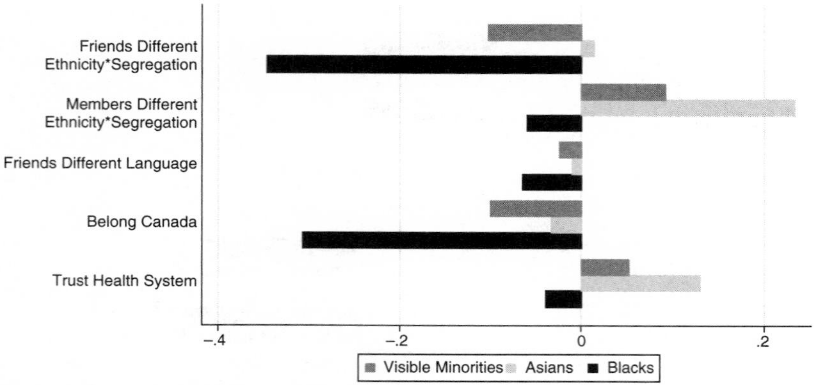

FIGURE 4.5. Probit effects for visible minorities, Asian, and black respondents for trust and segregation. General Social Survey 2008 Canada

These strong effects may be attributable to either: (1) differences stemming from small numbers of people at the highest and lowest values of the interaction terms; or (2) more likely, multicollinearity among the predictors. Under the first scenario, the gap in trust may be particularly large among Francophones who live in segregated neighborhoods and have no friends or group members from different groups. This is plausible but less likely since I also estimated a model with only the friendship diversity/segregation interaction. This model indicates that, counterintuitively, living in an integrated diverse neighborhood with all of your friends from a different ethnic group makes one 12 percent *less* likely to trust others.

The alternative explanation seems more likely. Since Francophones are the least likely to have friends and fellow members from other groups, the few who do have such bridging ties will also be more likely to live in more diverse neighborhoods and to extend these ties from one arena (friends) to another (group members): 95 percent of Francophones had either all (71.8 percent) or most (23.2 percent) of their friends from their same ethnic group – and only 2.9 percent had most or all of their friends from other groups. Of course, most people have most of their friends from their own group, and Anglophones are only somewhat more likely to have diverse ties. Asian immigrants have more diverse friendship networks – almost a quarter had most of their friends from different groups, while almost 30 percent of blacks' friends come from different groups. Even 11 percent of Southern Europeans' friends largely come from outside their ethnicity. The effect for Francophones may be positive or it may be negative. It is almost certainly less than that for Anglophones.

There are also large effects for Southern Europeans – increases in trust of about 35 percent for both friendship and group membership in integrated communities – and a further small increase (5 percent) for group members who speak different languages. Some collinearity may lead to spuriously high effects here but Southern Europeans do have far more variation in the structure of their networks. There are much smaller effects for Northern Europeans, 13 percent for diverse friendship networks in integrated communities and 7 percent for membership in heterogenous groups in similar settings.

For visible minorities, we see two different stories. Diverse friendship networks (which are common) in integrated neighborhoods (far less common) matter less for Asians on trust than they do for most other groups: only belonging to diverse groups and living in integrated neighborhoods leads to an increase in trust (23 percent). This effect seems large but few Asians are both group members and live in such diverse communities.

For blacks, there are powerful effects – larger than for any other group. Living in integrated neighborhoods (uncommon) with diverse friendship networks (the most common of any group) boosts trust among blacks by 35 percent. For Asians, the effect is a tiny drop in trust of 1 percent. For visible minorities overall, the results parallel the findings for Asians – since they constitute by far the largest share of minorities in Canada and especially in this sample.

The sense of belonging to Canada leads to higher levels of trust for the "charter groups," the English and the French. Belonging to Canada does not boost trust for either other European groups or visible minorities. Confidence in the health system has large impacts on trust (about 25 percent to 30 percent) for Anglophones, Francophones, and Southern Europeans and a more moderate effect for Northern Europeans (17 percent). A sense of attachment and positive attitudes toward the welfare state lead to greater trust for whites but not for visible minorities.

Why Contact Works – and Doesn't Work

Optimal contact in Canada works mostly as it does in Australia (see Chapter 6), but partially as it does in the United States (Chapter 2). This is not surprising since in many ways Canada and Australia are very similar: the former British colonies long gave preferential treatment to immigrants from the home country (although Canada had two founding peoples) and others who looked like them (Europeans). More recently, both countries shifted their immigration policies and embraced multiculturalism. Each had an influx of immigrants from Asia. Both invited professionals who already had the education, skills, and language ability that would make them fit into a middle-class society. Canada and Australia have lower levels of segregation and inequality than the United States, and Asian immigrants have levels of trust close to the dominant Anglo majority.

What makes Asians more trusting in Canada (and in Australia, see Chapter 6)? And why are they largely resistant to the positive effects of optimal contact? Canada and Australia both have points systems for immigrants. Canada's system is less demanding than Australia's but, nevertheless, it is not easy for most potential immigrants to gain entrance into Canada. But when they come, they are welcomed warmly (DeParle, 2010). As in Australia, the new system adopted in 1967 abolished racial quotas but replaced them with educational and professional tests. The new immigrants – with Chinese, Indians, and Filipinos being the most numerous – were required to bring savings of about 10,000 dollars with them, making the new Canadians "strikingly middle class" (DeParle, 2010).

Asian immigrants do face discrimination: about a third of Chinese and other Asians report biased treatment (Reitz and Banerjee, 2009, 128). Some Asians – notably Bangladeshis – are very poor and identify more with their local neighborhoods. Chinese immigrants have above average incomes compared to other residents of Toronto, with Indians only marginally below the overall average (Murdie and Ghosh, 2010, 302, 306). Asians, notably South Asians, have among the highest levels of belonging among Canadians (Reitz and Banerjee, 2009, 150).

For a people who do face some discrimination – but who nevertheless flourish economically and who are very optimistic about their own futures – trust reflects success more than social interactions. What is striking about the trust model for Asians is that only two noncontact variables are significant even at the $p < .10$ level: Catholicism (which likely reflects the fact that Filipinos are less prosperous than Chinese or Indians) and optimism. Asians in Canada are not as fully assimilated as they are in Australia – so the closer contact of membership in diverse groups in integrated neighborhoods does lead to an increase in trust.

Canada and the United States both have black populations – more than ten times larger south of the 49th parallel border than above it. Blacks in both countries are substantially less trusting than whites (except for

Francophones in Canada) or Asian immigrants. They report substantially more discrimination than do Asian minorities and are the least likely to live in integrated communities. Phan and Breton argue that "the experience of discrimination increases the likelihood that respondents will draw into their ethnic group" (2009, 111).

Forty-three percent of blacks say that they have faced racial discrimination in Canada, compared to an overall level of 24 percent for visible minorities. On a wider measure of discrimination – for any reason – half of blacks report facing such bias, compared to 35 percent for all visible minorities (Reitz and Banerjee, 2009, 128–9).[18] Blacks are not only low trusting; they are also less optimistic on most of the measures and they are the least likely to say that they trust strangers.[19] As with African-Americans, the relatively small number of Canadian blacks who live in integrated neighborhoods and have close friends of different backgrounds (either racial or linguistic) become significantly more trusting.

Optimal contact works in Canada, but, as in the United States and Australia, more for whites than for visible minorities. The evidence seems inconclusive as to whether Francophones become more trusting when they have more diverse social networks in integrated communities. Friendship across ethnic or linguistic lines is uncommon for most Canadians – especially for Francophones.[20] The simplest model I estimated showed optimal contact reducing trust among Francophones. Their geographical isolation (most are in the province of Quebec and most live in segregated neighborhoods) and their social seclusion are among the factors leading to their low level of trust.

Can you define identity through social welfare policy? In Sweden you can (see Chapter 6). The universal welfare state helps build trust among immigrants from countries with low levels of trust. The Canadian health care system is universal. It stands in sharp contrast to the private and very expensive medical care in the United States. It does build trust among Canadians – including Francophones – but only among white Canadians. The health system is not a universal social welfare regime. And it does not lead to greater trust among visible minorities (and not among Asians or

[18] The General Social Survey did not have questions on discrimination, so I could not include them in my analysis.

[19] On a five point scale, the mean for blacks is 3.09, compared to 3.91 for Anglophones, 3.61 for Francophones, and 3.49 for Asians.

[20] Among all Canadians, 88 percent have all or most of their friends with people of their (visibly) same ethnic group and 87 percent with people who speak the same language.

blacks). If it is a source of national identity, it only binds together people who look like each other.

Ironically, the groups with the most contact across ethnic/racial and linguistic lines – visible minorities – do not become more trusting as a result of those contacts. Canada's multiculturalism policy does not preclude some minorities from becoming trusting. But it doesn't create the bridging ties that build trust, at least for most visible immigrants (Asians). Nor does it eliminate discrimination. Multiculturalism is not a substitute for the unifying national identity that builds trust among diverse populations. Nor have any national institutions – especially national health care – filled the gap.

Canada may have had no choice, as Kymlicka and Soroka, Johnston, and Banting have argued. There is no common vision on which to build an overarching sense of national identity. Canada has avoided severe conflicts beyond the Quebec–Rest of Canada (ROC) divide not by socializing new immigrants, but by choosing who can come rather carefully. By doing so, Canada has created a society that is seen as fair, especially compared to its southern neighbor. Most Canadians are also optimistic about their own lives. Without a clear sense of national identity – and with modest levels of interaction among people of different backgrounds – social interaction may not be as strong a key to generalized trust as it is in its far less trusting and more segregated neighbor to the south.

5

The United Kingdom: Sleepwalking or Wide Awake?

From the day I was old enough to walk along the street by myself practically till now I have experienced [only] one month in my life that someone hasn't said something about my colour or my scarf or whatever, and I'm not feeling that I have to stay in the house because of it. But it's a natural part of life. It's just 'what are you doing here?', 'get back home'.

Asian British woman, quoted in Commission for Racial Equality (1998, 18)

The biggest problem is that the majority of white people have got preconceived ideas about black people. The attitudes of white people who live among blacks are completely different to those of people who have never lived among them. They know us better, they know we are human and not some alien from another planet.

African Caribbean male, quoted in Commission for Racial Equality (1998, 11)

It is the best of times, it is the worst of times.

Paraphrasing Charles Dickens, *A Tale of Two Cities*.[1]

Britain is a prime exemplar of the success of multiculturalism as the share of foreign born has risen from 1 percent (the average over 1,000 years until 1950) to 11 percent (Burns, 2010). Prime Minister Gordon Brown (2006) exulted that "we the British people should be able to gain great strength from celebrating a British identity which is bigger than the sum of its parts." A. Sivanandan, director of the Institute of Race Relations, said in 2006: "No country in Europe could be more proud of its multicultural experiment than Britain" (quoted in Cowell, 2006).

[1] Published in 1859, available online at http://www.online-literature.com/dickens/twocities/1/.

Others are not so sanguine. John Burns, a senior correspondent for the *New York Times*, himself British, wrote:

> Tony Blair's early years as prime minister have led to a net inward migration of about two million people since 1997, with a peak of 330,000 in 2007.... Britain, with 62 million people, is already one of the most heavily populated countries in the developed world; new settlers put pressure on schools, hospitals, public housing and a welfare system that are bending under the strain. Drawn by Europe's most generous welfare system, and by the status of English as the global lingua franca, illegal immigrants have shown inexhaustible resourcefulness in breaching the border controls of an island nation that Shakespeare vaunted as an ocean-bound redoubt – "This sceptred isle ... This other Eden ... This fortress built by nature for herself ... This happy breed of men, this little world, This precious stone, set in the silver sea."

Trevor Phillips, chair of the Commission for Racial Equality and a popular television broadcaster and writer, also drew a dire picture of race relations in Britain:

> America is not our dream, but our nightmare ... we are a society which, almost without noticing it, is becoming more divided by race and religion. We are becoming more unequal by ethnicity.... Residentially, some districts are on their way to becoming fully fledged ghettoes – black holes into which no-one goes without fear and trepidation, and from which no-one ever escapes undamaged. (2005, 3, 8)

And there is the old skinhead chant, reintroduced as a warning sign of racial tensions by a black academic working in cultural studies (Gilroy, 1991): "There ain't no black in the Union Jack."[2]

Brown's successor, David Cameron, charged that the "hands-off tolerance" of multiculturalism allowed immigrants – and Muslims in particular – "to live separate lives, apart from each other and the mainstream.... We have even tolerated these segregated communities behaving in ways that run counter to our values. So when a white person holds objectionable views – racism, for example – we rightly condemn them. But when equally unacceptable views or practices have come from someone who isn't white, we've been too cautious, frankly even fearful, to stand up to them" (Burns, 2011). Earlier, David Goodhart (2004), editor of *Prospect*, created a stir when he argued that "[a] generous welfare state is not compatible with open borders and possibly not even with ... mass immigration."

Is the United Kingdom "united" in its commitment to a multiracial, multicultural society? Or is it splitting apart at the seams as whites feel

[2] The Union Jack is the British flag.

threatened by increasing immigration and nonwhites feel left out? This is not a simple academic debate. It is also a central question of public policy in Britain, with a large number of studies conducted by government agencies (mostly the Home Office) as well as private think tanks about issues of "community cohesion" (Community Cohesion Panel [UK], 2004; Home Office of the United Kingdom, 2004a, 2004b; Home Office Research, 2004; Hudson et al., 2007; Laurence and Heath, 2008) and whether there is a "decline of Britishness" (ETHNOS Research and Consultancy, 2006). The studies include focus groups from different ethnic and racial backgrounds as well as large-scale surveys, one of which, the 2007 United Kingdom Citizenship Survey, I shall use here.

Much of the difficulty in describing the state of racial and ethnic relations in the United Kingdom stems from the nature of the questions asked and the measures used. The key term in both government and think tank studies is *community cohesion*, a catch-all term covering many distinct questions that I shall examine in this chapter:

- Are whites and minorities segregated from each other? More than any other question, the segregation issue is one of measurement. By the measures used in most cross-national studies (dissimilarity), Britain is *not* a segregated society. Another measurement technique paints a very different picture. Both tell part of the story.
- Do minorities see themselves as British? They do – more than whites do.
- Are whites proud of multicultural Britain? Most are, but they are critical of many (if not most) consequences of the policy.
- Are whites resentful of the level of immigration? Most are and a large share of the white population feels that minorities are straining the welfare system and do not adapt to British culture.
- Do minorities fare worse than whites economically? Emphatically yes.
- Do minorities perceive discrimination by white society? A large share do, even if they feel comfortable being British.
- Do positive feelings about belonging to Britain carry over to high levels of trust for minorities? No.
- Do minorities have friends of different ethnic and racial backgrounds? Yes.
- Do whites have friends of different ethnic and racial backgrounds? Generally not.
- Does living in an integrated neighborhood with friends of different backgrounds lead to greater trust? Yes, for both whites and minorities,

but a bit less so for Muslims than for other minorities. Optimal conditions matter far less in the United Kingdom than for whites, blacks, or Latinos in the more segregated United States.

Living Apart or Together?

Britain is not a high trust country as the Nordic nations are. But it is a *relatively* highly trusting society, tied for tenth (with Northern Ireland and Iceland) of 94 states/places in the 1995–6 World Values Survey, the most reliable cross-national measure.[3] In 1959, trust was much higher (56 percent). Hall attributes the decline most likely to a worsening economic situation (1999, 444–5). Britain's level of trust was approximately the same as America's during the boom years of the 1960s, but it did not fall as precipitously: the U.S. share of trusting responses was 36 percent in 1995–6. The most likely explanation for the divergence of trust levels for the two nations is the level of inequality: the United Kingdom ranked 31st of 101 countries on inequality in the Deininger and Squire (1996) inequality database, while the United States ranked 54th. The Gini index of inequality increased strongly in both countries as trust fell, but the overall level of inequality was much higher in the United States than in the United Kingdom (Weeks, 2005, 5–6).

Britain's inequality is relatively high at least in part because many of its immigrants are poor and have few skills – much as in the United States and Sweden. It is not surprising that immigrants to Britain have much lower trust than native whites – and the British story is thus different from two of its former colonies, Canada (Chapter 4) and Australia (Chapter 6). Canada and Australia have limited immigration to people who score high on a "points test" for skills, literacy, education, and English proficiency. Most of the immigrants to the United Kingdom come from former colonies, as was their right until a series of more restrictive bills was enacted in the 1960s and 1971, even as migration from Commonwealth nations continued at high rates throughout the twentieth century.[4] Britain adopted a tier system based upon qualifications, similar to the points systems in Canada and Australia, in 1983.[5] However, the Labour

[3] Later World Values Surveys, especially for the United Kingdom, give estimates that seem too low.

[4] Seehttp://www.nationalarchives.gov.uk/cabinetpapers/themes/immigration.htm#The%20Commonwealth%20Immigration%20Act%20of%201968 and http://www.migrationwatchuk.com/Briefingpaper/document/48.

[5] See http://www.workpermit.com/uk/uk.htm and the links from that page.

government relaxed many of the restrictions in the early twenty-first century, leading to considerable conflict over who should be admitted to the United Kingdom (Whitehead, 2009). Britain, as a member of the European Union, has less control over its borders (even as an island) than do Canada or Australia – once an immigrant finds entrance into one EU country, he or she can freely migrate elsewhere in the Union.

The problem of inequality, especially among the races, set the framework for the debates over community cohesion in Britain. Concern over cohesion stemmed from race riots in Brixton in 1981, followed by disturbances in Bradford, Burnley, and Oldham in 2001 (Finney and Simpson, 2009, 119), and bombings of the underground (subway) in London in 2005. These incidents were intertwined with claims that immigrants' anger was fueled by their isolation – segregation – from whites. Yet many people claimed that racial and ethnic provocations were exceptions to the norm of a society that had largely accommodated differences in race, religion, and ethnicity. The government commissioned a wide range of studies, quantitative and qualitative, on community cohesion and required each locality to develop a cohesion plan (Simpson, 2004, 679).

The plethora of studies on cohesion reflects the widely held belief that Britain, far more than many other societies, was succeeding in becoming a welcoming home for people of different races and religions. A BBC poll in 2005 found that 62 percent agreed that multiculturalism "makes Britain a better place to live," and the British rated their success at assimilating minorities very favorably, especially compared to the problems experienced by France (Cowell, 2005).

Three government-sponsored reports following the 2001 disorders attributed the conflicts to the isolation – the segregation – of minorities from the majority white population. The Cantle Report's authors were "particularly struck by the depth of polarisation of our towns and cities" and of "the acute problems of segregation of, and lack of contact between particular communities" (2001, 10, 28). They quoted two young people, one Pakistani and one white:

> When I leave this meeting with you I will go home and not see another white face until I come back here next week.
>
> I never met anyone on this estate who wasn't like us from around here. (Cantle, 2001, 10)

The authors of this report concluded: "The high levels of residential segregation found in many English towns would make it difficult to achieve community cohesion" (Cantle, 2001, 71).

The Ouseley Report included the argument that the key lesson of the Bradford disturbances was:

> [T]he high levels of residential segregation found in many English towns would make it difficult to achieve community cohesion.... At the heart of the self-segregation tendencies are issues of ignorance, fear and unfounded beliefs that affect attitudes and behaviour. These are deeply held attitudes and perceptions. They also restrict social interaction between different cultural groups, with the main casualties being young people who are discouraged by their parents and peer groups from mixing, interacting and socialising. (2001, 3, 28)

The Denham Report echoed these worries:

> Until this year, segregation was a term that was rarely used in discussion of community relations in Britain ... a trend towards segregation may be a symptom of deeper concerns, fear of racist attacks, or of deep seated prejudices and racism. (2001, 13)

The three reports all focused on social isolation as the underlying cause of the racial conflicts in British cities. Hudson et al. (2007) reported that black Caribbean and Somali immigrants found their own communities more welcoming than the larger society. They argued that "residential segregation between different ethnic communities ... is at the root of problems of social cohesion." The three government reports concluded that the failure to recognize segregation as a central problem was a major failure in social and political dialogue.

Or was it? Three years after the reports were issued, Ludi Simpson, a British academic who studies and measures segregation, challenged the claims that British communities were highly segregated and that different ethnic and racial groups were isolated from each other: "Increasing residential segregation of South Asian communities [the largest minority in Bradford] is a myth ... segregation is not the problem it is perceived to be" (2004, 668. 679).

Simpson argues that increases in segregation are temporary (2004, 664, 665). As new immigrants come to a community, they quite naturally flock to areas with people like themselves who speak the same language, eat the same foods, worship together, and provide social and economic support – the familiar argument about immigrant segregation. Seeming increases in segregation levels reflect influxes of new immigrants into communities. As groups become settled, they move out of ethnic enclaves and into more diverse communities. Moreover, Britain does not have ghettos as the United States does. No group is isolated as are African-Americans. Trevor Phillips's claim that no one ever escapes from

British ghettos, on Simpson's argument, is simply wrong: "The broad picture that can be painted from these data is one of dispersal of a growing South Asian population from the inner city. This does not result in lower segregation because the inner-city South Asian population is 'refilled' by natural growth (more births than deaths) and by immigration" (Simpson, 2004, 674).

Trevor Phillips's "Sleepwalking to Segregation" speech to the Manchester Council for Community Relations on September 22, 2005 kindled a larger debate throughout the country. Phillips is a black man who has clearly made it in Britain. His address drew upon an alternative academic perspective that pointed to a trend toward increasing segregation of racial and ethnic groups in Britain. Phillips argued: "Increasingly, we live with our own kind. The most concentrated areas, what the social scientists call 'ghettoes,' aren't all poverty stricken and drug ridden. But they are places where more than two-thirds of the residents belong to a single ethnic group" (2005, 10).

Phillips's claims stemmed from the work of Johnston, Poulsen, and Forrest (2005, 2007), who took strong issue with Simpson on the extent and consequences of segregation in the United Kingdom. It is rare that questions of measurement in academic research influence a public policy debate – much less get the attention (albeit indirectly) of the prime minister.

Simpson uses the familiar dissimilarity index. Johnston, Poulsen, and Forrest claim that this aggregate measure hides concentrations of minority groups. They construct six alternative measures based upon the dominance of a particular group in a neighborhood and the relative sizes of other ethnic or racial groups. The most extreme segregation occurs in areas where one group comprises 80 percent or more of the population. The most integrated neighorhood is where two groups contain between 50 percent and 70 percent of residents, with other ethnicities/races having substantial shares (Johnston, Poulsen, and Forrest, 2007, 718–19). Their measure is sensitive to the relative sizes of group populations, while the dissimilarity index used by Simpson and most other researchers is not. While Johnston, Poulsen, and Forrest argue that "[n]either index is right and neither is wrong" (2005, 1223), their measure "involves the degree to which it dominates the population of areas rather than shares those areas with members of other groups, and hence the degree to which it is encapsulated from the remainder of society."

I am not going to repeat the debates over measurement that I discussed in Chapter 2. What matters more here is how different measurement techniques: (1) tell different stories about segregation in Britain; and (2) shaped a public policy debate. Johnston, Poulsen, and Forrest argue that Simpson underestimates the negative consequences of segregation:

> If segregation has negative effects, on feelings of self esteem and identity among the minority population ... on conflict between them and the "others" who live elsewhere, and on educational and other opportunities ... then the pattern now is possibly more important to policy-makers than the emergent process. Segregation, as defined here, not only exists now but is becoming more marked. (2005, 1226)

Simpson (2005, 1230) responded that a preoccupation with high levels of minority group concentration is "partly a xenophobic response (highly White areas are not seen as a problem), partly a response consistent with global power relations, partly a diversion from real social issues affecting all groups including millions of White families."[6]

So who is right? There is no simple right or wrong answer to the question of British segregation. The hypersegregation of African-Americans means that blacks live apart from whites on multiple dimensions (see Chapter 2). The correlation of Iceland's multigroup entropy index and the P* measure of isolation of whites from African-Americans is strong (r = -.699; see Lieberson, 1981 and Racial Residential Segregation Measurement Project, n.d., 153 on p*). across 239 municipalities. But Britain (like most other countries) is largely free of ethnic ghettos (Clark, Putnam, and Fieldhouse, 2010, 29; Peach, 1996, 232; Poulsen, Johnston, and Forrest, 2007, 722). So measures of isolation are not as strongly related to dissimilarity indices.

The levels of segregation, as measured by dissimilarity indices, are much lower in the United Kingdom than in the United States. Across 12 major urban areas, values of the index were .35 for Caribbeans, .40 for Indians, .54 for Pakistanis, and .61 for Bangladeshis (Waters, 2009, 23). Fifty-six percent of blacks would have to move from their neighborhoods to make them more representative of larger areas – compared to 80 percent or more for African-Americans (Daley, 1998, 1715). The major exception is South Asians – especially Bangladeshis, who are the most segregated with dissimilarity indices approaching .75 (Peach, 1996, 224; Simpson, 2004, 669)[7] and are said to live in ghettos (Johnston, Poulsen, and Forrest, 2002, 609). Yet Pakistanis, and South Asians more

[6] He is careful to exonerate Johnston, Poulsen, and Forrest from these sentiments.

[7] Johnston, Poulsen, and Forrest maintain that South Asians live in a ghetto in Bradford (2002, 609).

generally, are considerably less segregated. Indians are even less isolated than Pakistanis (Peach, 1996, 225–6).

Peach explains why Britain does not have ghettos:

> [Minority] populations ... rarely achieve a majority of the population of urban wards and relatively low proportions of the ethnic populations are found at such high concentrations. Thus, if one accepts the dual definition of the ghetto – that all the inhabitants of the area are of that group and that all members of that group are in such areas – the British ethnic-minority populations do not conform to such conditions. (1996, 232)

While segregation is not as strong in Britain as in the United States, it is common to find clustering multiethnic neighborhoods that set minorities apart from the majority white population (Iceland and Weinberg with Steinmetz, 2002, 10; Johnston, Poulsen, and Forrest, 2005, 595). While most minorities live in majority-white areas, many live in mixed-minority enclaves (Johnston, Poulsen, and Forrest, 2002, 591, 601) where people of African and Asian descent live among the "host population" as well as "newer" white immigrants such as Poles, Greeks, Italians, and Turks, among others (Phillips, 1998, 1698). But even these communities are not the norm (Johnston, Poulsen, and Forrest, 2005; Peach, 1996).

The lower levels of segregation in Britain can be attributed to the smaller share of minorities in the British population, residential mobility among minorities, British housing policy, and a weaker tie between segregation and inequality compared to the United States.

A central factor in shaping lower levels of segregation is the smaller share of minorities in the United Kingdom (9 percent) compared to the United States (30 percent, see Goodhart, 2004). Two-thirds of all immigrants are white, mostly from Europe (Finney and Simpson, 2009, 57). Most minorities live: (1) in England rather than in Scotland or Wales; (2) in large cities; and (3) in a small number of wards. More than two-thirds of blacks and South Asians lived in fewer than 10 percent of wards in the United Kingdom in the 1990s. While half of African-Americans live in majority black neighborhoods, only 16 percent of minorities live in majority nonwhite areas in Britain (Clark, Putnam, and Fieldhouse, 2010, 29; Peach, 1996, 220). Most whites in the United Kingdom don't live near minorities, and are thus more segregated than minorities.

After a generation in an enclave, minority group members tend to move out and into areas dominated by majority whites (Finney and Simpson, 2009, 127; Simpson, 2004, 675). The level of segregation declines sharply over time for most minorities (Peach, 1996, 227; Simpson, 2004, 668).

Mobility itself is tied to British housing policy. Prior to 1970, minorities faced strong discrimination in obtaining housing, facing both racism and public policy. Many low-income people live in council housing (formerly owned and operated by local governments). Government policy initially restricted access to council housing to people who resided in an area for five years (Peach, 1998, 1670), as did the unwillingness of banks to give mortgages to minorities and, as in the United States, white opposition to having minorities as neighbors. The Race Relations Acts of 1967 and 1976 were designed to improve access to public housing for minorities, but, as with changes in the law in the United States, its effects on residential discrimination were weak. Estate agents continued to discriminate against minorities.

The Greater London Council introduced an experimental program in the borough of Tower Hamlets in the mid-1980s to try to attract Bengali-speaking immigrants, but with limited success. Birmingham adopted a program in the 1970s to make public housing more diverse and Bradford bussed students to white neighborhoods to attend integrated schools. Yet efforts to bring more minorities into council housing foundered upon the partial privatization of such residences in the 1970s. In the 1980s, the government stepped up enforcement of the Race Relations Act and made notable progress on integration (Phillips, 1998, 1693–6; Phillips and Karn, 1991, 67–9, 86).

The path to greater integration is eased by the weaker link between inequality and segregation in Britain compared to the United States (Johnston, Poulsen, and Forrest, 2007, 733; Peach, 1998, 1674). When segregation and poverty go together, minorities become trapped in the ghetto. The greater mobility of minorities in the United Kingdom is a clear sign that segregation of new immigrants does not lead to permanent isolation.

Phillips and Karn paint a more ominous picture of Britain:

> The prevailing trend for the South Asian and Afro-Carribean population has been one of continuing residential concentration, segregation, and deprivation, with a growing overrepresentation within the poorest areas.... Black minority segregation and deprivation is produced and sustained through widespread institutional discrimination against the South Asian and Afro-Carribean population in Britain. The process is one of cumulative disadvantage which arises ... from discrimination against black minority groups in the job market and the education system, by the police ... and the judiciary, as well as in the housing market itself.... South Asians and Afro-Caribbeans find themselves in a position of special disadvantage.... The whole trend of the British housing system is to become more like the U.S. system, with greater dependence on market forces and greater segregation

according to race and income ... attempts to introduce racial harassment legislation in 1985 and again in 1988 were thwarted in Parliament. (1991, 68, 74, 87)

The situation likely has improved substantially since Phillips and Karn wrote. More recently, only 25 percent of British respondents to a European survey preferred to live in a neighborhood where "almost nobody is of a different race, color, or ethnic group" than the majority – lower than in most other countries on the continent (Finney and Simpson, 2009, 103).

Whose Cohesion?

Why, then, so much worry about segregation? The nuances of the academic literature were lost on the public. As always, bad news (Johnston, Poulsen, and Forrest) travels faster and has a bigger impact than good news (Simpson, Peach). The stark language of Trevor Phillips's speech, as well as his status as a prominent black public figure, heralded a real crisis in British society.

There was more than a bit of reality – and a dose of discomfort – in some findings that both sides accepted. The two sides to the segregation debate agreed that South Asians are highly segregated, far more than other minorities. Muslim South Asians are isolated from the majority white population. Most of the racial disturbances involved young Muslims. They are perceived to be the minority that has not integrated well into mainstream society – and the least willing to fit in. For many British people, the riots were a clarion call to reassess what society was doing to help new immigrants. For others, it was an alarm that multiculturalism was not working, that British society was under threat, especially since most immigrants are now coming from Muslim countries.

Britain, like Canada, is committed to a policy of multiculturalism. Leaders (before Cameron) exulted in the island nation's diversity. This led to a redefinition of Britishness as a set of commonly shared values and institutions rather than a racial identity. Proponents such as Lord Biku Parekh wrote in a government-sponsored report:

> How is Britain's story imagined? ... In the dominant version ... there are several recurring themes.... People believe that Britain has been unified since time immemorial – hence the respect for tradition, for established social conventions and ancient institutions with roots in an ancestral past. (2002, 17, 38)

Instead, Parekh argued (n.d.):

> The sense of belonging cannot be ethnic and based on shared cultural, ethnic and other characteristics, for a multicultural society is too diverse for that, but must

be political and based on a shared commitment to the political community. Its members do not directly belong to each other as in an ethnic group but through their mediating membership of a shared community, and they are committed to each other because they are all in their own different ways committed to a common historical community. They do and should matter to each other because they are bonded together by the ties of common interest and attachment.

This, then, is the core of community cohesion, according to Phillips:

What makes us British: First and foremost, our shared values: for example an attachment to democracy, freedom of speech, and equality, values which anyone who expects to live in Britain must respect and abide by, both notionally and in practice. Second, we share common traditions which, whatever we do at home, we all agree to respect and observe in our everyday encounters. Central to these I would say are our common language, our good manners, our care for children. We also cherish a tradition of poking fun at politicians, priests and do-gooders. (2005, 6)

These demands are not demanding. The reassuring news is that minorities, including Muslims, *feel British*. They belong to Britain. Belonging is as slippery a concept as community cohesion. There is more than a bit of irony that minorities feel *more* British than do the majority whites, by 51 percent to 29 percent. Whites are more likely to identify as English, Scottish, or Welsh – by 52 percent compared to 11 percent for blacks and Asians. Belonging to Britain may simply reflect an acceptance of one's new country as home rather than identification with its culture. Even that veneer had become less shiny: In 1996, 52 percent called themselves British, but only 44 percent did so in 2005 (Taher, 2007). Phillips's idea of a national identity is ambiguous: democratic institutions and "good manners" are easy for people of different backgrounds to accept, but "shared values" and "common traditions" seem more connected to an integrationist model and at odds with British multiculturalism.

Manning and Roy find that immigrants from Muslim countries (especially Pakistan and Bangladesh) are *more* likely than other immigrants to see themselves as British and to adopt this identity faster (2007, 4, 5, 9, 13). Second-generation immigrants, whatever their background, are ready to say that they belong to Britain. Maxwell, using similar surveys, reports just the opposite: Muslims are *less* likely to see themselves as British, while Caribbean immigrants, who grew up with British institutions and the English language, feel *more* British (2006, 748; 2009, 1461).

Mason argues that the loose set of connections underlying belonging in a multicultural state may be too thin: commitment to a set of core values and practices such as good manners, taking care of your children, and speaking English won't bind people to any particular identity (2010, 867–8). One could be an American, a Canadian, an Australian, a citizen of Belize, or a Swede (almost all of whom speak English). A more demanding "thick" sense of identity, even if adopted voluntarily, "would threaten to be assimilationist in an oppressive or unjust way."

Mason makes a telling distinction between belonging and trust (2010, 871). Belonging is far less demanding. Britain is where immigrants live – and half of minorities were born there (Finney and Simpson, 2009, 57). They don't belong anywhere else. Belonging only demands a commitment to a country's customs and institutions (cf. Parekh, 2002). Acceptance of customs and institutions is not difficult, and even minimal (or no) contact with people of different backgrounds should be sufficient to achieve a sense of belonging (Mason, 2010, 867).

People can belong to Britain even if they have underlying feelings of discrimination and pessimism, which are recipes for mistrust. To get to trust, you need more than contact, even more than the "meaningful contact" among members of different groups urged by the Cantle Report and other government studies. You need to develop equality among different groups (Mason, 2010, 863–4, 872; Uslaner, 2002, chs. 2, 6, 8). Trust among citizens will develop "if and only if they believe that there is some reason why they should be part of the same polity, other than that they happen to live within its borders." These two types of attachment are different – and confidence in institutions generally does *not* lead to increased faith in one's fellow citizens (Uslaner, 2002, ch. 5), even as Mason believes that a sense that we share identification with national institutions can create bonds of trust among citizens.[8]

Yet minorities fare worse than majority whites – usually substantially so. Two-thirds of minorities, but only 37 percent of whites, live in the 88 most deprived districts in England (Home Office of the United Kingdom, 2004, 13). They "invoke a narrative of downward mobility" (Waters, 2009, 39–41). Caribbeans, who have achieved far greater financial and educational success than most minorities, nevertheless perceive persistent discrimination and feel that they may never be accepted as fully British (Maxwell, 2009, 1461). A third of black people and a fifth of Asians thought that the police would treat them worse than they would whites. And just a quarter of Asians and a fifth of blacks reported that people of different backgrounds "got on well together" in their neighborhoods (Home Office Research, 2004, 83, 109).

[8] I owe this interpretation to Andrew Mason (personal communication, March 11, 2011).

Muslims are the least likely of any ethnic/racial group to participate in the labor force and to hold professional positions, with 17 percent long-term unemployment compared to 3 percent for all Britons. Many Muslims perceive bias "from mainstream society that does not fully accept them as British" (Change Institute, 2009, 25, 32). Tony Blair, when he was prime minister, called upon Muslim women not to wear the veil, which he called "a mark of separation" and which David Davis, the Conservative Party's Home Affairs shadow minister, called a mechanism of "voluntary apartheid" (Cowell, 2006).

Economic discrimination and inequality lower trust. So does multiculturalism. The government has tried to integrate the Muslim community by funding community centers and programs as well as religious schools (Lyall, 2006). Yet despite – or perhaps because of – these institutions, Muslims are more likely to have dual identities and to identify as Muslim first and British second (Change Institute, 2009, 34; Mogahed, 2007, 3).

Overall, 66 percent of whites, 83 percent of nonwhites, and 88 percent of Muslims argue that a dual identity as British and one's home country or religion is possible.[9] Modood, reporting on the Fourth National Survey of Ethnic Minorities, argues that "[t]he majority of respondents had no difficulty with the idea of hyphenated or multiple identities," that religion is a common form of second identity – especially for Asian immigrants – and that "there was very little erosion of group identification down the generations ... there seems to be less subjective incompatibility between being British and Pakistani than being British and Scottish" (2008, 130, 127, 131). A strong sense of in-group identity should reduce generalized trust, especially if that dual identification is overlaid with economic distress.

The debate over how well integrated minorities are is marked by lots of accusations from each side. Whites, including leaders such as Blair and Cameron, put much of the blame on minorities who segregate themselves and may adopt extremist political views. Minorities counter that they want to see themselves as British but aren't really accepted as British (Change Institute, 2009, 31; Condor, Gibson, and Abell, 2006, 150). The overall result is at least partially one of tension: in a seven-nation survey of attitudes toward immigration in the West in 2008,[10] the British were most likely to say that immigration is a problem (62 percent) and to agree

[9] From the 2007 UK Citizenship Survey.

[10] The countries are the United Kingdom, the United States, France, Germany, Italy, the Netherlands, and Poland.

strongly that immigrants will raise taxes (43 percent), increase crime (34 percent), be involved in terrorist attacks (29 percent), take jobs away from those born in the country (29 percent); and that unemployed immigrants should be forced to leave the country (51 percent). The British were also the most likely to say that it is very important to be born in the country. Yet the picture is not all dire: more than any people other than Americans, the British were the *most* likely to agree strongly that immigrants are hard workers (29 percent compared to 45 percent for Americans and about 10 percent of Italians, Dutch, and Poles) and that Muslims respect other cultures (29 percent compared to 25 percent of Americans and 6 percent of Italians and Poles) (German Marshall Fund of the United States, 2008).

Minorities want to integrate, but they can't accept the almost thousand-year history of a white colonial power as their own narrative. Unlike settler societies such as the United States, Canada, and Australia, Britain is *not* a nation of immigrants. So there are not easily resolvable questions about what the common identity underlying trust should be. Lord Parekh argued, "Britishness, as much as Englishness, has systematic, largely unspoken, racial connotations. Whiteness nowhere features as an explicit condition of being British, but it is widely understood that Englishness, and therefore by extension Britishness, is racially coded" (2002, 38). Muslim scholars at the Policy Exchange think tank stressed the centrality of assimilation but blamed the government's policy of multiculturalism for creating barriers between peoples: "Stressing difference has pushed some people apart to the degree that they feel no empathy for the suffering of others who are 'not their own' ... promoting Britishness like this ends up treating an organic identity as if it were simply a public relations invention or a marketing ploy. You cannot re-name significant days in the calendar according to the whims of the latest focus group" (Mirza, Senthilkumaran, and Ja'far, 2007, 90–1).

Yet, given the task of integrating large numbers of people, Britain is hardly a bleak house. British minorities are neither as badly segregated nor as isolated as African-Americans.[11] While there is dispute over what integration or cohesion means to different groups (ETHNOS Research and Consultancy, 2006, 27), even most Muslims – widely believed to be the *least* integrated minority – say that they have as much in common with

[11] Waters argues that the levels of segregation of Britain's minorities are close to those for Hispanics and Asians in the United States (2009, 23, 26).

non-Muslims as with members of their own faith (Mirza, Senthilkumaran, and Ja'far, 2007, 39).

What, then, can we say about segregation, friendship networks, and trust in Britain?

Trust and Social Networks in the United Kingdom

I move now to an analysis of trust and the diversity of social ties in the United Kingdom. The data I employ are the 2007 UK Citizenship Survey conducted by the Home Office. The survey has face-to-face interviews with 14,095 respondents from England and Wales, including a large ethnic boost allowing me to estimate models for different minorities.[12] I look at the full sample and then at whites and nonwhites and minorities I label South Asians, Africans, and Muslims. The racial/ethnic classifications are straightforward. I focus on Muslims (who may come from more than one ethnic or racial group) because they are the minority group that has received the most attention in discussions of integration – and the more recent violence has involved Muslims. South Asians and Africans are two other major immigrant groups. I classify people of South Asian (African) heritage if either: (1) both parents came from South Asia (Africa) or (2) the respondent speaks an South Asian (African) language as his or her main tongue. The survey also had a modest number of immigrants from Caribbean countries. Caribbean respondents were virtually identical to Africans on most variables, so I included them in the African heritage category.

The data sets in use here, the Social Capital Benchmark Survey in the United States and the 2007 UK Citizenship Survey, show trust levels that are either too high (the former) or too low (the latter) compared to other surveys. Nevertheless, both surveys show that minorities are considerably less trusting than the majority white population (see Figure 3.1 in Chapter 3 for the United States and Figure 5.1 for the United Kingdom). Minorities are less trusting than whites: 43 percent of whites believe that most people can be trusted, compared to 29 percent of nonwhites, 31 percent of South Asians, 26 percent of Africans, and 28 percent of Muslims.

[12] The data in the 2007 UK Citizenship Survey, conducted for the Home Office, are described in Tonkin and Rutherfoord (2008). The data are available at http://www.data-archive.ac.uk/findingData/hocsTitles.asp (registration required). A description of the technical details of the survey can be found at http://www.esds.ac.uk/findingData/snDescription.asp?sn=5739. The survey is comprised of a core sample of 9,336 people and a minority ethnic boost of 4,759.

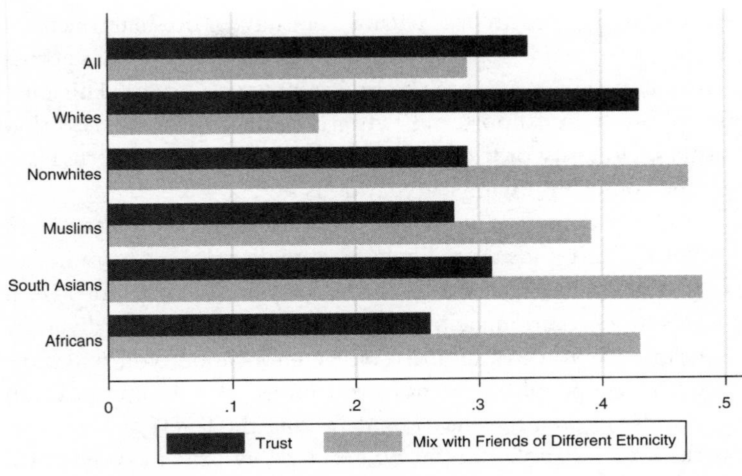

FIGURE 5.1. Trust and mix with friends of different background by ethnicity. UK Citizenship Survey 2007

These figures are substantially higher than the 13 percent among African-Americans, but comparable to the share of Hispanics who agree that "most people can be trusted."

More notable is the pattern of diverse friendships among majority and minority respondents, especially compared to the United States. While British whites are more trusting than minorities, they are substantially less likely than minorities to mix with friends of different ethnicities. Almost half of nonwhites – especially East Indians – socialize with people of different backgrounds. Almost 40 percent of the supposedly isolated Muslims do. Yet barely more than 15 percent of whites do so. While the question in the SCBS is somewhat different, the share of whites with diverse friendship networks is about the same in the United States as in the United Kingdom, but the far more segregated African-Americans have less heterogenous social ties. American Hispanics seem to have even more diverse networks (again noting the very different questions).

Whites are the most likely to be isolated socially and residentially – to have no friends of different backgrounds and to live in the most segregated neighborhoods (by their own perception): 83 percent of whites are so insulated, followed by Muslims (61 percent), South Asians (57 percent), all nonwhites (53 percent), and Africans (52 percent).

As elsewhere, minorities are less trusting but have more heterogenous social ties. The negative relationship between trust and diverse ties across the five groups is strong, even with the tiny sample ($r^2 = .760$). This puzzling finding shows why Allport and Pettigrew are correct to stress that context matters. Diversity of friendships alone does not lead to trust (see Chapter 2): the connection with segregation is key.

The low level of segregation in the United Kingdom makes contact with people of other backgrounds more likely. The smaller size of the minority population in the United Kingdom, especially when compounded with the lower levels of segregation, helps to explain the high levels of diversity in social networks. If you live in a diverse neighborhood, you will have more chances to meet people different from yourself. But the composition of neighborhoods is not sufficient to explain why the levels of heterogenous networks are uniformly low for whites, be they Brits or Americans.

How segregated are British neighborhoods? Aggregate data on segregation in the United Kingdom are not publicly available, so I have to rely upon a measure in the Citizenship Survey similar to that in the Latino survey in the United States: an estimate of the share of people of the same group who live within walking distance. This measure of segregation is distinct from the dissimilarity indices I use elsewhere, and is closer to the measure of group concentration of Poulsen, Johnston, and Forrest (2002). Their approach focuses on the share of each group living in an area relative to the percentage of other groups. Despite the differences, the two measures are complementary – and there is no alternative measure closer to dissimilarity available. I present the estimates for each group in Figure 5.2.

There is less segregation in Britain, but that does *not* mean that whites and nonwhites live next to each other. Almost 80 percent of whites estimate that more than half (or even all) of the people within walking distance of them are from the same ethnic group as they are (see Figure 5.2). Most nonwhites, including people of African and South Asia heritage – and most Muslims – say that less than half of the population within walking distance is from different groups. Yet this is not a simple picture of a fully integrated society. Almost 60 percent of whites believe that their environs are less than half minority. Almost 90 percent of South Asians, Africans, and Muslims say that their neighborhoods are 80 percent or more minority – and 70 percent of each say that 90 percent of their immediate neighbors are from minority groups.

The British pattern of integration is not a melting pot where people of all backgrounds live together (Johnston et al., 2002). The correlation

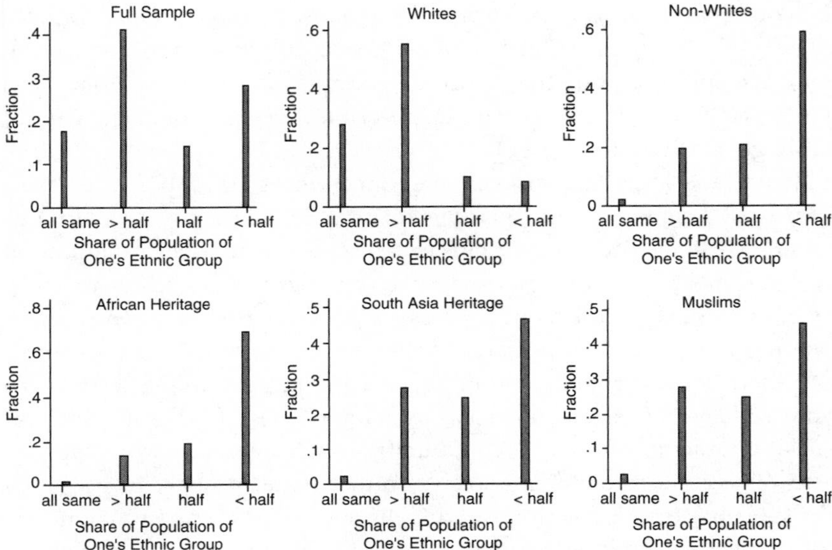

FIGURE 5.2. Diversity of population within walking distance

between the walking distance measure (closest to an indicator of segregation) and the minority share (which is an indicator of diversity) is modest: for the full sample, the tau-c correlation is modest (.484). For whites, it is .363; for nonwhites, the correlation is -.231; and for Muslims, it is only -.159. For minorities, living in an integrated community largely means living near other people of color. Yet since minorities constitute a small share of the British population, the prospect for diverse friendship networks to lead to the belief that "*most people* can be trusted" may be less than in the United States.

The evidence on diversity and trust in the United Kingdom is mixed. Clark, Putnam, and Fieldhouse find weaker, but still significant, negative effects of diversity on social capital (2010, 82, 90) (see also Fieldhouse and Cutts, 2010, 300). Pennant (2005) reports that people living in more diverse areas of Britain are less likely to trust others in their communities. However, Letki (2008), as I note in Chapter 2, finds initial support for a negative relationship between community-level diversity and a composite indicator of social capital – but the result becomes insignificant when she controls for the economic status of the community. Laurence and Heath argue that "far from eroding community cohesion, ethnic diversity is generally a strong positive driver of cohesion.... *It is ... deprivation that undermines cohesion, not diversity*" (2008, 41, emphasis in original). Bowyer (2009), analyzing multiple surveys, finds that more diversity leads to greater tolerance. Laurence finds that diversity builds *in-group* ties, but not social capital more generally (2009, 8, 14).

Do diverse social networks in integrated settings lead to greater levels of trust? I estimate probit equations for trust in Figure 5.3 for all groups except Muslims. Because Muslims are the focus of so much attention on integration, I present the results separately in Figure 5.4. The key variable, as in the model for the United States, is an interaction between whether one has close friends of different backgrounds and the share of people of different backgrounds within 15 to 20 minutes walking distance of your residence. I replace this measure with a series of other measures of social interaction in diverse communities, each interacted with the percent minority a respondent perceives rather than the share of people of the same background within walking distance. This is more of an indicator of diversity (heterogeneity) than of segregation, so it provides a rough test of the effects of segregation versus diversity. The social interactions I examine for the diversity measures are: (1) having diverse friends, close or not; (2) how often one mixes with diverse friends; and how often one mixes with diverse friends (3) in clubs; (4) in school (as parents); (5) in houses of worship; and (6) at home.

The balance of the model for trust is somewhat different from conventional models (esp. Uslaner, 2002, ch. 4), since the Citizenship survey did not include many of the questions I use for trust models elsewhere. The variables in the model, while less conventional, seem important for examining trust among minorities. The predictors include measures of local cohesion – do neighbors share your values and do they get on well with each other – as well as three questions about factors shaping one's identity. If you place a great deal of importance on your country of origin or your ethnicity,[13] you will be more likely to trust your in-group rather than out-groups. If, however, your identity is shaped by your interests, you may be more responsive to bridging ties. I have argued that trust presumes a common culture, so we might expect that support for the idea that everyone should speak English would lead to higher levels of trust (2002, 197). For minorities, demands that everyone speak English might be construed as an assault on their cultural heritage – so an argument

[13] For most whites, the country of origin is Britain or England, Scotland, Wales, or Northern Ireland.

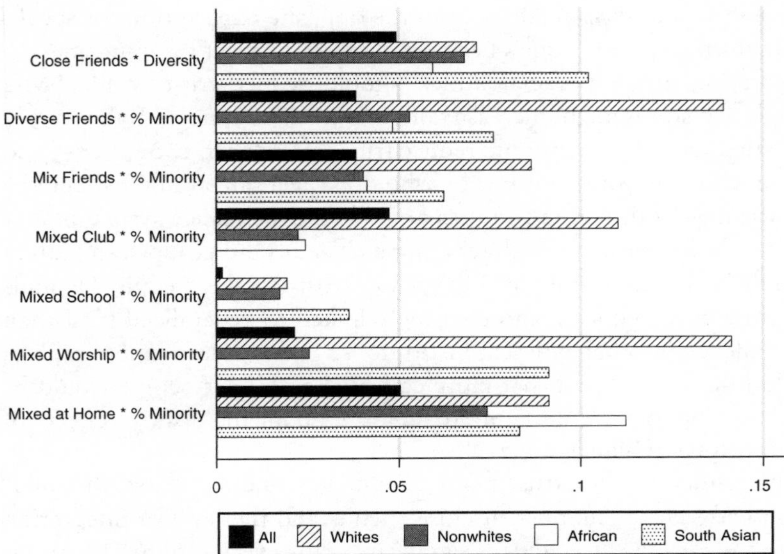

FIGURE 5.3. Probit effects for diverse friendship networks on trust by ethnic/racial group

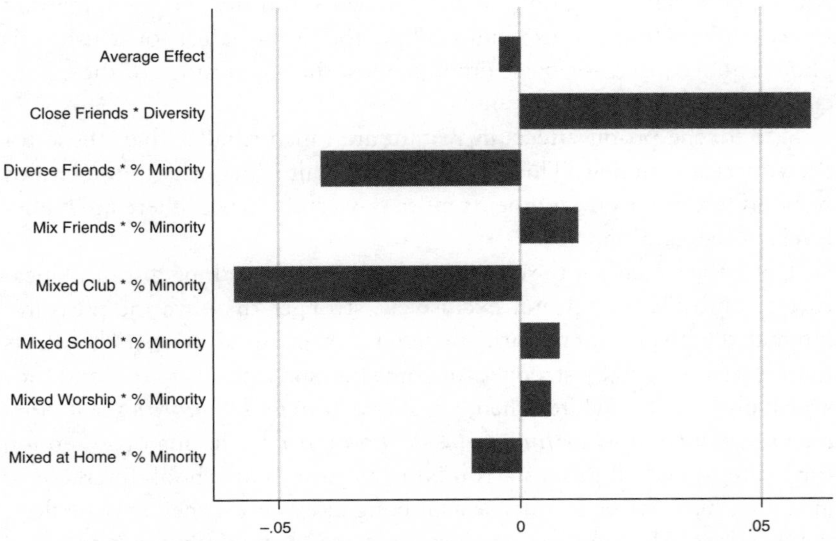

FIGURE 5.4. Probit effects for diverse social networks: muslims

from multiculturalism might lead to the opposite expectation for speaking English: respect for one's heritage might build trust for minorities.

Worrying about a racial attack should reduce trust, while being respected at stores might increase faith in others. Brehm and Rahn (1997) argue that fear of crime should reduce trust (cf. Uslaner, 2002, 128–9), so people who worry about crime or who don't feel safe at night should be less trusting. Rothstein (2000) has argued that the justice system is supposed to be a neutral, fair arbiter among citizens (and groups), so faith in the judicial system should lead to greater trust in other people. He finds that trust in the police is more strongly linked to generalized trust than is confidence in other political institutions. The standard demographics would lead us to expect that more educated and older people would be more trusting, but would be more agnostic about the positive effects of higher income (Uslaner, 2002, ch. 4).

The estimations for trust point to four key findings. First, the interaction between the number of close friends and the level of integration in one's environment is *always* significant – for every group. The probit effects are similar for most groups – with the exception of South Asians, for whom a diverse set of friends in an integrated environment matter most. South Asians are less likely than other minorities (other than Muslims) to have such diverse environments and ties – though still 3.5 times as likely to do so as whites. While the probit effect for Muslims is about equal to that for most other groups, the significance of the coefficient is less than for other groups.

Second, the probit effects in Britain are much smaller than those for the American models. This suggests that white (majority) populations respond to diverse environments more powerfully where there are higher levels of segregation.

Third, the effects for the close friends*diversity (walking distance) measure are mostly, though not exclusively, stronger than are the measures interacted with percent minority (a better measure of diversity). The effects for whites are actually stronger for some measures of diversity – and they are all positive. For whites, then, *any interaction with minorities in a more diverse or integrated setting seems to boost trust*. The major exception for whites – and all groups – is mixing as parents at school. Interactions at school may not be as intense as mixing elsewhere – they may be fleeting meetings. Meetings at church seem to matter mightily for whites and only for whites. Overall, then, interactions in an integrated setting seem to matter somewhat more for all groups in Figure 5.3 except for whites, for whom all interactions matter. For the groups in this figure, the effects of having close friends of different backgrounds in an integrated neighborhood matter most for South Asians and least for Africans.

The story changes in Figure 5.4, showing the results for Muslims. The results for Muslims are distinctive: the only strongly positive effect is for having friends of different backgrounds in an integrated setting. All of the other measures, employing estimates of diversity, are either tiny or even negative (mixed clubs, simply having diverse friends). If Muslims are the least integrated minority, then the path toward greater trust is through integrated neighborhoods and friends of diverse backgrounds. This result supports the argument that Muslims *want* to put their faith in fellow Brits – indeed, perhaps, even to assimilate while maintaining their religion as other groups have done. It is not quite time to exult in these findings: the effects for Muslims are still modest (about 6 percent).

On the other hand, the weakest effects for *any* of the measures are for Africans. Despite their longer ties to the British empire and their historical ties to British customs and the English language, the discrimination they report (34 percent say that they were denied a job because of their race, more than any other group) may make trusting others a more difficult task. Finally, the stronger effects for the close friends/diversity measure for South Asians and the weaker impact for Muslims suggest that the most powerful effect is for South Asians who are not Muslims – mostly Indian Hindus (and Jains and Singhs, among other minority religions). So the minority group that is already among the most integrated (if not *the* most integrated) becomes even more trusting as Allport's optimal conditions are approximated.

South Asians who have close friends from different races or religions and who live in diverse neighborhoods are 10 percent more likely to be trusting than those without such friends who live in more homogenous areas. The boost in trust is slightly larger for South Asians than for all respondents (5 percent), Africans and Muslims (6 percent), and both whites and nonwhites (7 percent). These effects are substantially lower than I reported for whites, blacks, or Hispanics in the United States or for majority groups in Canada. The effects for other measures – diverse friendship networks, mixing with people of different backgrounds in clubs, worshipping in mixed congregations (interacted with the estimated share of your community who are minorities) – are much greater, ranging from 11 percent to 13 percent. For Africans, mixing with people of different backgrounds at home (again interacted with diversity) boosts trust by 12 percent.

These closer, perhaps more intimate, contacts are a better approximation to the notion of optimal contact, so the stronger impacts on trust are not surprising. However, they are far less common than friendships – and the "close friends" questions in the Citizenship survey do reflect the equality that is important in Allport's formulation. The other forms of contact in diverse settings seem to matter mostly for whites, not for minorities. Indeed, for Muslims, friendship and mixing either don't increase trust at all, or perhaps (curiously) even reduce faith in others (Figure 5.4).

The roots of trust differ for majority and minority groups in Britain. Ironically, many of the factors I expected to shape trust for minority groups are significant *only for, or primarily for, whites*. Country of origin matters only for whites and for Muslims. The importance of ethnicity to your sense of identification matters *only for whites*, while concern about crime and the belief that everyone should speak English are more consequential for whites. The more isolated white majority seems to respond more to the demands of multiculturalism than do minorities. For South Asians, Africans, and Muslims, the key factors underlying trust are educational and economic status and especially confidence in the police.

Among minority groups, only Muslims' trust is shaped by identification with their home country and how well they feel treated in stores. Muslims are the most segregated of the minorities and have the fewest friends of different backgrounds. Africans, who are the most likely to live in integrated areas (in contrast to black Americans) and to have close friends of different backgrounds, are *least* affected by perceptions of safety and multicultural values. They are the only minority group for whom the importance of interests rather than ethnicity or country of origin shapes trust.

I also estimated an additional model for diverse friendship networks in integrated neighborhoods including the measure of whether where you live is the most important factor shaping your identity (see Chapter 2). For most samples, this variable was dropped because few people defined themselves by where they live. For the most segregated group – Muslims – residence as the source of identity *is the most important determinant of trust*. Muslims whose identity is shaped by where they live are 23 percent less likely to trust others. Only whether people share common values shapes trust almost much as this sense of identification.

Finally, familiarity by itself does not breed trust. I include a dummy variable for immigrating to the United Kingdom within the past seven years for each minority group. It is never significant in any of the estimations: people do not become more trusting simply by living in a higher-trust country. This finding reinforces data from Canada as well as Britain (Mirza, Senthilkumaran, and Ja'far, 2007, 39) that younger people have a stronger sense of ethnic identity than their parents – and this constitutes a threat to building trust.

Reprise

Diverse social contact in integrated settings matters in the United Kingdom as well as elsewhere. It matters for whites and nonwhites, though somewhat less for Muslims and people of African heritage.

And it matters less than in the United States and about the same as it does for whites in Canada. But this is not all bad news. With its higher levels of segregation and the greater link between segregation and inequality in the United States, this is not surprising. The optimal conditions matter, but they have a lot of mistrust, especially among minority groups, to overcome. A boost in trust of 6 percent (Muslims) or even 10 percent (South Asians) is a modest increment in relatively low levels of trust among minorities. The biggest boost for minorities who have close friends of different backgrounds and who live in the most integrated neighborhoods will still leave South Asians slightly less trusting than whites who might get no effect from their social ties in an integrated neighborhood. Fear for safety, distrust of the police, and low levels of education and income limit the impact of optimal conditions for minorities, even as inequalities are much lower than in the United States. For the majority, diverse friendship networks in integrated neighborhoods might matter more – if there were more of them. And the more segregated a group is (as with Muslims), the more likely its members are to maintain a sense of strong in-group identity, which in turn leads to lower levels of trust in people unlike themselves.

British minorities seem to become more trusting under "optimal conditions" than do Asians in Canada. Most likely this reflects the initially higher levels of trust of Asian immigrants in Canada – and perhaps their greater segregation than in the United Kingdom. The Canadian pattern is closer to that of Australia (see Chapter 6) because their immigration regimes are more similar. Britain does not impose as strict requirements for immigration as either Canada or Australia – in part because of the legacy of colonialism, which has led to large-scale immigration from countries formerly ruled by Britain. Canadian blacks, rather than Asians, seem more like British immigrants in terms of trust, economic distress, and perceptions of discrimination.

But social ties *do* seem to matter. How well the results hold up when I examine why people choose to live where they do I leave (as with the United States) to Chapter 8.

6

Sweden and Australia: Newer Immigrants, Trust, and Multiculturalism

with Susanne Lundåsen[1]

> Sure, we have immigrants at our school. I've heard there are more and more. I think it's good, really. But … how should I put this … I don't know if you can really call the people who go here "immigrants." This sounds stupid … but … they're really more like us.
>
> Cecilia, an eighteen-year-old Swedish student (quoted in Trondman, 2006, 432)

> [O]nly immigrants live where we live … you're not a problem when you walk around there.… [T]here isn't any contact between Swedes and immigrants.… Swedes don't dare to come to our neighbourhood because they're afraid to.
>
> Omar, a twenty-year-old from Somalia (quoted in Trondman, 2006, 439)

> The division that worked 30 years ago between Swedes and immigrants doesn't apply anymore.… Instead we see something new: an updated kind of Swedishness.
>
> Zanyar Adami, a journalist of Kurdish background (quoted in Ekman, 2006)

> You can't have a nation with a federation of cultures. You can have a nation where a whole variety of cultures constantly influence and mould and change and blend in with the mainstream culture, but a nation that doesn't have a core culture … and the core culture of this nation is very clear; we are an outshoot of western civilisation. Because we speak the English language our cultural identity is very heavily Anglo-Saxon. It doesn't mean

[1] The section on Sweden is co-authored with Susanne Lundåsen of Ersta Sköndal University College, Stockholm, Sweden. This explains the first person "we" in this section and "I" in the section on Australia.

> that it isn't distinctively Australian, but you have to recognise that there is a core set of values in this country.
>
> Australian Prime Minister John Howard, 2006 (quoted in Tilbury, 2007, 5–6)

> [M]any young people who live in Sydney's western and south-western suburbs feel ambivalent about calling themselves Australian.... A typical Aussie is still thought of as a sandy-haired surfer, or a square-jawed farmer, or a jocular beer drinker of impeccable Anglo stock. "The only time I see an ethnic person on the TV is when they've done something bad," a 25-year-old Australian-born woman of Lebanese-Greek background [said].
>
> Horin (2010)

Sweden and Australia are high trust societies. Trust in Sweden has been very high since the first World Values Survey in 1980 – 60 percent or higher, ranking second in the world in the 1995 World Values Survey. Faith in others has remained consistent over time (Kumlin and Rothstein, 2008, 12–13). Trust in Australia was moderate, around 40 percent in 2003 (Bean, 2003, 123), before rising significantly.

Sweden and Australia are more homogenous than most other countries. When I tell people, both academics and "ordinary people," of the high trust level in Sweden, their first response is: "Well, that's not surprising; they all have blond hair and blue eyes and they all look alike." Well, yes and no. Sweden is one of the least diverse countries on Alesina's ethnic fractionalization measure, ranking 13th out of 190 countries. It has become far more diverse in recent years. Yet trust has remained high (Holmberg and Weibull, 2009, 18). Kumlin and Rothstein argue:

> Sweden seems a puzzling case. Although the country has become much more ethnically diverse over the last twenty-five years due to immigration, the level of interpersonal trust remains, in a comparative perspective, very high and exceptionally stable ... support for welfare state policies remains high and stable throughout this period of significant increase in ethnic, religious, and racial diversity.

And Australia is even more, in the words of the king of Siam in the musical *The King and I*, of a "puzzlement."[2] A country that once had a racially exclusionary immigration policy now revels in its diversity. Trust has risen almost to Swedish levels (58 percent in 2007 and 2009; see Markus and Dharmalingam, 2007, 70).[3]

[2] The lyrics of "A Puzzlement" are available at http://www.lyricsondemand.com/soundtracks/k/thekingandilyrics/apuzzlementlyrics.html.

[3] Almost 70 percent of Australians of English-speaking background trusted others in the 2007 Scanlon Foundation survey (Markus and Dharmalingam, 2007, 83). Markus

Why are Sweden and Australia high-trust societies? Whiteness isn't the answer – especially since trust has either kept steady or risen in periods of increasing immigration from low-trusting countries. The answers lie in: (1) the levels of economic inequality; (2) low levels of segregation; and (3) the willingness to pull back from policies of multiculturalism and toward greater integration. Sweden is, according to the Wider inequality measures for 2000, the second most egalitarian society in the world – with a Gini index of .253, behind only Iceland. Australia is more unequal, with an index of .352, ranking thirtieth, just below Canada. However, by 2006, Australia's Gini index fell by 15 percent to .305.[4]

Sweden is the second least segregated country – behind only Germany, according to the Alesina index. Australia is more segregated on this index – ranking in the middle at 57th. However, other analyses of Australian residential patterns paint a very different picture of Australia as having ethnic enclaves, but little segregation (Grimes, 1993, 109; Poulsen, Johnston, and Forrest, 2004, 375; 2007, 733). Sweden and Australia resemble Canada in one critical respect. The overwhelming majority of immigrants live in the largest cities: Stockholm, Goteborg, and Malmö in Sweden and Sydney, Melbourne, Adelaide, and Perth in Australia (Burnley, Murphy, and Fagan, 1997, 34; Nesslein, 2003, 1274). Both Sweden and Australia were early converts to multiculturalism – and both came to reject it while seeking to incorporate immigrants into a common culture.

Here the similarities stop. Australia is a typical Anglo-American democracy with modest levels of segregation but with high levels of trust among minorities. Sweden is a welfare state with policies that provide benefits to all without regard to status. It has low levels of segregation and makes concerted efforts to equalize earnings for minorities and natives. Even as the income gap remains, immigrants believe that they are being treated fairly, which increases their level of trust. They also have more frequent close ties to whites – which, combined with lower levels of segregation, boosts trust even more. Immigrants in Sweden have higher levels of trust than the white majorities in the United States, Canada, and the United Kingdom.

Australian minorities have relatively high levels of trust – not as high as Sweden, but still higher than minorities elsewhere and whites in the United States. In both Sweden and Australia, as elsewhere, minorities

reports a substantial drop – to 45 percent trusters – in the 2009 Scanlon Foundation survey (2010, 16).

4 See https://www.cia.gov/library/publications/the-world-factbook/fields/2172.html.

have more contact with the majority population than whites have with them. Yet here we see another "puzzlement." In Sweden, minorities gain more from contact with people of different backgrounds in integrated communities than does the majority. In Australia, the majority white population gets a modest boost in trust from Allport's optimal conditions, but the minority is barely moved by living in integrated neighborhoods with diverse ties.

The most likely answer to these contrasting findings lies in who the immigrants in each country are and how the majority population views new citizens. Both Sweden and Australia early on embraced assimilationist visions. Both countries then moved away from integration and adopted multiculturalism. Ultimately Sweden rejected multiculturalism by an act of Parliament. Even though Swedes did not formally retreat to assimilation, the repeal of multiculturalism sent a clear message that the country's immigration policy would revert to emphasizing integration. Australia, like Canada and the United Kingdom, made a huge public commitment to multiculturalism. While the government stepped back from multiculturalism when opposition leader (later the prime minister) John Howard denounced the policy, Australians remain torn about what an integrationist identity might be.

While Sweden and Australia both make a great deal of welcoming immigrants, the new citizens coming to the two nations are different. While many of Sweden's immigrants come from other Nordic countries, especially Finland, the Swedes have increasingly welcomed refugees from nations in conflict. Australia did admit some refugees from conflict, but it has largely restricted entry to skilled immigrants. Despite similarities in levels of trust, inequality, diversity, and segregation, the experiences of minorities are quite different in Sweden and Australia.

Sweden: The Welfare State and Trust

Sweden is not a likely destination for immigrants. Swedish is not an easy language to learn. The winters are cold and dark, with the sun setting in Stockholm well before Londoners settle in for afternoon tea – and not long after they return from lunch.[5]

Until recently, few bothered to immigrate to Sweden or were allowed to enter. As late as 1940, only 1 percent of the population were immigrants. Almost all of them came from other Nordic countries. Sweden

[5] Allowing for an hour's difference in time zones.

then began to accept refugees displaced by World War II, including some Jews freed from concentration camps and Estonians and Latvians escaping Soviet domination. After the war, Sweden admitted a limited number of foreign workers, mostly from Finland and Southern Europe. Nordic immigrants were welcome: a substantial share of the Finnish population is Swedish-speaking. Many came across the border to work in their richer neighbor, eased by the common labor market in the Nordic countries. Estonians and Latvians were also welcome since they too shared a common culture (Bennich-Björkman, 2007).

The post-World War II economic boom fueled the demand for immigration in Sweden. No longer an agricultural nation, Sweden needed workers for its new industrial economy. By 1970, 7 percent of the Swedish population were born outside the country. A new wave of immigrants started coming from the Middle East, Africa, and Latin America – mostly political refugees. The share of immigrants born outside of Europe rose from .2 percent in 1970 to 4 percent in 2005. They constituted a third of the population born outside Sweden; in 1970, 90 percent of immigrants were born in Europe and 60 percent came from other Nordic countries. In 2008, 17 percent of all children in Sweden aged 18 and under were immigrants or had both parents born outside the country. The immigrant share of the population had risen to 14 percent, higher than the European Union average, with only a quarter of the foreign born coming from other Nordic countries and a slightly greater share, 27 percent, from Asia. The 70,000 immigrants coming to Sweden each year now account for all of the country's population growth over the past five decades (Andersson, 2007, 2008, 5; Demker, 2007, 6; Kumlin and Rothstein, 2010, 69–70; Statistics Sweden, 2008; Wadesnsjo, 2009, 13).

Sweden's generous immigration policy in part reflects its high level of trust. If you believe that most people can be trusted, you are more likely to have favorable views of immigrants and to favor greater levels of immigration (Uslaner, 2002, 196). There is also an element of guilt: Sweden was neutral in World War II and faced strong criticism both from outside and inside (Jordan, 2008). The later willingness to accept refugees from war and repressive regimes stems from such contrition.

People fleeing war – including large numbers of people from the former Yugoslavia as well as Ethiopians, Eritreans, and Iraqis – come to Sweden not just because they can. They come because Sweden is more welcoming than most other countries. When the number of immigrants from non-Western countries increased in the 1970s, Sweden signed on to multiculturalism, urging minorities to maintain their ethnic identity (Murdie and Borgegard, 1998, 1886). The parliament unanimously enacted the policy. The government expanded programs it had already started, funding libraries, newspapers, and periodicals in immigrants' languages (Dahlström, 2004, 301). Immigrants receive free public education in the Swedish language and the country's history and culture.

The preservation of ethnic identity was one of two fundamental premises underlying Swedish immigration policy. The other was economic equality: immigrants should be able to achieve the same standard of living of native Swedes (Andersson, 2008, 2). Multiculturalism, many worried from the beginning of this policy, might lead to the nominal equality of cultures. It might also isolate minorities and lead to social divisions, which would run counter to the Swedish policy and core belief in universalism (Crepaz, 2008, 226; Dahlström, 2004, 299; Murdie and Borgegard, 1998, 1886). Universalistic policies provide benefits by right rather than by status – as rich or poor, or white or black or yellow, or as Rothstein and I called them, programs that are "all for all." The principle underlying universalism is the equal worth of all Swedes – as well as the expectation, borne out in economic statistics, that such policies *promote* equality and trust. Universalism fosters a common identity because everyone is treated equally and the recipients of government services are not stereotyped as they are under means-tested welfare regimes (Rothstein and Uslaner, 2005).

Sweden's multiculturalism was different from policies toward immigrants elsewhere in Europe. Immigrants were "minorities" rather than guest workers, and Swedes regarded special institutions for ethnic groups dubiously. By margins ranging from three to one to four to one, Swedes have consistently argued that immigrants should assimilate rather than preserve their own cultures (Borevi, 2010, 14–15; Demker, 2007, 15). In the 2009 European Values Survey, 73 percent of Swedes held that immigrants should assimilate rather than maintain their own traditions.

Sweden, together with other Nordic countries, has among the most comprehensive welfare states of any advanced democracy (Scruggs and Allan, 2008). For more than two decades, Sweden's social welfare programs for immigrants and its policies were the most inclusive and generous among all European nations' – as well as providing the strongest legal protections (Koopmans, 2008, 10).

Universalistic social welfare policies are based upon fairness – especially fairness before the law and equity in how people are treated in the receipt of public services. Impartiality has two key benefits. First, it is based upon equity and leads to greater equality. Second, fairness leads to higher levels of generalized trust – although the causal mechanism is disputed.[6]

This commitment to fairness and equity led Swedes to vacillate between housing policies that promoted integration and those that treated immigrants as equals free to live wherever they wished (Crepaz, 2008, 225). Initially Sweden followed a strongly assimilationist policy and tried to avoid high levels of segregation by controlling rents and providing public housing available to all in what was called the "Million Homes Project" lasting from 1965 to 1974 (Joseph, 2007, 15–16; Murdie and Borgegard, 1998, 1886). A surplus of housing developed as the million home mark was met in 1975. More and more people were buying their houses and apartments. As the housing program ended, Sweden embraced multiculturalism and the idea that immigrants should be free to live wherever – and with whomever – they wished. But immigrants' options were restricted to what they could afford. The result was both economic and ethnic/racial segregation (Musterd, 2003, 628; Nesslein, 2003, 1274).

In the mid-1980s, Sweden moved away from multiculturalism and a laissez-faire approach to immigrant housing. In 1986, the parliament adopted a policy that largely reversed multiculturalism – an ongoing process that culminated in a policy of civic integration in 1997. A year earlier the government decided to disperse immigrants throughout the country, a program that lasted until 1994 (Borevi, 2010, 15–16; Crepaz, 2008, 227; Edin, Frederiksson, and Aslund, 2000, 8). Even as the program was terminated, 40 percent of immigrants live outside the big cities and are relatively evenly spread throughout the country (Statistics Sweden, 2008).

Neither multiculturalism nor assimilation prevented minority segregation. Segregation has increased dramatically over time as new immigrants cluster with their nationality group (Breton et al., 2006, 1132; Linden and Lindberg, 1991, 102–14). Yet new immigrants don't find themselves in a promised land of incomprehensible wealth readily available to all, an "Oleanna" (from a Norwegian satirical song of life in mid-nineteenth-century America) where "land is free [and] ... the cows all like to milk themselves and the hens lay eggs ten times a day."[7] Segregated communities are often marked by poor maintenance, vandalism, and high levels of unemployment (Brännström, 2006, 137).

6 Does generalized trust emerge from fairness per se (Rothstein) or because fairness leads to greater equality (Rothstein and Uslaner)?

7 For the lyrics of "Oleanna," see http://www.traditionalmusic.co.uk/song-midis/Oleanna.htm. For background on the song, see http://www.enotes.com/topic/Oleanna_(song).

The strong ties between inequality and segregation found in the United States and even the somewhat weaker relationships in other countries are largely absent in Sweden (Andersson, 2008, 20; Harsman, 2006, 1350). Some areas around the three largest cities (Stockholm, Gothenburg, and Malmö) have child poverty rates of almost 90 percent; Schierup and Ålund argue that "the urban multiethnic suburbs are places where otherness and poverty go together" (2011, 52, 51). Segregation may be increasing, but – as Alesina's cross-national measure indicates, it is not extreme.

Andersson argues: "Neither ghettos nor enclaves exist in Sweden, albeit local pockets of the enclave type can be found in a few cases.... Small colony-like clusters are quite common, and – as forecasted by the definition – they tend to depopulate when new immigration from the country of origin ends" (2008, 14). Kumlin and Rothstein add: "while immigrants are heavily concentrated in certain residential areas, they are not divided into specific areas by ethnicity. There is no equivalent to 'Chinatown' or similar ethnically pure enclaves" (2010, 70). The extensive welfare state means that immigrants will not be as poor in Sweden as they are elsewhere (but see Schierup and Ålund, 2011 for exceptions) and that immigrants escape poverty over time and especially over generations.

Sweden provides extra resources for schools with high shares of minority students – and students are not restricted to attending schools where they live. There are uniform expectations for students in all schools and there is no evidence that students in segregated schools perform worse until isolation becomes very high – and only 2 percent of all schools are so highly segregated (Szulkin and Jonsson, 2007, 29). As Szulkin and Jonsson argue: "Swedish welfare state policies counteract minority group poverty, and much governmental and municipality funds are invested in minority areas to keep them in good shape and their schools and social institutions on par with those in other areas" (2007, 35) (cf. Hällsten and Szulkin, 2009, 30). Even as welfare state retrenchment has been a worldwide trend since the 1980s and Sweden has moved from state to market solutions in some key areas,[8] the Swedish welfare state has remained largely intact, and child care, which arguably may be a key factor in promoting upward mobility, has become more extensive (Bergqvist and Lindbom, 2003; Lindbom, 2001).

[8] This is an argument made to me (personal communications) by Staffan Kumlin and disputed by Bo Rothstein.

The welfare state helps overcome the problem of low trust among immigrants that is prevalent everywhere else (including Australia). Minorities *are* less trusting, especially so when they live outside areas with large shares of Nordics. Unlike many other countries, minorities *do have* friendships with native Swedes. When minorities have many informal contacts with native Swedes – especially if they also perceive the state as fair – the differences in trust between minorities and whites drop significantly: "informal interaction and institutional fairness – under the right circumstances – have particularly bridging qualities for minorities" (Kumlin and Rothstein, 2010, 72–3).

Minorities, Social Ties, and Trust

To examine trust and social ties in Sweden, we use the Ersta Sköndal University College Social Capital Survey (ESSCS) of 2009, conducted by Statistics Sweden. The survey was conducted by mail across 33 municipalities (71 neighborhoods), with 6,463 respondents from an initial sample size of 12,621 (excluding 579 respondents who were ineligible because they were deceased, disabled, or unreachable at their address) for a response rate of 51.2 percent.[9]

The survey contained the standard trust measure, as well as questions about the ethnic background of respondents (where they or their parents were born),[10] whether they identify as a Swede or not, and whether they

[9] Statistics Sweden tested the questionnaire by using probing and cognitive interviewing on a small group of potential respondents. The sample was constructed in two different steps using a quasi-experimental design. First, all of the Swedish (290) municipalities were divided into 16 different groups according to variations in municipal level characteristics (diversity, church attendance, unemployment/dependence upon social welfare, reported crimes/inhabitants), where each municipality was categorized as high or low on the background variables. From this we got 16 different groups of municipalities ranging from high and low on the four municipality level variables. From the constructed 16 groups of municipalities, two municipalities were randomly drawn by Statistics Sweden from each group and one extra municipality was added (Malmö to include one of the three major cities. In a second step a random sample of 400 individuals aged 18 to 85 within each municipality was drawn from the total population register. The period of data collection administered by Statistics Sweden lasted from May 2009 to the end of November 2009. Three different mail reminders were sent out to increase the response rate.

[10] We classified a respondent as a minority if he or she or either parent was born in Asia or Africa; as of North American/European background if he or she or either parent was born in North America or in Europe outside the Nordic countries but neither parent is a minority; as Nordic if he or she or either parent is born in another Nordic country but is not a minority or a North American/European; and as a Swede if the respondent and both parents were born in Sweden.

have friends who speak a different language or practice a different religion. We also computed a dissimilarity measure of segregation, which we could estimate for only 50 neighborhoods. We may overestimate differences between native Swedes (and identifiers) and others since minorities are concentrated in three major cities: 84 percent of the respondents live in neighborhoods that are 90 percent or more ethnic Swedish. We thus also focus on the 544 respondents who live in "more diverse" (less than 90 percent Swedish) neighborhoods. While the samples are much smaller, they show more dramatic differences between Swedes and minorities. These estimates are more telling than the full models since testing for the impact of segregation in neighborhoods with virtually no minorities may be misleading.[11]

Eighty-one percent of respondents are Swedish, 7 percent other Nordic, five and a half percent European/North American, and six percent minority. Eighty-six percent say that they identify as Swedes, including 94 percent of native Swedes (the others remain a puzzlement), 64 percent of Nordics, and 46 percent to 47 percent of Europeans/North Americans and minorities.[12]

Who is segregated, and how segregated are they? Minorities are considerably more segregated, especially in "diverse neighborhoods" (see Figure 6.1). Native Swedes and other Nordics are the least segregated. People who don't identify as Swedes are more segregated than respondents who see themselves as Swedish – and again, the differences are much greater for diverse communities. The overall levels of segregation are small, especially by comparison to the other countries examined. Minorities are more segregated, but hardly isolated.

What about trust and social networks? Three results stand out in Figure 6.2. First, native Swedes and people of other Nordic background are the most trusting. Almost 70 percent say that "most people can be trusted." Second, minorities are also highly trusting: 60 percent, greater than we find for majorities in most other countries, have faith in others. Third, Swedes of all backgrounds have friends of different backgrounds – but immigrants from Europe and North America and especially minorities

[11] Only three municipalities in our data set have fewer than 90 percent native Swedes: Malmö, Sundbyberg (in Stockholm County), and Växjö.

[12] In an open-ended question, 28 percent mainly identified as Nordics, 25 percent as Europeans, 14 percent from "outside Europe," 13 percent as internal minorities (Saami and Tornedaling, a Finnish minority), and 3 percent as "regional Swedish"; the rest of the responses were scattered (including 8 percent saying "citizen of the world").

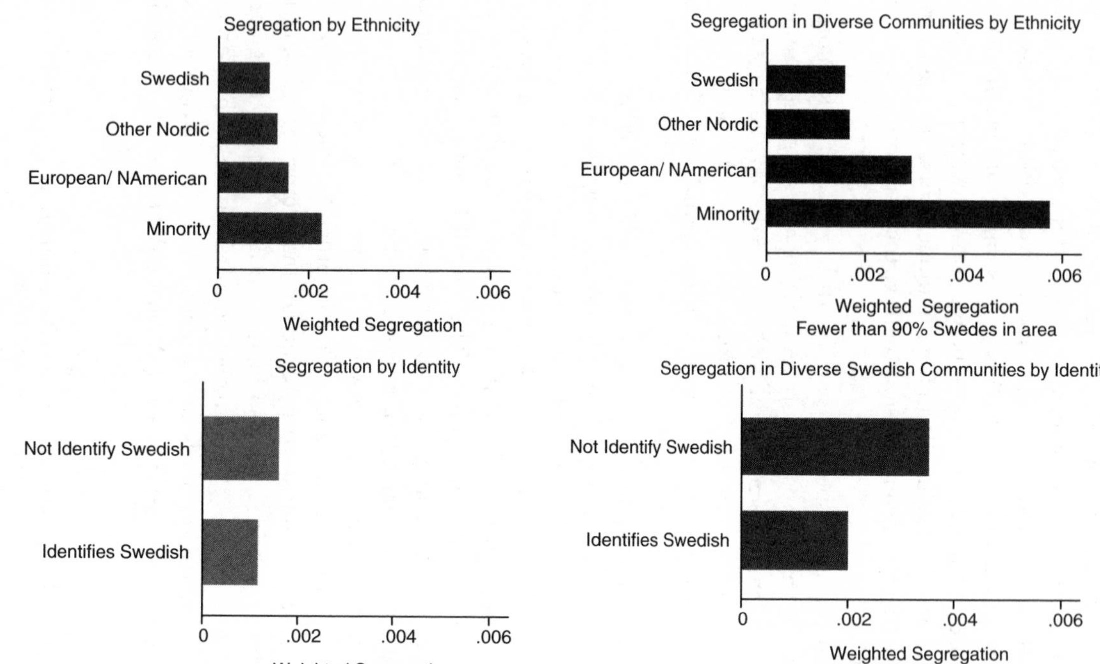

FIGURE 6.1. Swedish segregation by ehtnicity and identity. Ersta Skondal Social Capital Survey 2009

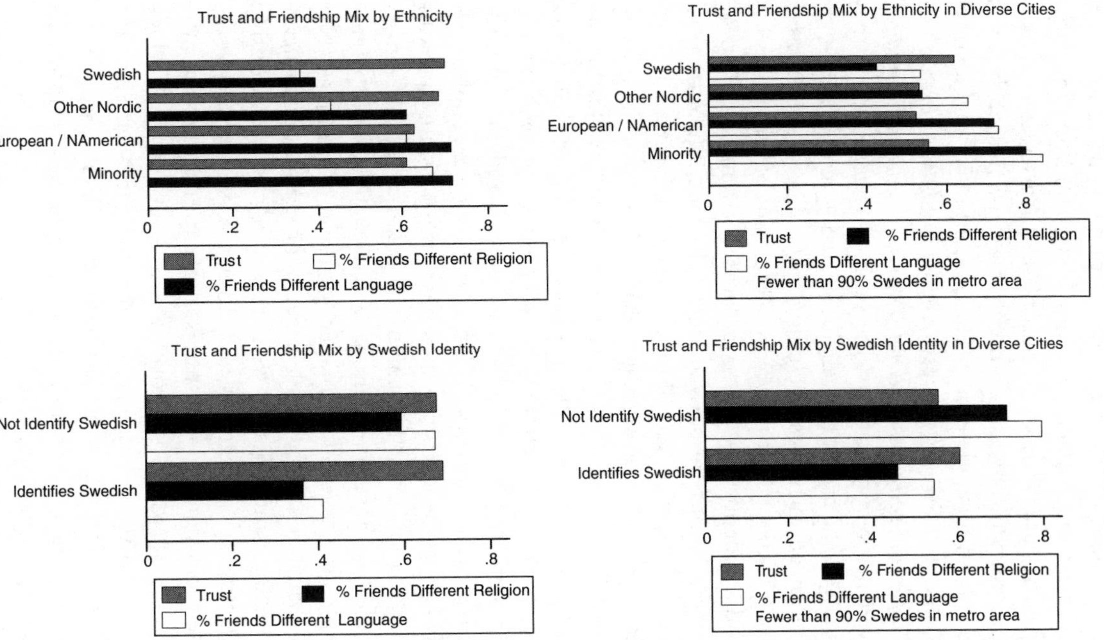

FIGURE 6.2. Trust and friendship mix by ethnicity and identity. Ersta Skondal Social Capital Survey Sweden 2009

are *more* likely to have such bridging ties than are Swedes and other Nordics.

We also examine trust and friendship mixes by whether respondents identify as Swedes. Where your roots are does shape your identity, but the relationship is far from perfect. Trust levels are the same for those who identify as Swedes and those who do not see themselves primarily as Swedes, and non-Swedes have substantially more friends of different backgrounds than do Swedish identifiers. For both ethnicity and identification, minorities and non-Swedes are *less trusting but have substantially more friends of different religions and who speak different languages*. Minorities in Sweden are connected to the larger society. Even if they don't identify as Swedish, they are well integrated – and increasingly they are taking on Swedish names, including the unlikely combination "Mohammedsson" (Tagliabue, 2011). Only 38 percent of minorities say that they have a dual identity as a Swede and something else, and 98 percent who primarily identify as a Swede reject dual identification.

Do diverse ties in integrated neighborhoods lead to more trust? We estimate three sets of models for all respondents, those who identify as Swedish, and those who do not identify as Swedes. The samples for different ethnicities are small, so we focus on identity rather than ethnic origins. The three sets of models are: (1) a "full model" for each sample/subsample; (2) the same full model but excluding respondents from the town of Övertorneå, which borders Finland – and where people work and marry across borders – and who thus have more friends speaking a different language; and (3) a "truncated" model for the full sample and each subsample for those communities with fewer than 90 percent Swedes. The sample sizes are much smaller for these subsamples (N = 340 for all respondents, 263 Swedish identifiers, and 77 non-identifiers). As in Chapter 2 for the United States, we expect a *negative* relationship between the interaction of segregation and diverse friendship networks and trust (because the residential measure is segregation or lack of integration). We focus on friendship networks based upon language, which are more common than those based upon different religions. Since the survey does not have information on respondents' religions, we cannot separate Muslims or adherents of other minority religions from others who might follow different religions.

For all respondents and Swedish identifiers, the full models show that living in an integrated neighborhood with friends who speak different languages boosts trust by about 20 percent (see Figure 6.3). However, once we drop the municipality of Övertorneå, the effects fall by half for

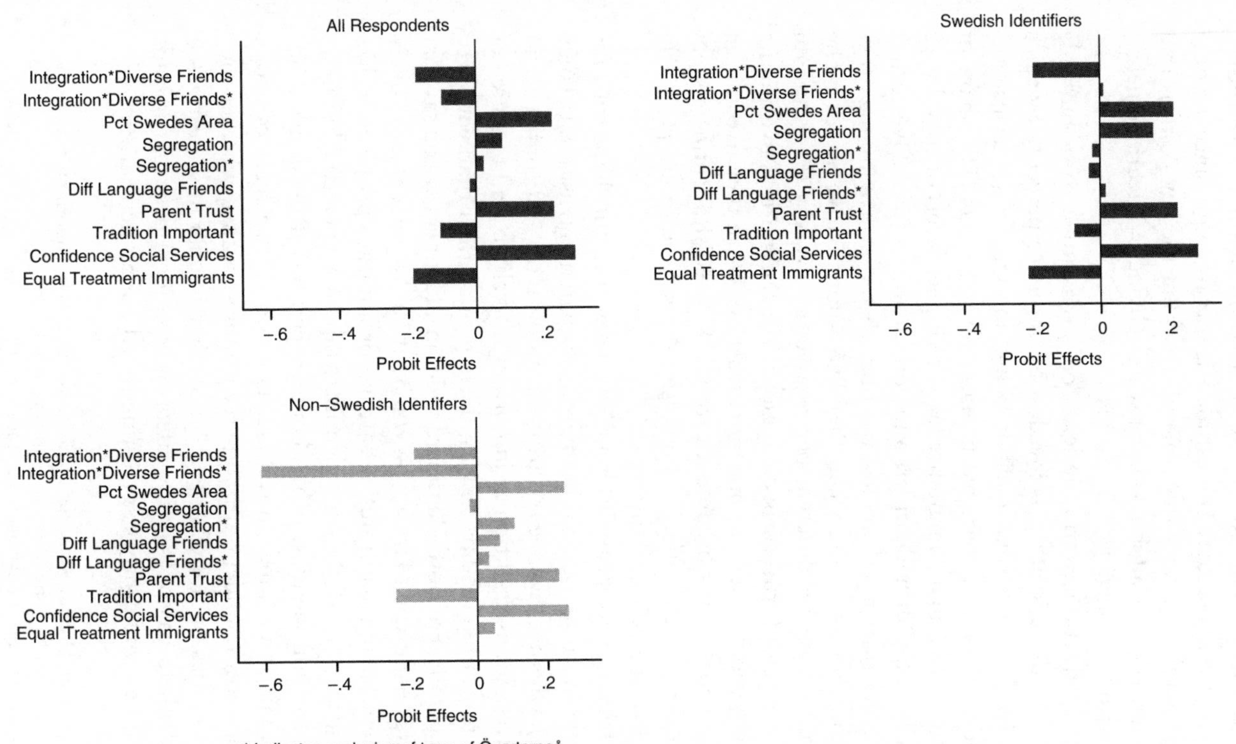

FIGURE 6.3. Probit effects for full models Sweden. Ersta Skondal Social Capital Survey 2009

all respondents and are virtually zero for Swedish identifiers. We initially see similar results for non-Swedish identifiers, but without Övertorneå, trust increases by 60 percent! This estimate is way too high, since it would lead to a probability greater than one of trust. But the key point is that non-identifiers get a strong boost in trust from living in integrated neighborhoods with heterogenous friendships.

Diversity (a fractionalization index) *does* drive down trust, but only for people who *don't* identify as Swedes (by about 10 percent). Swedish identifiers (with Övertorneå excluded) are marginally (and insignificantly) *more* trusting if they live in more diverse areas. The share of native Swedes living in a community leads to higher levels of trust by 20 percent for *both* Swedish identifiers and non-identifiers (with Övertorneå excluded). Minorities, then, are less trusting when they live among other minorities but more trusting when they live among native Swedes. The Swedish case presents a different perspective on diversity than Putnam might argue: levels of trust seem contagious. When minorities live among more trusting people, they become more trusting. When they live among less trusting people, they become less trusting. Swedish identifiers seem immune to any negative effects of diversity – but do respond positively when they live among high trusters.

Having friends who speak different languages does not shape trust for either sample. What matters for both groups is parental trust (cf. Uslaner, 2002, ch. 6), whether they see tradition as important,[13] and confidence in social services. Seeing tradition as important is likely to lead to a greater sense of identification (and trust) with the in-group rather than with people more generally. For both identifiers and non-identifiers, if you say that your parents taught you to trust, you will be about 20 percent more likely to trust others. Saying that traditions are important leads people to be less trusting in strangers – slightly for identifiers (about 10 percent) but more powerfully for non-identifiers (by about 20 percent). Rothstein's argument that a fair and competent welfare state boosts trust receives strong support: the most confident are 30 percent more trusting, whether they identify as Swedes or not. The perception that immigrants are treated better than others has only a tiny effect on non-identifiers, but it leads identifiers to be significantly *less* trusting (by about 20 percent).[14]

[13] The question, from Shalom Schwartz's value typology, is how important it is to follow the customs handed down by one's community or family.

[14] The models also include life satisfaction, education, income, and age. Life satisfaction is a strong determinant of trust for all samples (with effects between .35 and .4), education somewhat less so (effects of .18 for Swedish identifiers and .50 for non-identifiers),

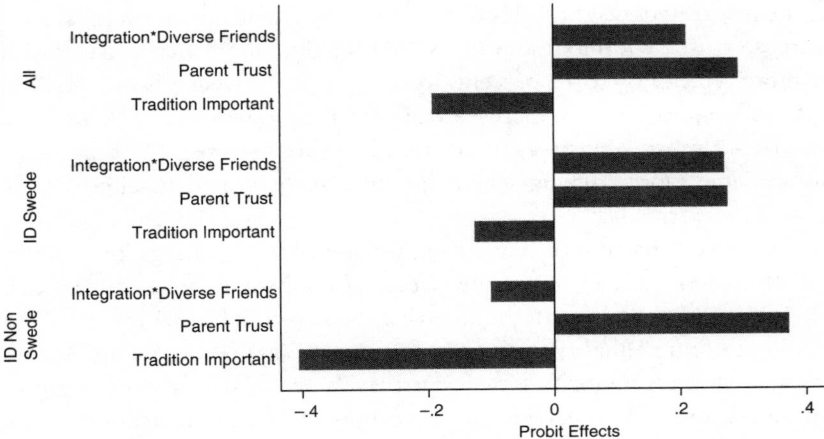

FIGURE 6.4. Probit effects for truncated models for diverse cities. Ersta Skondal Social Capital Survey 2009

The truncated models (Figure 6.4) tell a slightly different story. For all respondents and Swedish identifiers, having diverse friends in integrated neighborhoods seems to *decrease* trust by about 30 percent. However, these coefficients are not even close to standard levels of statistical significance (with t ratios below one). For non-identifiers, the optimal conditions lead to a 10 percent increase in trust, substantially less than the 37 percent increase from having trusting parents and the 51 percent decline if you say that traditions are very important. Both parental trust and tradition shape trust for Swedish identifiers, but again the effects are smaller than for non-identifiers.[15]

The truncated models give a more realistic picture than the full models. They confirm that Allport's optimal conditions matter for minorities who don't identify as Swedish but do not shape trust for anyone who sees himself or herself as a Swede. In one way, the Swedish results confirm other results: outside the highly segregated United States, living

income (effects of .370 for identifiers and not significant for non-identifiers), and age (effects of .10 for identifiers, .17 for non-identifiers). Older people are more likely to trust others, as are more satisfied, more highly educated, and higher-income respondents for Swedish identifiers.

15 The models also include life satisfaction, education, and age. Life satisfaction is a strong determinant of trust for all samples (with effects between .35 and .4), education somewhat less so (effects of .20 for Swedish identifiers and .12 for non-identifiers), and age (significant for identifiers, not for non-identifiers). Older people are more likely to trust others, as are more satisfied and more highly educated respondents.

in an integrated neighborhood with diverse friendship networks does increase trust by a maximum of 15 percent (for minorities in Australia) or more typically 5 to 10 percent. In another way, Sweden is distinct: the optimal conditions *only* increase trust for people who don't identify as Swedes – almost exclusively minorities. Identifiers – mostly Nordics – do not become more trusting when they live in integrated neighborhoods with diverse friends.

The effects for minorities strongly support the findings of Kumlin and Rothstein (2010). So do the effects of confidence in social services. The universal welfare state builds trust, be it through institutions or by leading to more equality. Not only do the optimal conditions build trust among Sweden's minorities, their trust levels are relatively close to those for native Swedes: 60 percent for minorities of African or Asian heritage overall and 55 percent for these minorities in more diverse communities, compared to 70 percent and 62 percent of native Swedes, respectively.[16]

The principal causal mechanisms are likely greater equality and lower segregation. Across 71 neighborhoods, the correlation of trust and average income is just .17. For the 33 municipalities, the correlation between average trust levels and the Gini index is -.38, and with median income only .08. Segregation is only moderately linked to lower trust (r = -.35) and lower average income (r = -.25, both N = 50). Inequality is not great across Sweden's municipalities: the median Gini index across the 33 communities is .30 and only one city – Malmö – has a Gini above .4 (just barely). Only two municipalities have average trust levels below 50 percent (including Malmö). Without Malmö, the correlation between average trust and inequality falls to -.16.

The welfare state goes hand in hand with low segregation and it helps understand Sweden's march away from multiculturalism.[17] It is far easier for minorities to identify with the larger culture when they are optimistic

[16] The results are not much different if we break the data down by Swedish identification: 61 percent of those who identify as Swedes are trusters, compared to 60 percent who do not identify as Swedes. For the most diverse neighborhoods, the respective figures are 60 percent and 55 percent.

[17] One component of multiculturalism remains strong in both Sweden and Australia: the status of the original settlers in each country. Even as Sweden moved away from multiculturalism, it reiterated in its constitution (the *Regeringsformen*, §2) in 2002 and 2010 a commitment to encouraging" the Saami people and other ethnic and religious minorities to "maintain and develop their own cultural and associational life." Policies toward non-Saami minorities and Swedish attitudes are far more assimilationist. Similarly, in Australia, there is an acknowledgment of the role of centrality of Aboriginal culture in Australian identity and there are public acknowledgments of Aboriginals as the original owners of the land at public ceremonies, cultural events, and lectures. In Australia as in

about their own life chances. Life satisfaction is, for both the majority and the minority, the major determinant of trust. Unlike many other countries, minorities in Sweden are both satisfied with their life chances and not very different from natives in their levels of optimism – even in the most diverse cities. This doesn't mean that immigrants are living in a winter wonderland. They are more likely to be unemployed and to remain on welfare (Månsson and Olsson, 2009). While the generosity of the welfare state may reduce the incentive to find work, it does provide a social safety net against the extreme poverty found elsewhere in the West.

The remaining puzzle is why native Swedes get no boost in trust from diverse friendship networks in integrated communities. Two explanations seem plausible. First, there may be, as Forbes has argued, a two-way street: people who have friends of different backgrounds may be high in trust in the first place (1997, 111–12). This is a reasonable argument – and there is substantial evidence for it (see Chapter 8). However, it doesn't explain the positive effect of the optimal conditions elsewhere and for Swedish minorities. This suggests an alternative account: native Swedes are very high in trust – now and as far back as we have survey evidence. This high level – 70 percent in this survey – may be a ceiling.

Sweden thus stands out as a case study of how low levels of inequality may lead both to low levels of segregation and to high levels of trust. It is also a case study on why multiculturalism didn't fail – it just proved superfluous. Many immigrants may not identify as Swedish, but their high level of generalized trust, especially compared to their home countries (Uslaner, 2008a), provides evidence that with the right social situation you can build trust.

Sweden is not without problems. The social solidarity of Sweden has been tested by the rise of an anti-immigrant party, the Sweden Democrats, that received almost 6 percent of the vote nationally and 10 percent in Malmö, one of the most diverse cities. Unemployment is rampant among recent immigrants from conflicted lands. There are immigrant communities that have begun to resemble the ethnic ghettos found elsewhere in Europe, leading some Swedes to express frustration about supporting them through the country's generous welfare state.

Yet others see the economic distress and crime waves in these poor neighborhoods as temporary problems that have already begun to wane

Canada (among First Nation people), multiculturalism is more likely to be seen as conflicting with the standing of native peoples as the original inhabitants of the land with claims to the land.

as immigrants become more settled. The immigrants are not a homogenous lot: many from Iran have high levels of education, while Somalis do not (Andersson, 2007). The response by native Swedes is tempered by a low level of support for right-wing parties in comparison to other European countries (Andersson, 2007; Daley, 2011). A substantial majority of Swedes (60 percent in the 2009 European Values Survey) dispute the claim that there are too many immigrants in the country, and there are few calls to end the welfare state or to cut the level of immigration.

Australia: From "White Australia" to Multiculturalism to Assimilation (?)

Australia – like the United States and Canada – is a nation of immigrants. The people who came to Australia were almost entirely British. The "White Australia" policy, adopted as the first act of the parliament of the newly independent country in 1901, was designed to ensure that Australia remained culturally British (Kukathas, 2008, 31). "[T]he Australian type was constructed in terms of the white, masculine, outdoor person originating from the British Isles" (Castles et al., 1988, 8).

The sparsely populated nation accepted mass immigration after World War II to ease labor shortages (as did Sweden). Most of the early wave of immigrants came from the traditional English-speaking nations, who received financial incentives to move Down Under. Immigrants from outside the English-speaking world were "expected to accept the ideals and values of British parliamentary democracy, Christian belief, and acculturate into the 'Australian way of life' ... Migrant cultures were considered to have less values and to ... pose a long-term threat to the preservation of the Australian national character" (Lopez, 2000, 48). The White Australia policy began to unravel with the Migrant Act of 1958, which removed references to race as a condition for immigration. The White Australia policy itself was repealed in 1973 (Kukathas, 2008, 31; Tilbury, 2007, 2).

Increasing immigration from non-English-speaking countries led to a reimagining of Australia. The new wave of immigrants came from nearby Asia, especially Vietnamese refugees, or "boat people," who fled the communist regime in dinghies. Australia adopted the discourse of multiculturalism in 1973, two years after Canada, and it became official policy five years later (Jupp, 2002, 105; National Multicultural Advisory Council, 1999, 34).

Multiculturalism was a response to the failure of assimilationist policies as many immigrants felt uncomfortable and returned to their home countries or charged that they faced discrimination (The Committee to Advise on Australia's Immigration Policies, 1988, 58). It was also an attempt by successive governments of both the left and the right to develop an Australian identity that placed neither race nor British heritage at its center (Markus, 1988, 6–7, 18).

Australian multiculturalism was conflicted from the start. On the one hand, it was said to be less concerned with "cultural maintenance" of minority groups than the Canadian variant (Jupp, 2002, 84–5). It grants immigrants the right "within carefully defined limits to express and share their individual heritage" (Department of Immigration and Citizenship, Government of Australia, n.d. [a]), "to be accepted as an Australian without having to assimilate to some stereotyped model of behaviour" (Department of Immigration and Citizenship, Government of Australia, n.d. [b]). The core values of the Australian multicultural value system were "civic duty," respect for all cultures, equality of opportunity, "productive diversity," a "fair go," democracy, the rule of law, tolerance, and a "commitment to Australia" (National Multicultural Advisory Council, 1999, 9, 42) on one account. Another list includes democracy, individualism, courageousness, loyalty to mates, egalitarianism, suspicion of the powerful, intolerance toward oppression, pragmatism, and secularism (Markus, 1988, 8–9).

As Mason (2010) argues, there is little here that identifies a distinctive *Australian* culture. So alternative visions arose as to whether multiculturalism has led to either a thoroughly assimilated immigrant population (Galligan and Roberts, 2004, 14, 75–6) or a struggle to cope with Australia's Anglo-Saxon colonial heritage (Tilbury, 2007, 13). Jupp called the search for an Australian identity a "conceptual muddle" (2008, 238).

The most prominent manifestation of multiculturalism is the SBS radio and television network created in 1975. SBS (the Special Broadcasting Service) provides programming in almost 70 languages with a promise of seven digital television channels in addition to the two broadcast networks.[18]

[18] The main web site is http://www.sbs.com.au//. On the multiplicity of languages and services, see http://www.sbs.com.au/future/article/108205/Media-Release:-SBS-submits-plans-to-Government-for-more-services.

Multiculturalism was controversial from the start. A 1988 survey by the Office of Multicultural Affairs, the FitzGerald Report, found widespread dissatisfaction with the policy, including the belief that it has led to favoritism toward immigrants from non-English-speaking countries in employment and government benefits, leading to "injustice, inequality, and divisiveness" (Foster and Seitz, 1990, 287; Healy, 2007, 110). The survey results marked the beginning of the decline of multiculturalism. It marked the shift to a skills-based point system for immigration even stricter than Canada's.[19] To qualify as a skilled immigrant with a permanent resident visa, one must be under 45 years old, know enough English to speak it on the job, have at least a high school degree, and have work experience or two years of study in a profession that is on the "Skilled Occupations List."[20] The point system is more demanding in Australia than in Canada. Two-thirds of immigrants come from the "Skill Stream," mostly sponsored by employers. Most of the rest come to Australia under family unification, overwhelmingly spouses (Australian Government Department of Immigration and Citizenship, 2010, 3, 16).[21]

John Howard, as leader of the Liberal Party, repudiated multiculturalism in 1988. As prime minister in 2006, he specifically rejected it (quoted in Tilbury, 2007, 5–7):

> Our celebration of diversity must not be at the expense of … ongoing pride in what are commonly regarded as the values, traditions and accomplishments of the old Australia.

While critical of multiculturalism, Australians are not of one mind on immigration. On the one hand, only 16 percent (1997) and a third of Australians (2007) favored government aid to support the customs of minority groups.

As in Sweden an overwhelming share of the population agreed that ethnic groups should blend into the larger society. Substantial minorities said that you cannot become fully Australian if you don't share national customs (40 percent), don't have Australian ancestry (37 percent), or are not a Christian (31 percent) (Goot and Watson, 2005, 185, 188).

[19] Banting argues: "Australia relies more heavily on residency requirements largely because its core social programs are means-tested … in Canada, universal programs attract less political controversy about immigrant utilization" (2010, 812).

[20] See the "points calculator" at http://www.workpermit.com/australia/point_calculator.htm.

[21] For the specifics of the immigration policy, see http://www.immigrationandvisas.com/australia/aus_perm.htm#Independent%20Category. A small share of immigrants are refugees (in contrast to Sweden). See http://www.immi.gov.au/visas/humanitarian/onshore/866/.

Even as Muslims comprise less than 2 percent of Australians,[22] a third of Australians said in a 2007 survey that Muslims constitute a threat to the Australian way of life (Tilbury, 2007, 12). Nevertheless, Australians remain conflicted over whether the level of immigration is too high or too low (Markus, 2010, 20; Markus, Jupp, and McDonald, 2009, 131). Fewer than a fifth of Australians disagreed that immigration has made Australia stronger and has been a positive force for the economy (Markus and Arnup, 2009, 69; Walmsley et al., 2007, 54).

Multiculturalism faded from much of public discourse until the government reaffirmed it in 2007. The renewed commitment to multiculturalism seems strained in comparison with debates in Canada and the United Kingdom. The Acting Race Discrimination Commissioner held that the policy would lead to a "harmonious integrated society" and that minorities such as Muslims would "integrate into mainstream Australian society" (Calma, 2007, 12–13). The government also introduced a new citizenship test that Member of Parliament Petro Georgiou (2008) from the governing Liberal Party saw as an attempt to impose an "idea of Australian national identity" through an "institution or code that lays down a test of Australianness" and devalues diversity.[23] In 2011, the Labor government announced a new multiculturalism policy that appears more aimed at combating racism than at rejecting assimilation (Australian Multicultural Advisory Council, 2010, 7–8; Weinreb, 2010).

The commitment to multiculturalism is ambiguous.[24] The main instrument of cultural diversity, the SBS Networks, continues to expand its multilingual offerings. Yet their programming includes such multicultural shows as the *Newshour* (news and interviews from the Public Broadcasting System in the United States), *Mad Men* (the popular series about a 1960s advertising agency in New York City from an American cable network), and BBC travelogues. Public policy seems to want to eat your cake (advance multiculturalism) and have it too (forge a common identity).

Immigration continues to rise – over half of Australia's population was born overseas or have at least one parent born abroad, with figures even higher in the Sydney and Melbourne urban areas (Birrell, 2003, 111;

[22] See http://www.islamicpopulation.com/Ocenia/oceania_general.html for 2001 estimates.

[23] The test is a mixture of questions about Australian history and general knowledge of democratic practice, with nothing about the distinctiveness of national culture. See the practice tests at http://www.citizenship.gov.au/learn/cit_test/practice/.

[24] To be sure, the Council did call for additional funding for arts and sports for minorities (Australian Multicultural Advisory Council, 2010, 8).

Menadue, 2003, 81). The share of Australians with an Anglo-Saxon heritage has fallen to 82 percent (Jupp, 2008, 226). Australian immigration policy has not been free of conflicts: in 1996, Pauline Hanson won a seat in the federal parliament in a protest movement called "One Nation." Her party won ten seats in Queensland two years later and Howard refused to condemn her or her movement. But Hanson and her party faded into oblivion by 2001 (Galligan and Roberts, 2003, 13). Australia has largely been free from the racial disturbances that have been prominent elsewhere (the United States in the 1960s and Britain in the early twenty-first century). There have been sporadic acts of violence, most notably the racist riot against Lebanese immigrants in Cronulla Beach in 2005 (Tilbury, 2007, 10), and throughout Australian history, mostly in the early years, violence was common against Aboriginals, who have excluded themselves from multicultural Australia (Menadue, 2003, 86) even as the government sought to bring them into the mix (Department of Immigration and Citizenship, Government of Australia. n.d. [a]).[25]

Immigration has been relatively free of conflict, even as multiculturalism has come under widespread criticism largely because the new citizens of Australia have not been a burden on the state as they have elsewhere.[26] The point system for skills means that most immigrants come to Australia ready to participate in the marketplace and not become dependent upon welfare. Their higher education and income also means that they more quickly move into integrated neighborhoods and that what segregation remains is not strongly linked to inequality, as it is in the United States and to a lesser extent in the United Kingdom.

Across between 2,321 and 2,489 neighborhoods,[27] the mean level of segregation (using a dissimilarity index ranging from zero to one) is just .09, half the level across American metropolitan areas. The top 10 percent of neighborhoods in diversity are no more segregated, and even the most

[25] As with Canada's First Nation people, Australian Aboriginals do not see themselves as one people among many, but as the original inhabitants of the land.

[26] Illegal immigration from people arriving by boat has increased dramatically in 2009 (2,726) and 2010 (6,535) from just 161 in 2008 (Siegel, 2011). These numbers are not very large by themselves and amount to about 10 percent of the family immigration total for 2010.

[27] The data are arranged by postal codes, as is typical with Australian data. The varying numbers reflect some missing data. I am grateful to Mike Poulsen of Macquarie University for generating the segregation data; to Steven McEachern, deputy director of the Australian Social Science Data Archive, Australian National University, for generating the diversity data from Australian Census data; and to Andrew Leigh, on leave from the Australian National University to serve as a member of parliament, for diversity and inequality data.

diverse 5 percent only have a segregation average of .18. Across states, the levels of segregation don't vary dramatically, except for the very low value for the Australia Capital Territory (Canberra) at .06. The sparsely populated New Territories, home to many Aboriginals, is the most segregated state, but even here the dissimilarity index is just .20.

The average level of inequality is .44, higher than reported in cross-national data sets for Australia but it does not vary at all for the neighborhoods with the most diverse populations. The simple correlation between segregation and the Gini index is only .026 across all 2,489 postal codes, but is somewhat higher among the most diverse communities (r = .191 for the most diverse 10 percent and -.177 for the most diverse 5 percent). Segregation and inequality are only weakly related in Australian communities, even those with the greatest diversity.

These snapshots of data comport well with what others have argued about Australia, and especially its level of integration. American cities are 20 times as segregated as Australian metropolitan areas – and the white majority and the minorities in Australia live in much more integrated neighborhoods than do people in other Anglo-American democracies (Johnston, Poulsen, and Forrest, 2007, 722–8). There is some segregation in Australia: in Sydney the Australian-born (mostly whites) tend to be more isolated than are other groups (Poulsen, Johnston, and Forrest, 2004, 367). But minorities are widely dispersed across the city and almost no ethnic minority group forms more than 20 percent of the population in any neighborhood (Poulsen, Johnston, and Forrest, 2002, 2004, 367).

A few ethnic groups are isolated in various cities, but even the most concentrated minorities – such as Vietnamese – move out and into integrated neighborhood over time (Burnley, Murphy, and Fagan, 1997, 34, 38; cf. Poulsen, Johnston, and Forrest, 2004, 375 and Jayasuriya and Pookong, 1999, 36). Initial segregation seems to depend upon language proficiency (Foster, 1995, 103; Walmsley, McInotsh, and Rajaratnam, 2007). As the skills point test becomes more central to immigration in Australia, language barriers fall and so does segregation. Groups admitted as refugees – Vietnamese in the past and Sudanese in recent years – do face the prospect of greater isolation. Yet planners in Toowoomba, Queensland proactively dispersed Sudanese refugees throughout the city to prevent segregation from 2001 onward. Even so, half of the refugees were proficient in English (Carrington and Reavell, 2007, 116, 121).

Immigration did not become a flashpoint issue in Australia because it did not increase social strains. The country had a long period of economic boom, even missing the worldwide financial crisis beginning in 2007. It has a sparse population and thus can absorb more people into the workforce. The new immigrants came with skills and language proficiency – and either moved into integrated neighborhoods immediately or as their economic situation improved. In recent years, a consensus arose that people need to develop a common identity, even though they were uncertain on how to frame it. Now two-thirds of second generation immigrants marry outside their own groups and 40 percent of all Australians are of mixed backgrounds (Menadue, 2003, 81). All of these conditions bode well for trust. In the first decade of the twenty-first century, there has indeed been a significant increase in levels of generalized trust among Australians. Can we attribute this rise to Allport's optimal conditions?

Trust and Social Ties Down Under

Australians and their government have put a lot of effort into understanding how citizens think about their social and political worlds. However, only one survey asks about both trust and the diversity of social ties: the Scanlon Foundation Mapping of Social Cohesion 2007 survey. The telephone survey of 2,000 Australians was conducted between June and August 2007 using a sample stratified by state (Markus and Dharmalingam, 2007, 8).[28]

I initially divided the population into five groups based upon the slightly more elaborate ethnic variable in the survey. The categorizations I use are similar to those in Chapter 5 (the United Kingdom) and divide respondents who were:

- born in Australia and whose parents were born in Australia and who are white (Australians)
- born in Australia or in English-speaking countries (the United Kingdom, the United States, Canada, Ireland, New Zealand) or whose parents were born in English-speaking countries (Anglos)
- born in Northern Europe or who had at least one parent born in Northern Europe (Europeans)

[28] See http://www.scanlonfoundation.org.au/socialcohesion.html for the program in general. See http://www.globalmovements.monash.edu.au/publications/reports.php for the report on the 2007 survey with technical specifications on sampling design. There were also five regional surveys that are restricted. I am grateful to Andrew Markus of Monash University and the Scanlon Foundation for access to the national survey.

- born in Central and Eastern Europe or in Southern Europe or who had at least one parent born in these countries (CEE/Southern)
- born in the Middle East or Asia or of Aboriginal background or who had at least one parent born there or of Aboriginal background (Minority).

As with the UK analysis, a respondent with any minority connection is classified as a minority – even if he or she has an Anglo or CEE/Southern European parent. Each category working upward becomes more demanding, so a European cannot have a CEE/Southern or a Minority parent but can have an Anglo or Australian mother or father. Then I further divided the ethnicity category into majority (Australians, Anglos, Europeans) and minorities (CEE/Southern and Minority) for the multivariate analyses to ensure sufficient cases. Some CEE/Southern Europe immigrants are refugees from the conflicts in the former Yugoslavia. All are from non-English-speaking backgrounds – a common distinction made in Australian writing – academic, governmental, and journalistic. As I shall show, the CEE/Southern European respondents are more disadvantaged than are Minorities (at least in this sample).

What can we say about trust and social ties in Australia? The Scanlon Foundation survey did not ask a simple question about the diversity of one's social networks, but rather about how often one visits or hosts friends of different ethnicities and religions. These are stronger ties than simple friendships – and perhaps better suited to test for Allport's optimal conditions. I present the results for trust, social ties, and segregation levels for all respondents in Figure 6.5 and for majorities and minorities in Figure 6.6.

The immediate story of Figure 6.5 is that Australians are a trusting people: 58 percent believe that "most people can be trusted," in this survey. They also have diverse social ties: almost 60 percent visit friends of other ethnicities and religions and host friends of other religions; more than half host friends of other ethnicities at their residences. As I noted above, they are also unlikely to live in segregated communities. The mean segregation index for all survey respondents is less than .10. Minorities are less trusting and more likely to live in segregated neighborhoods than the majorities – but these differences are small. Sixty-one percent of majority respondents believe that "most people can be trusted," but so do 54 percent of minorities. The mean segregation levels are .08 for majority groups and .12 for minorities (Figure 6.6). Minorities are, as elsewhere, more likely to visit and host people of different ethnicities than

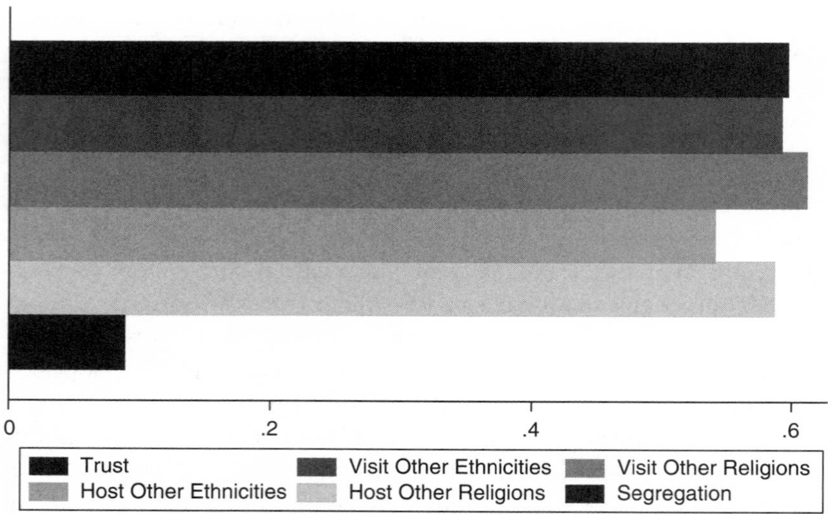

FIGURE 6.5. Trust, friendship mix, and segregation all respondents. Scanlon Foundation Survey 2007

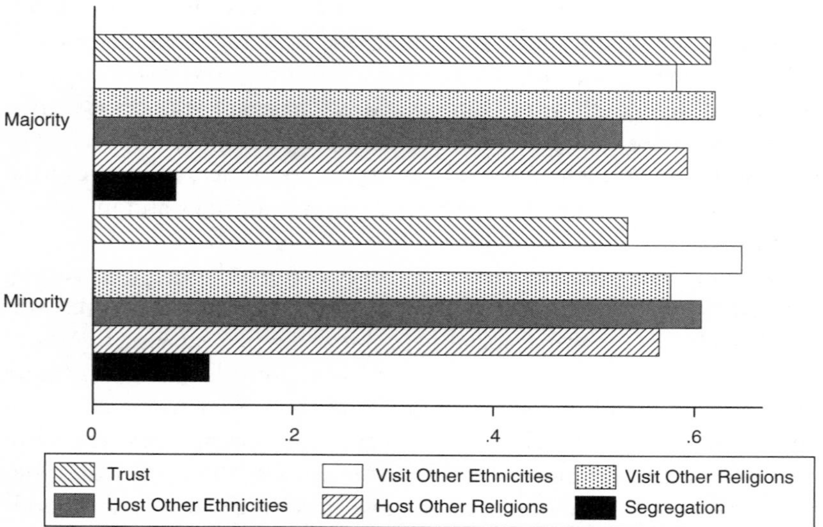

FIGURE 6.6. Trust, friendship mix, and segregation by ethnicity. Scanlon Foundation Survey 2007

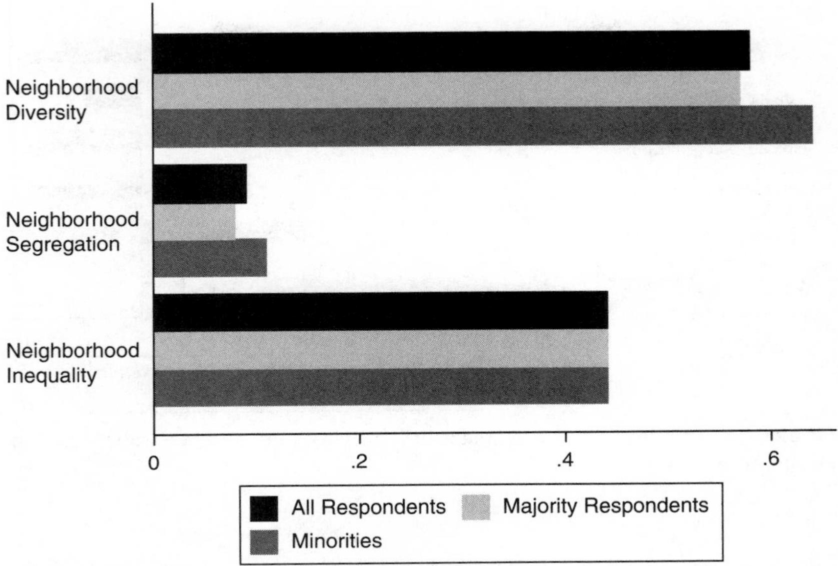

FIGURE 6.7. Neighborhood segregation, diversity, and inequality in Australia. Scanlon Foundation Survey 2007

majority respondents, but less likely to visit and host people of different religions. Again, these differences are small and statistically insignificant. Majorities and minorities look pretty much alike on these key measures of social interaction and values.

I put neighborhood demographics in context in Figure 6.7. I include segregation to show that it is *not* distinctive. Minorities do live in more diverse neighborhoods, as measured by a fractionalization index elsewhere computed from census data. This is hardly surprising, but again the differences are not large, even if significant: .64 for minorities and .57 for majority respondents. As in the United States, diversity and segregation are not the same thing. The correlation seems a bit higher for Australia than for the United States across 2,481 neighborhoods (r = -.386), but it is in the wrong direction! This stems from an a somewhat scattershot pattern in neighborhoods low on both segregation and diversity, with outliers high in both far from the regression line. The relationship turns positive for the 71 neighborhoods with segregation above .3, but the relationship is weak (r^2 = .234). Only for the 10 percent of neighborhoods with segregation at .4 or above (N = 25) is there a strong positive relationship (r^2 = .485).

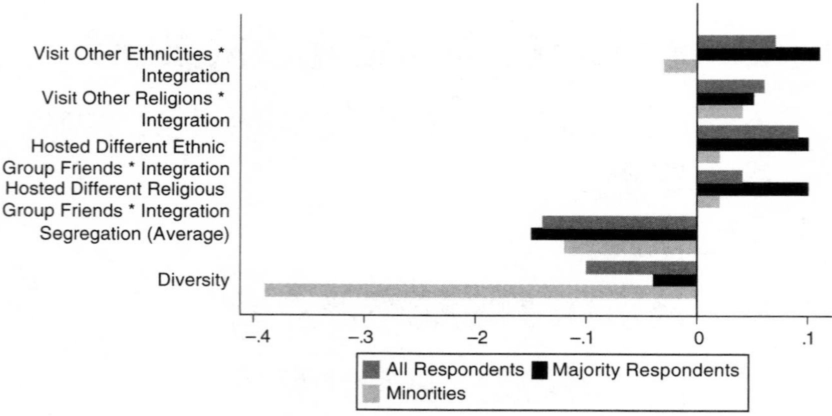

FIGURE 6.8. Probit effects for segregation, diversity, and trust Australia. Scanlon Foundation Survey 2007

Do diverse social ties in integrated neighborhoods lead people to be more likely to trust others? I estimated a series of models for all respondents and for majorities and minorities (see Figure 6.8). These models included visiting and hosting people of different ethnicities and religions interacted with the measure of segregation (reflected to measure integration). Each indicator of diverse ties is estimated separately. I also include the simple measures of segregation and diversity in all models as well as the interaction terms,[29] The models also included neighborhood level inequality as well as individual measures: is the economic gap between the rich and the poor too large; will life be better for the next generation (see Uslaner, 2002, 98–107); will your life get better over the next three or four years; have you experienced discrimination because of ethnicity or religion; level of education; and age.

The key results for diverse social ties and levels of segregation and diversity are reassuring for all respondents and majorities. Diverse ties build trust. It doesn't seem to matter whether you visit or host people of different ethnicities if you are a majority: if you have such ties *and* live in an integrated neighborhood, you are about 10 percent more likely to believe that most people can be trusted (averaged over the four

[29] As in Chapter 3, I estimate the changes in probabilities for the interaction terms by setting the interaction terms first at their minimum value holding segregation at its median and then replacing the interaction value at its maximum, letting all of the other values take their observed values. I then did the same for segregation. See Chapter 3 for details.

estimations). These impacts are similar – indeed a bit larger – than I found for Canada and the United Kingdom, which may reflect the lower level of segregation, the greater frequency of heterogenous social ties, or both. Hosting people of different religions also boosts trust by a similar amount, although simply visiting friends of other religions has a smaller effect, about half the size.

More striking are the results for minorities. Diverse social ties in integrated neighborhoods have almost no effect on building trust. Visiting people of other ethnicities has a marginally negative effect. Only visiting people of other religions produces any appreciable effect – boosting trust by .04. Segregation by itself depresses trust for both majority and minority respondents. Living in the most segregated neighborhoods lowers the probability of trust by about .15 for majority respondents and .12 for minorities. But the real culprit seems to be diversity, but only for minorities. Contrary to Putnam (2007), Australian majority respondents don't become less trusting (or at least not by much) if they live in a heterogenous neighborhood. But the effect for minorities is substantial: minorities become more trusting when they live in the least diverse neighborhoods. These neighborhoods are *composed of people different from themselves (whites)*, not people like themselves. The effect is very powerful. Living in the most diverse neighborhood reduces the likelihood of trust for minorities by 40 percent.

The determinants of trust beyond these measures of social contact, integration, and diversity are different for majority and minority respondents. For the majority, education has by far the biggest impact, while perceptions that life will be better in three to four years and for the next generation also lead to greater trust. Older people are more trusting while people who say they have faced religious discrimination are less likely to have faith in their fellow citizens. For minorities, outside of segregation and diversity, the only factors that matter are education and whether life will get better for the next generation.[30]

It may seem surprising that discrimination does not lead to less trust for minorities – but does for majority respondents. Minorities *do* perceive discrimination. There are modest correlations between trust and discrimination based upon religion (tau-b = -.09) or nationality (tau-b = -.18). But they are not significant in the probit analyses of trust. Only 9 percent

30 For majority respondents, the average effects are: education (.40), life better for next generation (.13), life will get better in the next three to four years (.15), religious discrimination (-.11), and age (.12, scaled from 18 to 75). For minorities, the effects are: education (.37) and life for the next generation (.21).

of minorities say that they have faced discrimination because of religion – likely because there are few Muslims in Australia and only 14 among the survey respondents. But half of people of non-English-speaking backgrounds say that they have faced discrimination because of their nationality (Markus and Dharmalingam, 2007, 85). Perceptions of discrimination against your group are likely to be far more prevalent than personal experiences of mistreatment – and this would likely depress trust. But there is no perceived measure of prejudice toward groups.

Why, then, do diverse social ties in integrated neighborhoods not boost trust for minorities? A likely answer is that the self-selection of immigrants to Australia may lead to higher levels of trust among immigrants in the first place. The point system rewards one's education level and professional skills and demands that immigrants have a working knowledge of English.

Minorities, at least as reflected in this survey, already possess the key demographic factor underlying trust – education. The mean level of education in the survey is 6.1 – a bit above a secondary school degree. Anglos average 6.5 on the ten-point scale (with ten being a postgraduate degree), Europeans 6.3, and native Australians only 5.9. The least educated come not from Asia and the Middle East, but from CEE/Southern Europe at 5.3. Minorities are *the most educated with a mean score of 6.9*. Thirty-nine percent of minorities have a college degree or higher, more than any other ethnic group. Minorities (from Asia and the Middle East as well as Aboriginals) *are* less trusting than the average Australian – by 54 to 60 percent. But their faith in others is only marginally less than that of Europeans (56 percent) and higher than trust for CEE/Southern Europeans (48 percent). The most trusting ethnicity is not native Australians (58 percent), but Anglos (68 percent).

If these data are reliable, they explain the relatively high level of trust among minorities (54 percent) compared to minorities elsewhere. Education and living in a neighborhood with lots of native Australians are by far the strongest predictors of trust for minorities in Australia. Minorities seem so well integrated that diverse social ties may not add anything to their levels of trust.

Reprise

Australia and Sweden have two different roots to developing trust among minorities, and they seem to have done so rather well. Sweden does it the hard way – by an extensive and fair welfare state designed to combat inequality. Australia does it by an easier path: recruit immigrants who already have both human capital (education) and social capital (trust).

Sweden is a society based upon equality and optimism – optimism based upon the old Scandinavian notion of *Jante Law*, based upon a 1930s book by Axel Sandemose in Danish and Norwegian. Under *Jante Law* you are not supposed to believe that you are better than anyone else and certainly not to boast about it. But you also realize that you belong to a society, you must contribute to it, and in turn people will stand behind you.[31] It is this commitment to equality and mutual assistance that makes Sweden and the other Nordic countries so trusting. *Jante Law* is now reputedly in decline (so my friends in the Nordic countries tell me). But as I travel in Sweden, I meet few who challenge the universalistic welfare state and there is little political conflict between the left and the current more conservative government about Sweden's commitment to equality and to the integration of immigrants.[32] On one recent trip, I asked two taxi drivers what they liked most and liked least about Sweden. The drivers, one from Afghanistan and the other from Madagascar, both immediately said that the best thing about Sweden was its universal social programs – that their children could go to university for free and that everyone was equally entitled to benefits from the state. (The downside of the country, both agreed, was the weather.)

Australia has not worked out the longer-term strategy of whether it can return to an integrationist policy that was its official plan before the repeal of the White Australia Act (Levey, 2008, 5). Aside from such universal values as democracy, the rule of law, good friends, and a "fair go," Australia has not developed a larger vision an inclusive national culture. There are some signs of strain in the social fabric. Young minorities in Sydney, according to a survey by Jock Collins, are unlikely to call themselves Australian and a fifth don't feel Australian at all (cited in Horin, 2010). But overall, the vast majority of Australians identify with the country, both majorities and minorities (cf. Markus, Jupp, and McDonald, 2009, 111). Two-thirds of minorities identify "to a great extent" with the country and just 6 percent not at all. Half of minorities are very proud of the Australian way of life and 9 percent are not proud; only 5 percent of minorities under 35 years old are not proud of Australia.

31 See http://www.foreignersindenmark.dk/display.cfm?article=1000552&p=1000549&page=Jante+Law.

32 Rice (2011) makes a similar argument about Finland.

Australia has relied upon a sentiment I came upon again and again in my four months in Canberra: the belief that life is good and is going to get better Down Under, especially compared to one's homeland. Optimism is a central factor shaping trust and the Aussies seem to have it endlessly. From Vietnamese cab drivers to Polish scientists to Indian waiters, immigrants seemed thrilled to be in a land where, as Little Orphan Annie sang in the musical *Annie*: "The sun'll come up tomorrow." Even if I face discrimination and a lower wage than I might hope for now, things will be better for my children (another significant predictor of trust, especially for minorities). And they will likely move into a neighborhood and perhaps marry a native Australian. This is the story of the American dream that seems to have eluded many Americans these days and flowered on the other side of the Pacific Ocean.

The results for Australia are strikingly similar to those for Canada. Both countries use point systems for most of their immigrants and those who do enter are mostly highly educated and skilled. They are more trusting than minorities elsewhere but in neither country do they develop more faith in others through optimal contact. Australia has less segregation and more equality and a more demanding point system for immigration. Unlike Canada, it does not have a strong linguistic or ethnic divide, so it has been easier for Australia to adopt effectively (if not officially) an assimilationist worldview. But these differences seem less consequential than the similarities in the levels of trust, the effects of integration and diverse networks on majorities and minorities, and the method of admitting immigrants.

Sweden and Australia have taken different routes to increasing trust among immigrants. And this leads to different outcomes for social interactions in integrated neighborhoods. Swedish immigrants become more trusting under Allport's optimal conditions. Immigrants from low trusting countries inherit their trust from their home country (Uslaner, 2008b). The fair treatment of migrants from low trusting countries in Sweden stands out as an exception to this transmission belt from the old country to the new. And the self-selection of educated and skilled immigrants by Australia means that you can't infer trust levels by ethnicity alone. Add to this high-trusting native whites who are generally tolerant and welcoming of immigrants and you have a recipe for higher trust among the new citizens – and the possibility that social interactions can lead to greater trust either for the majority or the minority or both.

7

Altruism and Segregation

> [I]f any provide not for his own, and specially for those of his own house, he hath denied the faith, and is worse than an infidel.
>
> Timothy 5:8, *King James Bible*[1]

> Second Degree (of charitable giving on an eight-degree ladder): "The Giver and Receiver Unknown to Each Other": One who gives charity to the poor without knowing to whom he gives and without the poor knowing from whom they take. This is how it was done in the Lishkat Hashaim (Chamber of Charity) in the Temple of Jerusalem.
>
> Moses ben Maimonedes, *Maimonides' Ladder of Tzedakah (Charity)*[2]

Joining civic groups may not depend upon trust or create it (Claibourne and Martin, 2000; Stolle, 1998; Uslaner, 2002, ch. 5). However, there are two civic activities that *both* draw upon trust and lead to greater faith in others in turn – giving to charity and volunteering (Uslaner, 2002, ch. 5). Volunteers reject materialistic values in favor of ideals such as a world at peace, inner harmony, and true friendship (Mahoney and Pechura, 1980, 1010; Williams, 1986, 167). They don't expect anyone to repay their kindness (Gerard, 1985, 237). Their acts of altruism have a spiritual rather than an economic payoff, what Andreoni (1989) calls a "warm glow." Such acts of kindness are part of the same value system as trust (Rahn and Transue, 1998, 551). So the conditions that lead to trust, including living in diverse, integrated neighborhoods with friends

[1] Available at http://kingjbible.com/1_timothy/5.htm.

[2] Available at http://www.bookonlife.com/pdfs/jewish_charity.pdf. The lower the number of the degree, the more praiseworthy is the action.

of different backgrounds, should also increase the likelihood of doing good deeds such as giving to charity and volunteering time.

Not all forms of charitable giving and volunteering time are the same. You can spend time at your child's school: As Sara Mosle wrote: "a lot of what passes for volunteering used to be called simply 'parenting': people helping out in their own children's schools or coaching their own children's soccer teams" (2000, 25). Or you can volunteer at your church, your synagogue, your mosque, or your temple, or donate money to them. In each of these cases, you are doing good deeds and following the dictates of your faith.

Every religion exhorts followers to give of themselves, especially to the needy (Cnaan et al, 1993, 37): Jesus fed the poor and hungry, priests and nuns take vows of poverty and work in missions in poor countries, Jews and Muslims are required to give to charity (*tzedakah* in Hebrew, *zakat* in Arabic, from the same root). People with faith participate more in civic affairs – especially in the more demanding activities such as volunteering their time (Hodgkinson, Weitzman, and Associates, 1992, 203; Uslaner, 2001; Verba, Schlozman, and Brady, 1995; Wuthnow, 1991). Faith leads people to put less emphasis on materialistic values and more on how to help others (Harris, 1994; Rokeach, 1973, 128).

Not all volunteering or charitable giving is the same or stems from the same values. Giving to people of your own background – much less volunteering at your own child's school – does not depend upon or produce trust in people who may be different from yourself (Uslaner, 2002, ch. 5). Almost half of volunteering in the United States occurs through religious organizations (Greeley, 1997, 590). Even in the United Kingdom – universally seen as less religious than the United States – most volunteering occurs through houses of worship.[3]

Helping people who are close to you or similar to you is praiseworthy. In doing so, we don't reach out to people who are different, which is the basis of trust. Rabbi Moses ben Maimonedes, one of the most important Jewish theologians, established in the twelfth century an eight-degree ladder of charitable giving. The first and most praiseworthy is to make someone self-sufficient – something that lies beyond what most of us can afford. The second, cited here, is reaching out to strangers anonymously – a form

[3] In a cross-national survey of the importance of religion conducted in 105 nations by Gallup in 2009, two-thirds of Americans said that religion was very important in their lives (ranking 64th) while only 29 percent said so in the United Kingdom (ranking 96th). See http://www.gallup.com/poll/142727/Religiosity-Highest-World-Poorest-Nations.aspx#2.

of giving that transcends boundaries of who the donor and recipient are (see also Sonderskov, 2011a, 2011b; Uslaner, 2002, 128–35). This is the sort of altruism that rests upon trust.

Although the distinction is far from perfect, religious beneficence depends more on in-group trust, religious faith, and attendance in houses of worship (Uslaner, 2002, ch. 5; Wuthnow, 1991). In part this distinction stems from who the beneficiaries of such charity and volunteering are. Religious beneficence may target people of the same faith, or it may come with a message to those outside the faith who receive the charity or other services. Secular good deeds are more likely to focus on the poor, education, literacy, or disaster relief – with beneficiaries unknown.

The distinction also reflects who the donors are. Many strongly religious people, especially fundamentalists or evangelicals in the United States, are high in in-group trust and low in generalized trust. Putnam sees religion as an alternative to social trust rather than as part of its foundation (1993, 107). People may identify so strongly with their faith that they become suspicious of others. Religious fundamentalists will regard people outside their own circle as heathens. Fundamentalists believe that the Bible is the literal word of God and hold that a key tenet of the Scriptures is that humans are born with original sin. This view of human nature stands at odds with the optimism that underlies trust in others (Schoenfeld, 1978, 61; cf. Smith, 1997, 189).

Fundamentalists may withdraw from contact with unredeemed "sinners" and retreat into their own communities. Throughout American history, they have been active in nativist organizations that sought to restrict immigration and immigrants' rights. They fear that people who don't believe as they do are trying to deny them their fundamental rights. When they participate in civic life, they restrict their activities to their own faith's organizations (Uslaner, 1999; Wuthnow, 1999). Since much volunteering and charitable giving stems from faith, it is not surprising that evangelicals overall do *more* good deeds than do members of mainline Protestant denominations. Yet evangelical churches "do not embrace social service provision as an essential part of their mission [and] concentrate their energy on evangelism on meeting the immediate needs of congregational members" (Greenberg, 1999, 19–20). Mainline Protestants are more likely to be generalized trusters than are fundamentalists or evangelicals (Schoenfeld, 1978, 64).[4] According to the Social Capital

[4] Schoenfeld's fundamentalist group is Baptists; his mainline denominations are Episcopalians, Presbyterians, Congregationalists, and Unitarians.

Benchmark Survey, 65 percent of mainline Protestants believe that "most people can be trusted" compared to 53 percent of evangelicals. They are *more* likely to give their time and money to secular causes than are evangelicals.

There is little evidence on the impact of diversity (or segregation) on altruistic deeds. Putnam reports a negative correlation between diversity and volunteering and charitable giving in the United States (2007, 150–1). Clark and Kim (2009) report similar results for New Zealand. These findings are based on sparse models and should be taken as preliminary at best.

I posit that segregation leads to lower levels of secular charitable giving and volunteering and provide support for this in aggregate analyses of altruistic deeds across American communities. Yet this is just part of the story – and not the most telling. Living in a diverse, integrated neighborhood and having friends of different backgrounds should lead to an increase in the sort of altruistic acts most clearly associated with generalized trust – secular giving and volunteering – while religious good deeds should be greater when people don't have diverse friendship networks and live in segregated communities. The effects should be more pronounced on religious giving and volunteering among people with stronger in-group identities: evangelicals and African-Americans in the United States and Muslims in the United Kingdom. Adherents of mainline religions should be more likely to engage in good deeds under Allport's optimal conditions and the effects should be greater for volunteering than for giving to charity since the former involves us in directly helping people of different backgrounds while we can remain comfortably isolated as we donate funds. I focus on the United States and the United Kingdom for a practical reason: The SCBS and the UK Citizenship Survey are the only ones that allow me to examine both secular and religious altruism.

Living in racially segregated neighborhoods may lead to greater in-group trust, but it is not the only type of segregation or diversity that might shape charitable giving or volunteering. If you live in a community with many adherents of your faith, you may be more likely to engage in altruistic deeds helping those who share your faith and less likely to give time and money to those who are different from yourself. I examine this in the United States using data on the share of believers of different faith traditions in American communities from Jones et al. (2000).[5]

[5] I am grateful to Dale E. Jones, Director of Research and Centennial Projects at the Global Ministry Center, for providing the estimates of adherents at the SMSA level.

TABLE 7.1. *Segregation, diversity, and volunteering rates across American communities: instrumental variable estimation*

Variable	Coefficient	Std. Error	t Ratio
Segregation/Diversity Interaction	−.282****	.081	−3.49
(Segregation)	(−.200)***	(.067)	(−2.97)
(Diversity)	(−.125)**	(.056)	(−2.21)
Mean age of community	−.010****	.002	−5.78
Mean level of education in community	.036****	.009	3.93
Population/(100,000)	−.005	.050	.01
Minority homeowner percentage	−.002**	.001	−2.75
Overall home ownership percentage	−.014***	.004	−3.33
Constant	.637****	.109	5.84

RMSE = .378 R^2 = .378 N = 145
* p < .10 ** p < .05 *** p < .01 **** p < .0001 (all tests one tailed except for constants)

Segregation, Diversity, and Altruism

Are acts of beneficence higher in communities that are both diverse and integrated? The answer, at least for the United States, is simple. Yes. The combination of integration *and* diversity is more important than either segregation or diversity alone.

I examine volunteering across 145 American communities and charitable donations across 223 metropolitan areas in Tables 7.1 and 7.2. The data on volunteering come from the Corporation for National and Community Service; the data on charitable contributions come from the Urban Institute.[6] The volunteering data are percentages of people in each community who give their time. The charity data represent mean contributions as a percentage of adjusted gross income. I estimate two-stage least squares instrumental variables to account for possible endogeneity of beneficent acts and segregation.[7] For both charitable giving and volunteering, I present models for the segregation/diversity interaction and for segregation and diversity separately. The coefficients for the latter two

6 I am grateful to Nathan Dietz of the Corporation for National and Community Service for providing the volunteering data and to Tom Pollak and Katie Uttke of the Urban Institute for providing the charitable contributions data.

7 These effects would be indirect through trust, which I cannot measure at the community level and are based on the argument of Andreoni (1989) that good deeds are rewarded with a "warm glow" (which is a form of optimism that underlies trust). The instruments are percent white in the central city, percent black with a high school degree or higher, percent Hispanic living in suburbs, and the percentages of African-Americans and Hispanics. All except percent white in the central city are significant at p < .01 or better.

TABLE 7.2. *Segregation, diversity, and rates of charitable giving across American communities: instrumental variable estimation*

Variable	Coefficient	Std. Error	t Ratio
Segregation/Diversity Interaction	−.023**	.011	−2.20
(Segregation)	(−.013)**	(.008)	(−1.82)
(Diversity)	(−.005)	(.005)	(−1.06)
Mean age of community	−.001****	.000	−4.85
Mean level of education in community	.002**	.001	3.02
Population	.016***	.005	2.93
Minority homeowner percentage	.000	.000	.96
Overall home ownership percentage	−.000	.000	−1.09
Percent Jews in community	.066***	.026	2.53
Percent evangelicals in community	.028****	.004	6.68
Constant	.550****	.078	7.14

RMSE = .083 R^2 = .251 N = 223
* p < .10 ** p < .05 *** p < .01 **** p < .0001 (all tests one tailed except for constants)

measures are in parentheses in the tables; the other coefficients are for the model with the interaction term.

These measures of altruism do *not* distinguish between types of charity or volunteering (religious or secular), so these estimates simply tell the first part of a larger story. But they provide strong support for the argument that living in an integrated and diverse neighborhood matters: the probability of volunteering is 14 percent greater in the most integrated neighborhoods, but the effect on charitable contributions is tiny (.1 percent). The effect of the segregation/diversity interaction on volunteering is greater than that for either segregation (10 percent) or diversity (6 percent with a negative coefficient) alone. The same holds for charitable contributions, where living in the most diverse integrated neighborhood is more important than simply living in the most integrated neighborhood (.08 percent) or the least diverse neighborhood (.03 percent).[8]

[8] These effects were calculated by multiplying the regression coefficients by the ranges of volunteering (from .14 in Miami, Florida to .64 in Provo-Orem, Utah) and charitable contributions adjusted for gross income (from .007 in Laredo, Texas to .07 in Provo-Orem). For both volunteering and giving to charity, communities with a lower mean age gave more to charity and volunteered more, as did areas with higher levels of education. Home ownership rates – both overall and for minorities – were, perhaps surprisingly, *negatively* related to volunteering (but unrelated to charitable giving). In the model for charity, I also included measures for two religious groups noted for their high levels of charitable giving: the percentage of Jews and evangelicals in the community. Both were significant, Jews at p < .01 (b = .066) and evangelicals at p < .0001 (b = .028). Only the percentage of Jews in a community had a stronger impact than did the segregation/diversity interaction.

Segregation and Altruism

Do Allport's optimal conditions matter for altruism at the individual level – and, if so, for whom and for what types of volunteering and charitable giving? I turn first to the United States, where the data are the most comprehensive. I estimate probit models for volunteering and charitable giving from survey data from the Social Capital Benchmark Survey – and, as in Chapter 3, I merge aggregate data on segregation and diversity with the survey data. I also include aggregate measures of the shares of membership in three faith communities (mainline Protestants, evangelicals, and Catholics) to test whether the density of your religious environment shapes the types and levels of altruism.

I estimate models for all respondents, mainline Protestants, white evangelicals, and African-Americans.[9] The SCBS estimates of altruistic deeds seem to be too high, but no other survey has as many respondents who can be matched to their communities. With that caveat, 78 percent of Americans claim to volunteer at their houses of worship. Not surprising, white evangelicals are the most likely to give their time at their churches (84 percent). Mainline Protestants and African-Americans volunteer at church only slightly less (82 percent, see Figure 7.1). The church and religious life more generally is central to the African-American community. Church attendance is strongly linked to altruistic deeds, and this strong commitment to the church explains the high level of African-American religious volunteering. Religious charitable donations are common for most groups: 73 percent overall (and for whites), 78 percent for mainline Protestants and white evangelicals, and 56 percent for African-Americans.

Secular volunteering is much lower, overall and for African-Americans and white evangelicals. These two groups have the *lowest* levels of secular volunteering (at 48 percent and 50 percent), though the difference is small (51 percent overall and 52 percent for whites). Secular volunteering

[9] The SCBS asks respondents about their Protestant denomination. Following the advice of Geoffrey Layman (now of the University of Notre Dame), I categorized as mainline people who are members of Episcopalian, Methodist, United Church of Christ, Wesleyan, Lutheran Evangelicals, and Reformed churches and most others (nondenominational, community church, Seventh Day Adventists, Baptists, Mennonites, Christian Missionary Alliance, Church of the Nazarene, the Salvation Army, independent churches, Pentecostals, Disciples of Christ, and Christian churches) as evangelicals. I used the same basic categories for developing the aggregate measures (which Dale E. Jones calculated for me). The SCBS does not specify what types of volunteering and charitable giving fall under the rubric "secular." It divides each into religious and "other."

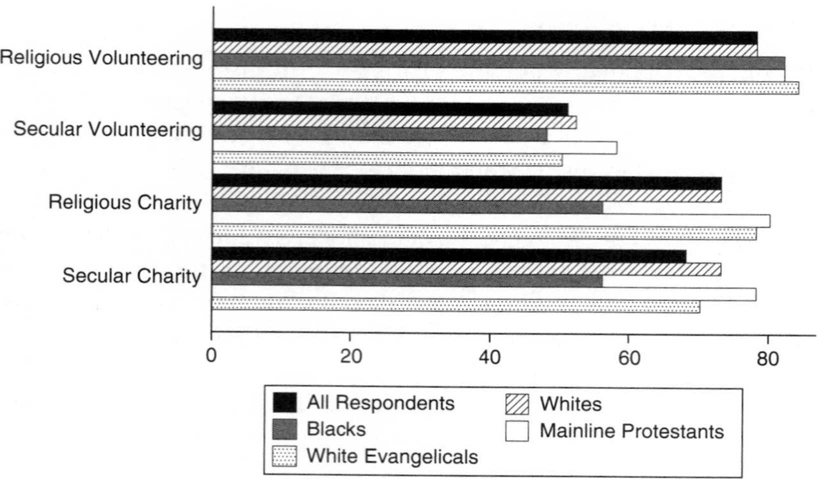

FIGURE 7.1. Percentages of altruism in the U.S. Social Capital Benchmark Survey

is highest among mainline Protestants (58 percent). There is a similar pattern for secular charitable giving: overall, 68 percent say that they give money to secular causes, 73 percent of whites, as well as 70 percent of white evangelicals (65 percent) and blacks (56 percent). More mainline Protestants (78 percent) give money to secular causes than others.

These patterns reflect both resources and priorities. The wealthy are more likely to donate money while the poor are more prone to give of their time, especially to their houses of worship (Verba, Schlozman, and Brady, 1995, 202). Mainline Protestants are relatively wealthy (with an annual income estimated around $50,000 from the SCBS coding), compared to evangelicals (estimated income about $30,000 a year) and African-Americans (estimated income less than $30,000 a year but considerably less than evangelicals). The donation data are all dummy variables – do you donate or don't you – rather than the amount given. However, wealthier people – notably mainline Protestants – are more likely to make *any* donation than are the poor. African-Americans, evangelicals, and mainline Protestants all give to secular charities. But evangelicals are *far more likely to give to religious charities than to secular causes*. Together with African-Americans, their gap between religious and secular volunteering is considerably greater than we find for mainline Protestants. Mainline members give their time and money to a wide range

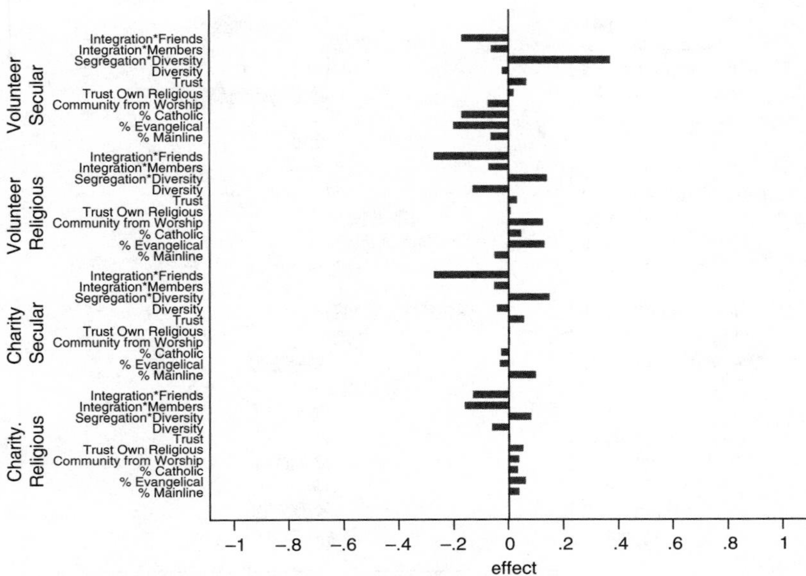

FIGURE 7.2. Probit effects for altruism: all respondents. Social Capital Benchmark Survey

of causes – both religious and secular. Blacks and especially evangelicals do most of their good deeds with their own kind.

The Sources of Altruism in the United States

What drives volunteering and charitable giving in the United States? I estimate four models for each type of altruistic acts – for all respondents, mainline Protestants, evangelicals, and African-Americans. I include the measures of living in diverse integrated communities with heterogenous networks of friends and group members (as in Chapter 3), the interaction term for segregation and diversity, the simple measure of diversity, and the percentage of evangelical, mainline, and Catholic adherents in the community. The models also include a variety of factors shaping giving and volunteering, most notably generalized trust, trust in one's co-religionists (a measure of in-group trust), and whether one believes that his or her sense of community mostly derives from his or her worship network. I present the results in Figures 7.2 through 7.8.

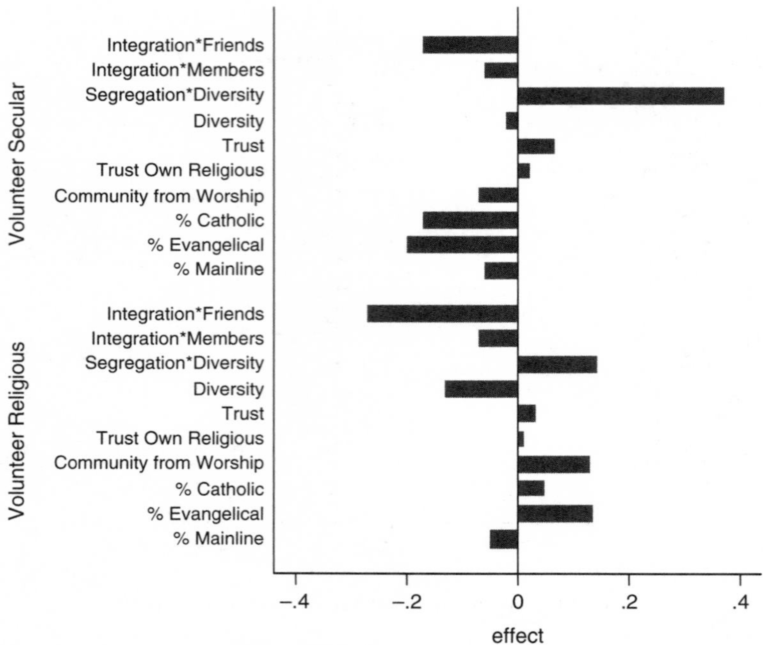

FIGURE 7.3. Probit effects for volunteering: all respondents. Social Capital Benchmark Survey

The forces leading to altruistic deeds thus fall into four core components: (1) Allport's optimal conditions of living in an integrated diverse community with heterogenous friendships and group membership networks; (2) the ethnic and racial demographics of a community (segregation and diversity); (3) the religious demographics of an area; and (4) the values (generalized and in-group trust and the source of community). I also focus on whether ethnic/ racial or religious diversity matters more.

More specifically, I argue that under Allport's optimal conditions, people will be more willing to reach out to help those who may be different. If you are surrounded by people like yourself, ethnically, racially, or religiously, you are more likely to concentrate your giving and volunteering to people of your own kind. Heavy concentrations of co-religionists may lead people to focus their good deeds among their own kind But so may large contingents of members of *any* religious denomination. Living among many religious people may lead to more religious good deeds and fewer secular acts of altruism. So I include measures of both evangelical

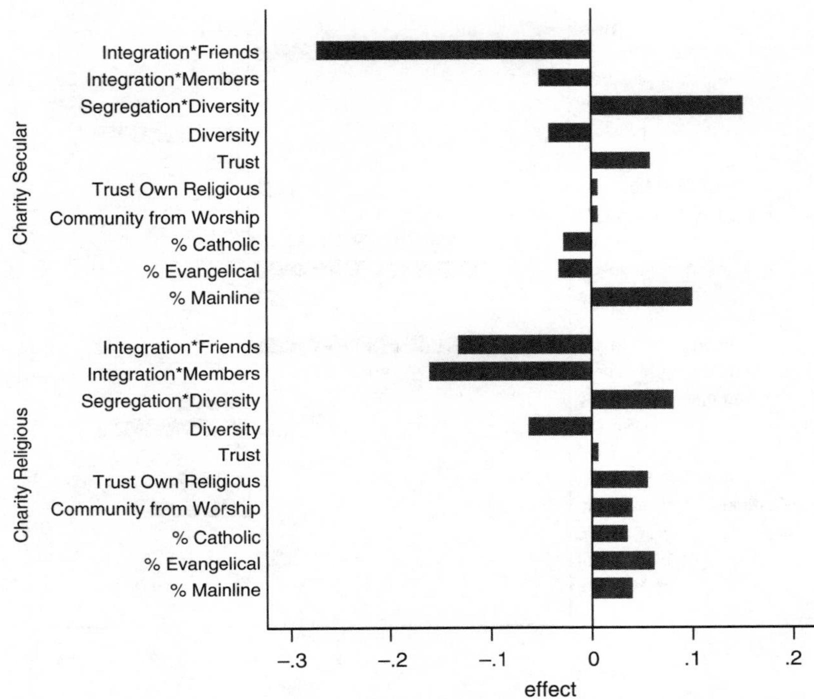

FIGURE 7.4. Probit effects for charitable giving: all respondents. Social Capital Benchmark Survey

and mainline adherents in the models for both groups. I also include the share of Catholics in each community, because Catholics have a long tradition of religious giving and volunteering.[10]

Finally, I examine in-group trust (trust in one's co-religionists), which should increase altruistic deeds based upon faith and generalized trust, which should matter more for secular good works. If you see your community as stemming from your worship network, you should give more through your house of worship and less to secular causes.

[10] The models also include income, education, age, and gender (always significant) as well as the frequency of attendance at religious services (always significant, less so for secular volunteering for evangelicals), inequality (rarely significant), the importance of religion (not significant), whether people running your community care about what happens to you (significant for religious charity for evangelicals), and the Gini index of inequality (not significant). The same pattern holds for the African-American models summarized in Figure 7.5.

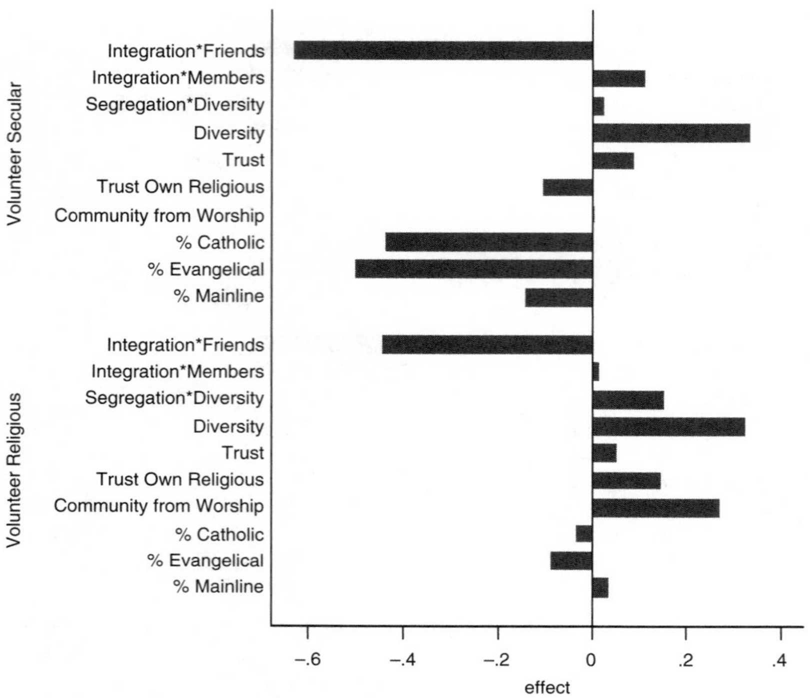

FIGURE 7.5. Probit effects for volunteering: mainline protestants. Social Capital Benchmark Survey

Allport's optimal conditions for diverse friendship networks matter for volunteering for secular causes – but not for white evangelicals. If you live in an integrated diverse community and have a heterogenous friendship network, you are 17 percent more likely to give your time to a secular cause. If you are a mainline Protestant, you are 63 percent more likely to volunteer for a secular cause. Evangelicals seem to withdraw from secular volunteering by a large amount (68 percent) if they live in integrated and diverse neighborhoods with heterogenous friendship networks. This estimate is implausible and may reflect collinearity among the predictors since the zero-order correlation between this measure of Allport's optimal conditions and secular volunteering is higher (-.259) than the correlation for mainline respondents (-.205). At the least, there might be no appreciable effect for white evangelicals.

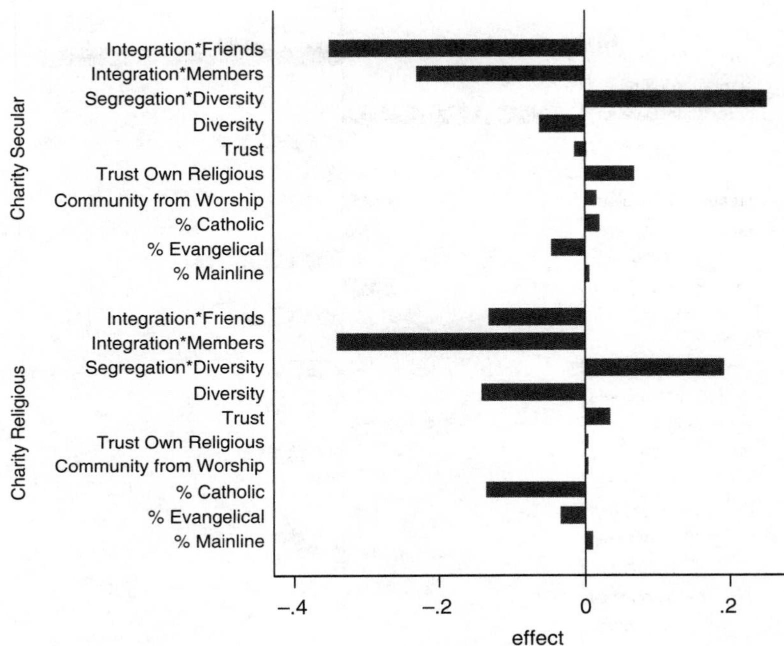

FIGURE 7.6. Probit effects for charitable giving: mainline protestants. Social Capital Benchmark Survey

For all respondents, the optimal conditions are stronger for secular donations and even for religious volunteering (27 percent) – and almost as well for religious contributions (13 percent). For the mainline respondents, the effects are not quite as powerful for other forms of altruism, though they are substantial: a 44 percent rise in religious volunteering for mainline Protestants, a 35 percent rise in the likelihood of secular donations for mainline Protestants (27 percent for all respondents); and a 13 percent to 14 percent boost in religious giving for mainline and all respondents. *The optimal conditions lead to greater acts of kindness for both secular and religious altruism, but only for mainline Protestants.* Across all forms of beneficent deeds, white evangelicals seem to withdraw from good deeds under the optimal conditions.

One reason why there might be large effects on religious volunteering for mainline Protestants is that such activities are more likely to involve social activism – together with Jews, mainline Protestants were among the most active white volunteers in the civil rights movement in the

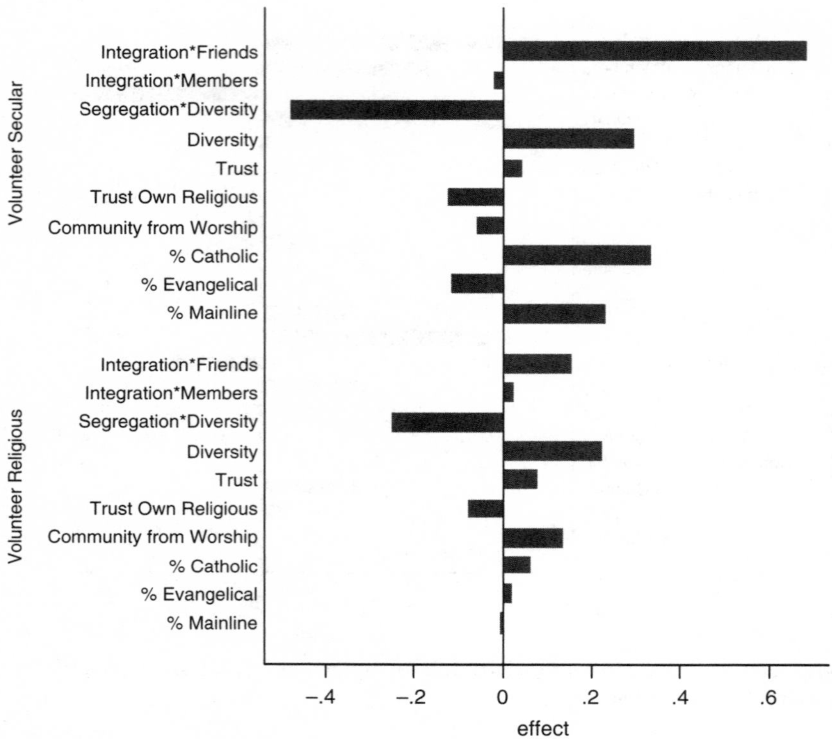

FIGURE 7.7. Probit effects for volunteering: evangelicals. Social Capital Benchmark Survey

1950s and 1960s and have continued to work on interfaith and interracial causes since then. So religious volunteering and religious charity may benefit others even more than in-groups.[11]

The optimal conditions for group membership are much smaller than those for friendship networks. There are substantial effects only for charitable contributions for secular and religious causes by mainline Protestants (effects = -.23 and -.34, respectively) and for secular contributions by evangelicals (effect = -.13). Friendship networks matter more than group membership. There is no way to unpack how or why group membership matters for mainline members and only for charitable giving,

[11] Every major Jewish charity, which I know best, has opportunities to donate funds that would help non-Jews – and some (such as the American Jewish Society for Service) focus almost exclusively on helping non-Jews.

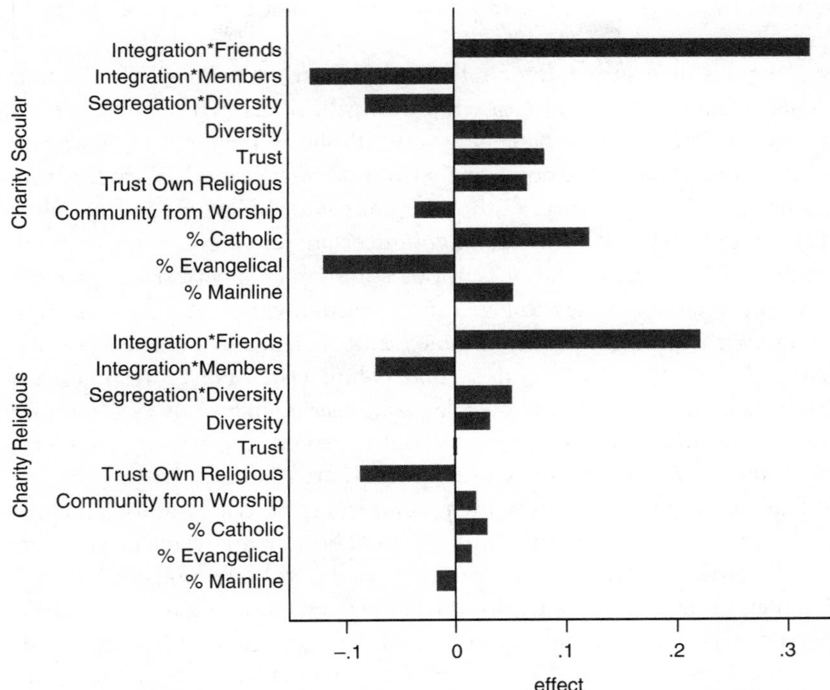

FIGURE 7.8. Probit effects for charitable giving: evangelicals. Social Capital Benchmark Survey

not volunteering – it may reflect the specific groups they join or who the beneficiaries of the contributions might be.

The segregation/diversity interaction is also important only sporadically – and not consistently – and with inexplicable signs. Mainline Protestants living in segregated communities that are not diverse are *more* likely to give money to either secular or religious causes (by 25 percent and 15 percent) and to volunteer for religious causes (by 15 percent). For evangelicals and all respondents, segregation *increases* secular volunteering – by a lot (35 percent). I have no ready explanation for these results other than possible confounding effects of multicollinearity.

Diversity matters more. While Putnam (2007) argues that diversity leads to fewer good deeds, I find the opposite. Mainline Protestants are about 33 percent *more* likely to volunteer either for secular or religious causes if they live in a more diverse area, and 14 percent less likely to give to religious causes. White evangelicals are 24 percent more likely to volunteer for secular causes and have a 22 percent greater probability of religious volunteering.

Religious diversity matters only for volunteering, primarily for secular volunteering – but again not for white evangelicals. Even though Figure 7.4 shows large effects of the percentage of Catholic and mainline believers on secular volunteering, the coefficients from the probit models are far from significant. However, large faith communities of all types lead mainline Protestants to focus less on secular volunteering. A mainline Protestant living in a heavily evangelical or Catholic community is between 44 percent and 50 percent less likely to give time to secular causes. Living in a community with a large share of mainline members leads to a smaller (14 percent), but still notable, drop in secular volunteering. For all respondents, there are moderate declines in secular volunteering in heavily Catholic and evangelical communities (17 percent and 20percent respectively), but a far more modest effect for a large evangelical share (6 percent).

Faith communities thus crowd out secular activities among people whose religious ties are more bridging than bonding. Diverse ties encourage all forms of altruism, most notably secular volunteering. As I argued (Uslaner, 2002, ch. 5), generalized trust leads to more secular volunteering: by 7 percent for all members and evangelicals and 9 percent for mainline Protestants. There is also a boost of 8 percent in secular charitable giving for evangelicals (but not for mainline members). There are only minimal effects for trust in members of one's church (a 7 percent boost in secular donations, but a 10 percent decline for secular volunteering, both for mainline Protestants).

There are also small effects for defining your community as the people you worship with: a drop in secular volunteering for all respondents (7 percent) and for evangelicals (4 percent) – but more substantial increases in the likelihood of religious volunteering (27 percent for mainline Protestants and 9 percent for evangelicals). These latter effects (for trust in co-religionists and defining your community) are smaller than one might expect because people overwhelmingly trust members of their church, and over 80 percent of respondents (90 percent of evangelicals) say that their place of worship gives them a sense of community. Nevertheless, high levels of in-group trust boost religious *and* secular volunteering among white evangelicals (by 8 to 9 percent) and has an even greater effect (13 percent) on secular volunteering.[12] The sense of community

[12] The negative effects in the figures stem from the coding of the variables for prejudice and for choosing friends of your own religion.

through worship increases religious volunteering by 13 percent among white evangelicals.

Overall, where you live and who your friends and group members are matter, but for mainline Protestants and not for white evangelicals. Allport's optimal conditions are powerfully important for volunteering, much more so than for charitable giving. And this makes sense since you volunteer with others while you are more likely to give to charity in the privacy of your own home (or house of worship). The simple presence of large faith communities is associated with less secular volunteering for mainline Protestants. Faith in others boosts volunteering, especially for mainline Protestants but also for white evangelicals – as well as for secular charitable giving for this group.

There is no neat and simple picture for the various types of altruism and the different faith groups. White evangelicals don't respond to the diversity of friendship networks. They *do* volunteer more in racially diverse communities, though they are not affected by religious diversity. The main factor underlying all forms of good deeds is how often one attends church. For mainline Protestants, the largest effects are for Allport's optimal conditions. Racial diversity and segregation seem to matter more than the religious composition of one's neighborhood. How do segregation and diversity affect altruistic acts among African-Americans? I estimate the same model for blacks and focus primarily on the indicators of segregation and diversity (see Figure 7.9).

The pattern of effects are familiar and not surprising: when African-Americans live in diverse and integrated communities and have heterogenous friendship networks, they are 63 percent more likely to volunteer for secular causes (the same effect for mainline Protestants and evangelicals), 45 percent more likely to donate to secular causes, and have a 25 percent greater probability of doing each type of religious good deeds. As in Chapter 2, the optimal conditions for group membership (rather than friendships) are generally not significant – except for donating to religious causes. Segregation seems to increase (substantially at 48 percent) secular volunteering.[13] Diversity (mostly the share of non-whites in a municipality) drives down all volunteering by about 30 percent, much as Putnam suggests. The main negative effects for diversity come not for most people, but for minority respondents only. For many African-Americans, this might be the inner city where hypersegregation leads residents to withdraw from civic life.

[13] These are also unlikely effects, which could be attributable to collinearity.

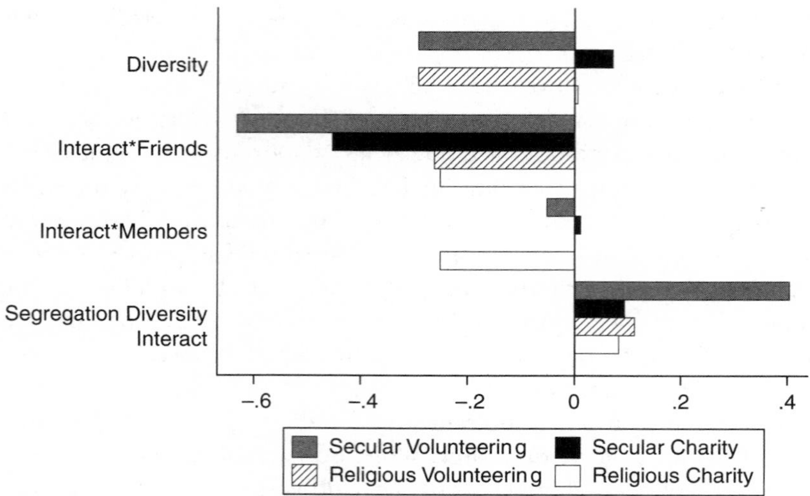

FIGURE 7.9. Probit effects for African-Americans on altruism in the U.S. Social Capital Benchmark Survey

For African-Americans, as for whites, trust leads to more secular good deeds – by 8 percent for volunteering and 6 percent for giving to charity. The central role of faith in shaping civic behavior in the African-American community is reflected in the strong impact of the evangelical share of a municipality's population. It leads to increases in religious volunteering of 29 percent and of both religious and secular donations of 12 to 13 percent. This is not surprising since 49 percent of African-Americans identify as evangelicals, compared to 21 percent of whites. Evangelicals comprise 15 percent of the population in communities where African-American respondents live, compared to 13 percent for whites. Secular volunteering is the only realm of altruism not affected by the evangelical share.

But the overall story is that living in a diverse and integrated community with friends of different backgrounds is the most important factor shaping good deeds, and especially secular good deeds. Across religious and racial groups in the United States, this factor stands out above others. Does it apply elsewhere?

Altruism in the United Kingdom

The British, who have a stronger social safety net through the state, are less likely to volunteer or give to charity than are Americans. For the full

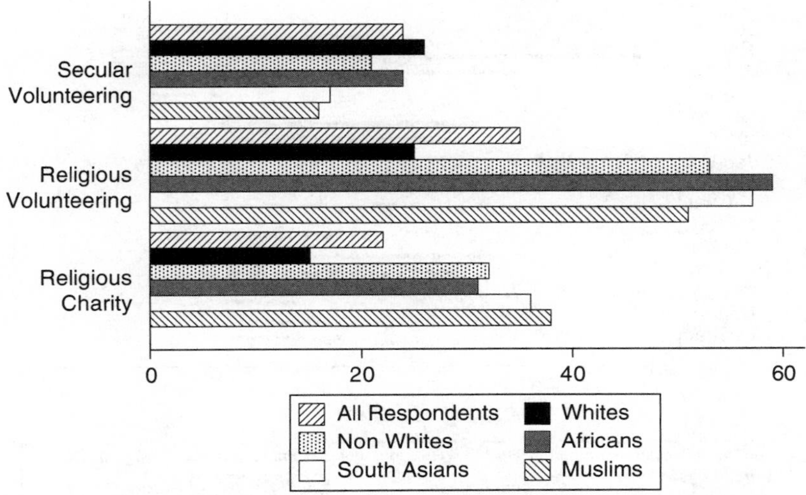

FIGURE 7.10. Percentages of altruism in the U.K. UK Citizenship Survey 2007

population, 24 percent volunteer for secular causes, 35 percent through their houses of worship, and 22 percent contribute to religious charities (see Figure 7.10).[14] White Britons give little money or time to religious causes – just 15 percent donate through their houses of worship and only 25 percent give time to religious volunteering. Minorities are far more faithful to their religions – with between 51 percent (Muslims) and 59 percent (Africans) volunteering through houses of worship, and between 31 percent (Africans) and 38 percent (Muslims) donating to religious charities.

I examine the roots of giving and volunteering in the United Kingdom for all respondents and members of ethnic/racial/religious groups as in Chapter 5. The models are more sparse than those for the United States because the 2007 Citizenship Survey has fewer relevant variables. I focus on four possible determinants of altruistic behavior: generalized trust, the interaction of diversity/segregation (the share of people of your own background within 15 to 20 minutes walking distance), how important someone's religion is to selecting friends, and whether there is a lot of

[14] The 2007 UK Citizenship Survey asks about religious volunteering and charity. The secular volunteering question I use asks about giving time to adult education, the elderly, health and welfare, and safety. I dichotomized the latter measure. The only charity question asked is for religious giving.

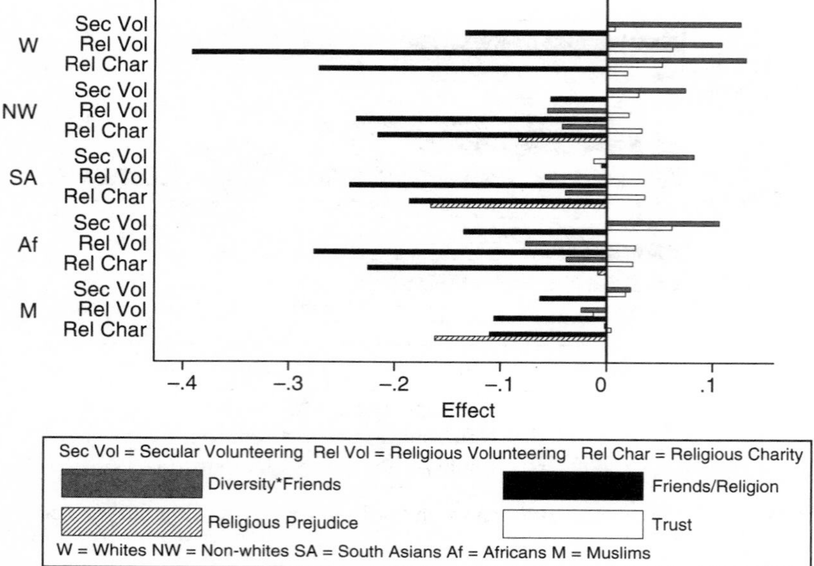

FIGURE 7.11. Probit effects for UK by ethnicity/race. UK Citizenship Survey 2007

prejudice in Britain today. People who say that their friendship networks depend strongly on religion should be less likely to volunteer for secular causes and more likely to engage in religiously-based good deeds. If you believe that there is much prejudice in the country, you would likely focus your attention on your own group.[15] I present the results in Figure 7.11.

Diverse friendship groups in integrated communities matter less than they do in the United States. For secular volunteering, there are consistently significant effects of between 2 percent (for Muslims), 5 percent (all respondents), and 11 to 13 percent (for Africans and whites). The biggest effects are for whites, who are the most segregated. The effects are equally strong for whites on religious volunteering and charitable giving (about 13 percent). So living in integrated communities with diverse friendship networks promotes altruism as well as trust for white Britons. Minorities are stimulated to do good works by the optimal conditions only for secular volunteering. The effects for religious good deeds are

[15] Other variables in the models are education, income, gender, marital status, and ability to influence decisions in your area.

either insignificant (in most cases) or even negative (for all nonwhites and Africans for religious volunteering). Minorities are less likely to target their good deeds through their religious institutions and more likely to engage in secular volunteering if they have diverse friendships in integrated neighborhoods. This optimal condition promotes trust among most groups in the United Kingdom (see Chapter 5), but trust in turn has little impact on altruism. The only exceptions, and they are not powerful effects, are for Africans on secular volunteering and for whites on religious charitable contributions.

If you believe that Britain has a lot of prejudice, you will be more likely to give to charity through your religion *if your background is from South Asia or are a Muslim*. Muslims and others from South Asia who believe that there is a lot of prejudice in Britain are 17 percent *more* likely to give to religious charities. Whites and Muslims who see a lot of prejudice have greater probabilities of volunteering through houses of worship.

But the most powerful determinant of religious giving and volunteering is whether you choose your friends based upon their religion. Whites who base their friendships on common faith are 39 percent more likely to volunteer and 27 percent more likely to donate through their houses of worship. This in-group favoritism is almost universal for religious altruism. But the effects vary across groups: a 28 percent increase for Africans, 24 percent for nonwhites generally and South Asians, but just 11 percent for Muslims. For religious donations, the effects range from 29 percent for the full sample to 11 percent for Muslims (27 percent for whites, 22 percent for Africans and nonwhites generally), and 19 percent for South Asians.

The overall story for Britain is more straightforward than it is for the United States: Allport's optimal conditions promote secular volunteering for virtually all groups. A strong commitment to socializing with people of your own background leads you to focus your volunteering and charitable contributions within your own faith community.

Reprise

Integrated communities have higher levels of charitable giving and volunteering. And people who live in such communities and have diverse friendship networks are more likely to give of themselves – and the effects are greater for good deeds that are more bridging than bonding, for secular rather than religious activities. The effects are greater in the United States, where there is more segregation than in the United Kingdom.

There is some modest evidence – mostly for mainline Protestants in the United States – that communities with large numbers of religious adherents have lower levels of secular altruism. But there is little evidence that diversity *per se* isolates people and leads to fewer good deeds. Only African-Americans seem adversely affected by such isolation. Mainline Protestants and white evangelicals are more likely to reach out to help people who are different from themselves if they live in diverse communities, above and beyond any benefit that they might get from Allport's optimal conditions.

There is some evidence that in-group trust may lead to more religious altruism in the United States, but there is far stronger evidence that perceptions of racial prejudice and especially choosing friends of your own faith will lead to sharply higher levels of religious good deeds. This may be wholly praiseworthy since it seems that in-group friendship patterns also boost secular volunteering, though at a much lower rate. To the extent that there is a trade-off between secular and religious good deeds,[16] a strong sense of identity may lead to fewer altruistic acts that help people of different backgrounds. These findings may suggest that caution is in order in promoting policies that reinforce a group's identity – including multiculturalism.

There is also some irony in these results. In both the United States and the United Kingdom, groups with a strong sense of in-group religious identity – white evangelicals and Muslims – seem largely unaffected by their surroundings and having close friends of different backgrounds. White evangelicals' good deeds are largely a function of how often they attend church; Muslims' good deeds are not well predicted. Prejudice and choosing friends based on religion matter for religious giving (*zakat*), but not for any type of volunteering. The only variable that consistently matters is gender.[17] Allport's optimal conditions are not restricted to the majority – they lead to more good deeds by African-Americans as well as mainline Protestants in the United States. However, the largest impacts seem to be for the majority (or dominant) groups.

Or do they? In the next chapter I examine the foundations of residential choice in the United States and the United Kingdom.

[16] The zero-order correlations among the measures are slight.

[17] Men do most of the volunteering and make most of the charitable contributions.

8

Where You Sit Depends Upon Where You Stand[1]

"They'd think you're crazy if you had a colored woman visit you in your home. They'd stare at you and there'd be a lot of talk."

"I started to cry when my husband told me we were coming to live here.... I didn't want to come and live here where there were so many colored people. I didn't want to bring my children up with colored children, but we had to come; there was no place else to go. Well, all that's changed. I've really come to like it. I see they're just as human as we are. They have nice apartments, they keep their children clean, and they're friendly. I've come to like them a great deal.... I'd just as soon live near a colored person as a white; it makes no difference to me."

Whites living in segregated and integrated housing projects in New York City and Newark, New Jersey, 1951, quoted in Deutsch and Collins (1951, 66, 98–9)

"They're so prejudiced; I'd be afraid to live among them."

African-American living in a segregated housing project, 1951, quoted in Deutsch and Collins (1951, 117)

The [housing] projects in Harlem [the predominantly black section of Manhattan] are hated. They are hated almost as much as policemen, and this is saying a great deal. And they are hated for the same reason: both reveal, unbearably, the real attitude of the white world, no matter how many liberal speeches are made, no matter how lofty editorials are written, no matter how many civil-rights commissions are set up ... for the

[1] An "inversion" of "where you stand depends upon where you sit" – a description of how military strategies for the American armed forces reflect the branch of the military in which one serves: Air Force officers prefer airborne attacks, the Army ground forces, the Navy battles at sea.

> Northerner, Negroes represent nothing to him personally, except, perhaps, the dangers of carnality. He never sees Negroes.
>
> James Baldwin (1961, 60, 65), *Nobody Knows My Name*

Living in a diverse integrated neighborhood and having friends of different background from yourself leads to higher levels of trust across both countries and ethnic/racial groups, though not evenly. Can we "reshuffle" people to create the sort of neighborhoods that are conducive to a greater civic spirit?

Alas, creating such communities is difficult. Moving large numbers of people from one place to another in the highly segregated American cities is a logistical nightmare. But convincing their potential new neighbors to welcome there would be even more difficult. The quotes above indicate that many Americans were racially biased and did not want to live among African-Americans – and that blacks in turn feared living among whites. While such direct expressions of racist views are now rare, many whites still hold negative views of African-Americans but express them differently. Segregation persists because many whites – and not just in the United States – don't want to live among blacks.

The desire to live in overwhelmingly white neighborhoods reflects both negative stereotypes of African-Americans *and* low levels of generalized trust. If you believe that African-Americans are lazy and not law abiding, you will not want to live among them; if you see blacks as honest, hard working, intelligent, honest, and generous, you would welcome them as neighbors. Generalized trusters have faith in people who are different from themselves – and thus should be more welcoming of people of different backgrounds as neighbors.

So we have a vicious circle: low trust leads to greater segregation, which in turn (together with homogenous social networks) leads to low trust. Trust and segregation are endogenous – they cause each other. The positive effects on trust of Allport's optimal conditions may be exaggerated. High trusting people may sort themselves into integrated neighborhoods and will be more likely to have diverse friendship networks. Looking at these neighborhoods and finding lots of trusting people may confound cause and effect.

And it does. When I examine trust and housing preferences in both the United States and the United Kingdom, the positive effects of Allport's optimal conditions either fade dramatically (for most groups in the United Kingdom and for African-Americans) or fall dramatically (whites in the

United States). The question then becomes whether one can "create" integrated neighborhoods in the absence of a desire of many whites to accept African-Americans. I estimate simultaneous equation models for residential preference and trust in the United States and for the interaction of segregation and friendship diversity and trust in the United Kingdom. If trusting people prefer to live in integrated communities (or actually live there and have diverse friendship networks), then the "causal" power of Allport's "optimal conditions" comes into question. The "optimal conditions" may work because trusting people may select themselves into integrated neighborhoods (and have diverse networks). I estimate simultaneous equation models for the United States and the United Kingdom and find that such selection effects cast doubt on the positive effects I have reported so far. Before I turn to this question, I consider how integrated neighborhoods with diverse friendship networks leads to greater satisfaction with your community and to more tolerant attitudes on race.

The Benefits of Integrated Neighborhoods

People who live in integrated diverse neighborhoods with friends of different backgrounds are more satisfied with their communities and are less likely to have negative views of people of different races. These claims are supported by data from a special survey on race conducted by the Pew Research Center in October/November 2009 with a large oversample of African-Americans.[2] I examine satisfaction with communities and racial stereotypes for whites, African-Americans, and Hispanics in the Pew data, merging the survey results with measures of segregation and diversity (see Chapter 3).

Allport's optimal conditions make your neighborhood a more pleasant place – for whites and especially for African-Americans.[3] I estimate probit models for how satisfied people are with their communities for all respondents, whites, and African-Americans. The two principal predictors are the three-way interaction of diversity/integration/friends of different backgrounds and the simple fractionalization (diversity) index.

[2] I am grateful to Scott Keeter of the Pew Center for providing me with an early release of the data and for helping match the geocodes in the data set he sent me with a master list. For details on the survey, see http://pewsocialtrends.org/2010/01/12/blacks-upbeat-about-black-progress-prospects/.

[3] The key groups here are blacks and whites, so I don't focus on Hispanics for satisfaction.

I also include a measure of racial stereotypes, how well whites and blacks get along in the community, whether the police treat African-Americans and whites equally, age, income, and education.[4]

The stereotype measures play a central role in explanations of the determinants of residential choice. The standard ways of framing stereotypes is by asking respondents which of two traits they believe characterize most members of a race. They rate people of each race on seven-point scales such as lazy-hardworking, violence prone/not violence prone, etc. The stereotype measures tap prejudice of one group against another (Bobo and Kluegel, 1993, 462). Negative stereotypes of African-Americans are a key reason why whites don't want to live among African-Americans (Charles, 2006, 139; cf. Bobo and Massagali, 2001, 131; Charles, 2007, 49, 72; Ellen, 2000, 71, 124).

The Pew survey asks somewhat different stereotype questions than the norm. Respondents are asked whether blacks (whites) are hard working, intelligent, honest, generous, and law abiding – without a corresponding negative reference. I create an index of stereotype bias by a factor analysis of the five measures – black stereotype measures for whites and white stereotype measures for African-Americans. In Figure 8.1 I present estimates for the diversity/segregation/friendship interaction and the simple diversity measure.

All respondents, whites, and blacks all are less satisfied in more diverse communities. However, the effects are very small: ranging from a .02 decline in the probability of being very satisfied for African-Americans to a .05 decline for whites. The three-way interaction has stronger effects. The optimal conditions raise the probability of being very satisfied with your community by about 10 percent for whites and all respondents – but by 35 percent for African-Americans.[5] Bradburn et al. (1970, 361) report in their comparison of 50 segregated and 50 integrated communities in 1967 that "... economic factors are more important for happiness than are neighborhood factors." However, African-Americans in integrated

[4] For all respondents, the key predictors (by t ratios) are equal treatment by the police (more equal treatment leads to greater satisfaction), age (older people are more satisfied), and income (wealthier people are more satisfied), and whether whites and blacks get along well. For whites, equal treatment by the police, age, and income are the only significant predictors of being very satisfied. For African-Americans, how well blacks and whites get along is the most important predictor of strong satisfaction with your community, followed by age and income.

[5] The coding for the three-way interaction for the Pew data leads to the expectation of a positive, rather than a negative relationship.

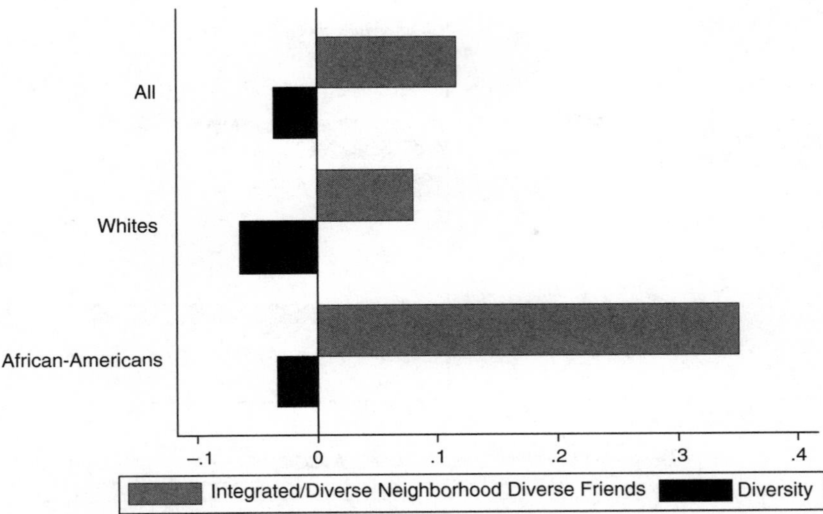

FIGURE 8.1. Probability very satisfied with community by ethnicity. Pew race survey 2010

neighborhoods who socialize with their white neighbors are substantially happier than those who do not.

While Allport's optimal conditions boost trust more for whites than for blacks, they have much greater effects on community satisfaction for the highly segregated minority. Most likely the powerful effect for African-Americans does not represent the strong bonding needed for trust – but rather it reflects dissatisfaction with life in the ghetto and all of the problems associated with hypersegregation. It is notable that diversity itself matters little – blacks don't react negatively to living among other African-Americans. It's the context, not the neighbors that matter.

Stereotypes don't effect community satisfaction for all respondents or whites. They have a small effect ($p < .10$) for African-Americans. However, they do have powerful effects on residential choice (see below), so it is useful to examine what drives prejudice. In Figure 8.2, I present regression models for stereotypes for all respondents, whites, and African-Americans – and I also include Hispanics. The dependent variable is a composite measure: the stereotype factor score for whites minus the same measure for blacks. Thus it is a measure of bias toward whites. I focus on the three-way interaction and three variables connected to race relations. I expect fewer negative stereotypes if one believes that blacks and whites are treated equally by the police, if blacks and whites share

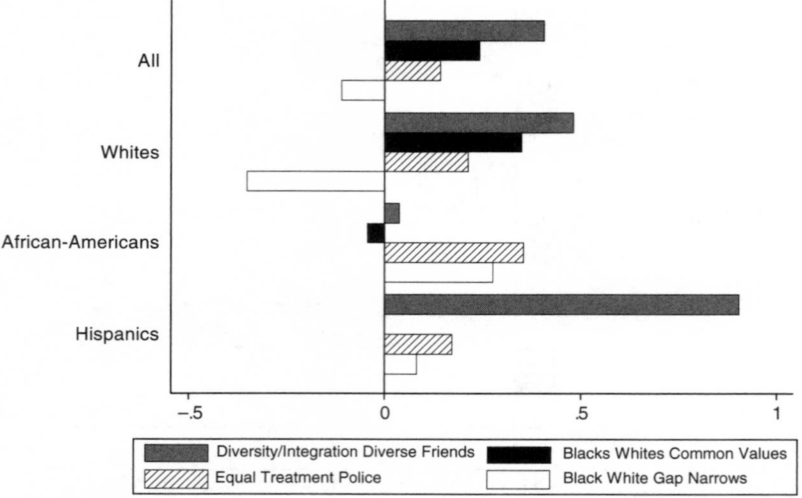

FIGURE 8.2. Racial stereotype bias determinants by ethnicity. Pew race survey 2010

common values, and if the economic gap between blacks and whites is narrowing.[6]

Racial stereotypes have smaller effects for whites, and especially for Hispanics, if they live in integrated diverse neighborhoods with diverse friendship networks. Deutsch and Collins (1951, 91–2) found that white housewives living in integrated projects in New York City and Newark were substantially less likely to harbor negative stereotypes about blacks compared to their peers in segregated apartment complexes. They also echo the findings of Bradburn et al. (1970, 250), who showed that whites who moved from segregated to integrated neighborhoods more strongly endorsed pro-integration views than did whites living in segregated communities. There is virtually no effect for African-Americans. The big effects for whites and Hispanics reflect two dynamics of community life in America: The optimal conditions matter more for whites and Hispanics because they are more prejudiced than African-Americans. Hispanics' mean score on the overall prejudice measure is .45, largely reflecting negative views of African-Americans. Whites are the least biased (with a mean

[6] Since these results come from regressions, the entries in Figure 8.2 are marginal effects (using the margins routine in Stata 11) rather than changes in probabilities. Also included in the models are what shapes success in life, age, income, and education. I did not include simple diversity to reduce collinearity.

score of .06), but they are the least likely to have friends of different backgrounds. They are more likely to rate both blacks and whites highly on each of the five measures, often by substantial margins. African-Americans rate themselves and whites less favorably than do whites – but are more skeptical of whites (especially on honesty) than they are of other blacks. These stereotypes don't change much if blacks live in diverse integrated communities and have friends of different backgrounds.

For African-Americans, the nature of social ties doesn't matter as much as perceptions of justice: Equal treatment by the police and the perception that the black–white income gap is narrowing are the key to positive evaluations of whites. For whites, on the other hand, perceptions of narrowing income gaps leads to more racial resentment. The positive effect of living in a diverse and integrated neighborhood (.479) more than outweighs resentment over a declining income gap (-.351) for whites.

The foundations of stereotypes are quite different for whites, blacks, and Hispanics. For Hispanics, it's all about social networks. For whites, social networks and the perception of common values (a change of about .35) lead to less prejudice. A narrowing income gap leads to a less pronounced bias against blacks by whites (by about .35) and to more favorable views of whites by African-Americans (by about .2) – with almost no effect for Hispanics.

For whites and Hispanics, where you live and who your friends are matter a lot for how you view people who are different from yourself (cf. Rothwell, 2010, 24). For African-Americans, who are by far the most segregated in the United States, it's less where you live and who you friends are than how you are treated that shape racial stereotypes.

The Bases of Residential Choice

Why do people choose to live where they do? The most common story, which holds for most people in most countries, is economic: People want the best housing they can afford. They look for nice houses with plenty of space, perhaps a garden, in neighborhoods that are quiet and safe and have good schools and easy access to transportation.

The bases of segregation, on this view, are economic. Whites shun heavily black neighborhoods because poverty, poor schools, crime, and disorder more generally are higher in areas with larger populations of African-Americans (Ellen, 2000, 99–100, 121–2; Frey, 1979, 439; Harris, 1994, 476). In 100 segregated and integrated neighborhoods in 1967,

Bradburn et al. (1970, 136) found that most white residents of integrated neighborhoods did not choose to live among blacks because they had more liberal views on race: These poor neighborhoods were all they could afford.

For most minorities in the United States and elsewhere, this economic account works well. For Hispanics and Asians in the United States, for most groups in the United Kingdom and Canada, and for virtually every minority in Australia and Sweden, economic success leads to better and less segregated housing.

But there are at least two groups that remain relatively segregated: African-Americans in the United States and South Asians (especially Muslims) in Britain. There is strong evidence that simple economics doesn't explain residential choice, at least between blacks and whites in the United States. Many American whites have an aversion to living among African-Americans. In 1942, 84 percent of whites held that there should be separate sections of each city for blacks and whites. In 1962, six out of ten Americans believed that whites could keep African-Americans out of their neighborhoods (Massey and Denton, 1993, 49). So it is *not* just the socioeconomic character of the neighborhood that determines who wants to live where. It is also the racial composition of the people around you. Even a leading advocate of the economic basis of urban housing choice, Ellen (2000, 57), admits:

> ... while black clustering undeniably accounts for some amount of racial segregation, the segregation levels of blacks are so much higher than that of other ethnic groups that we would have to assume, implausibly it seems, that their desire for clustering is exceptional – far beyond that of even recent immigrants, such as Mexicans and Koreans, whose foreign language and customs make such clustering natural and perhaps even advantageous.

As the American civil rights leader and politician Jesse Jackson said of whites' opposition to busing children across town to achieve racial balance in the public schools in the 1970s: "It's not the bus, it's us" (quoted in Davis, 2007, 60).

Segregation persists because whites don't want to live among many blacks. African-Americans today, as in the quote from Deutsch and Collins's 1951 study, feel unwanted in white communities. Charles (2006, 54) argues: "... active racial prejudice is a critical component of preferences for integration and therefore the persistence of racially segregated communities."

It is no longer fashionable to say that you don't want to live among people of a different race in a segregated community. Farley et al. (1978)

formulated a more sophisticated measure of housing preferences. They show respondents neighborhood cards, with 15 houses surrounding one's own hypothetical house in the center. The cards vary in the share of other races who live in the neighborhood – and by the proximity of people of different races to your own house. Respondents are asked how comfortable they would be living in each hypothetical neighborhood. This has become a standard way of measuring the preferences for integration in American communities – and I shall use it below. Farley et al. (1978, 336–338) found that 40 percent of whites in the Detroit area said that they would move out of a neighborhood that was a third black and two-thirds would leave a majority African-American community. When a neighborhood reaches 30 percent black, more whites begin to move out than to move in.

A quarter of whites are willing to buy into a neighborhood that is just 15 percent black – but no whites would move in to a neighborhood that is two-thirds African-American, regardless of the level of crime, school quality, or housing values. High shares of Asian and Hispanic neighbors do not lead to a widespread out-migration of whites (Emerson, Chai, and Yancey, 2001, 929–30). The "ideal" neighborhood for whites (in the 2000 General Social Survey) has a majority of whites and just 17 percent blacks; a quarter of whites preferred no blacks at all in their immediate area (Massey, 2007, 71–2).

For blacks, the ideal neighborhood is half African-American and half white (Zubrinsky and Bobo, 1996, 358). African-Americans who favor neighborhoods with greater shares of blacks are not expressing strong in-group loyalty, but rather fear that whites will "treat them as unwelcome intruders" (Charles, 2006, 55; Krysan and Farley, 2002, 969–70). They are also more likely to believe that whites discriminate against them and, especially in mostly white areas, will subject them to intimidation (Bradburn et al., 1970, 364–5; Krysan, 2002, 535, 539; Timberlake, 2000, 437). This fear begins even before African-Americans move into a white neighborhood. Blacks still face discrimination when they seek houses – they are far more likely to be steered away from white neighborhoods now than they were in the recent past Charles, 2006, 60).

It's not simply that whites want to live among whites. Positive feelings about your own group play a small role in shaping housing preferences for all racial groups (Bobo and Zubrinsky, 1996, 892, 897). Views of out-groups are what matters – and blacks are the least liked group for whites, Asians, and Hispanics. Whites, on the other hand, have positive views of Asians and want them as neighbors (Charles, 2006, 127, 139).

Whites are the group with the highest favorability ratings among minorities – and thus are the most desirable neighbors (Bobo and Massagakli, 2001). But all minorities see whites as dominant and not welcoming (Charles, 2006, 181).

Whites don't simply say that they don't want minorities as their neighbors. This is "old fashioned" racism, now widely frowned upon. Instead, whites say that they fear what an integrated neighborhood might become. And this is generally reflected in a more nuanced prejudice, as reflected in negative stereotypes of blacks (see above). The view that African-American neighborhoods are marked by poor schools, high crime, general disorder, and lower house prices may well reflect hyper-segregated inner-city neighborhoods, but many middle class (and higher) segregated neighborhoods are not marked by this litany of problems. Whites who see African-Americans as lazy (as opposed to hard working), poor (as opposed to wealthy), unintelligent (as opposed to intelligent), and committed to strong families (as opposed to not so committed) are more likely to be expressing stereotypes.

The 2000 General Social Survey allows me to examine the reciprocal relationship between residential preferences, trust, and racial stereotypes for both whites and nonwhites (blacks).[7] The GSS presented respondents with "neighborhood cards" representing 15 houses (see Figure 8.3). The respondent was told that his (her) house was number 8 and was asked to fill in the blank center of each of the 14 houses with the race of your preferred neighborhood ("A" for Asian, "B" for black, "H" for Hispanic, and "W" for white). I created scores for the three groups of houses: The homes immediately next door and above and behind you (houses 3, 7, 8, and 12 in Figure 8.3), those on a diagonal to your house (houses 2, 4, 11, and 13), and houses a bit farther out (1, 6, 9, 10, and 14). For each house, I coded the race of the respondent and the choice of race of the occupant of each house within each group. For each of the three groups, I assigned a score ranging from zero to four (for the first two groups) or six (for the further houses). I then created an index for the three groups of diversity preferences by factor analysis.[8] I label this the "neighbor closest" factor.

The key question is whether residential preferences lead to trust or depend upon trust. To examine this possible interdependence, I estimate a

[7] All nonwhites in this subsample are African-American.

[8] The three indices formed a single factor, with the loadings for the three groups of houses being almost identical (ranging from .59 to .61).

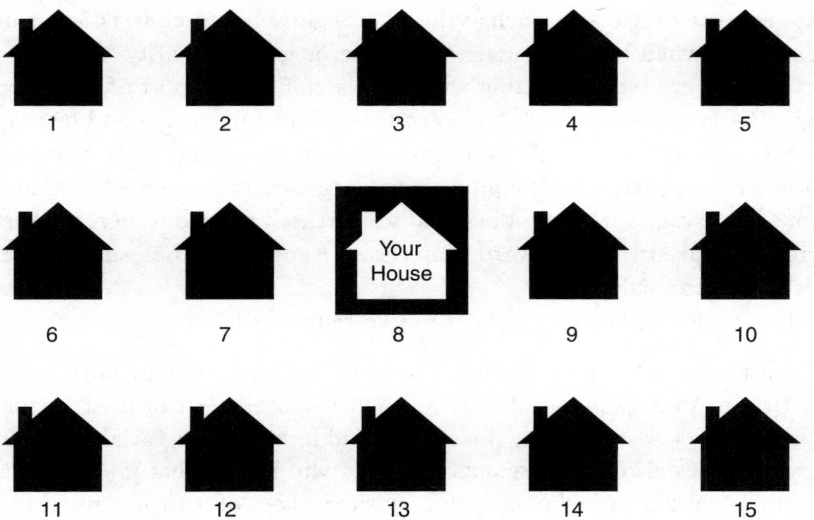

FIGURE 8.3. The Neighborhood Card. General Social Survey

two-stage least squares non-recursive model. In simpler terms, this model allows residential preferences to shape trust and trust to determine residential preferences. I also created indices for stereotypes based upon the questions of being hard-working, wealthy, intelligent, and committed to strong families for whites, blacks, Asians, and Hispanics. I use the African-American stereotypes in the analysis for whites and the white stereotypes in the model for blacks. Hispanic and Asian stereotypes are also important since the residential preference factor is based upon preferences for Hispanic and Asian neighbors as well as for whites and blacks – and also because whites have very different attitudes toward Asian-Americans as neighbors than they do toward blacks or Hispanics (Charles, 2007, 49).

The model for the "neighbor closest" factor includes trust and the three stereotype measures. For the trust model, I focus primarily upon residential choice as the key predictor of interest. One could argue that the stereotype indices should also predict trust – and this might constitute a threat to the specification of the model. In Uslaner (2002, 193–197) I argue that if you believe that most people can be trusted, you are more likely to be sympathetic to minorities and immigrants and to believe that the society has a moral obligation to fight discrimination against them. Civil rights volunteers in the United States had higher trust when they entered the struggle – as much as the "warm glow" (Andreoni, 1989) that people get when they volunteer their time or give to charity, the activists became even more trusting after their actions in support of minority rights (Uslaner, 2002, 161). We learn trust at an early age – and having friends of a different race as a child leads adults to be more trusting (Uslaner, 2002, 105–6). Changing attitudes toward minorities – becoming more favorable over time – does lead to increased trust, but there is little evidence that attitudes toward minorities at any given time shape trust (Uslaner, 2002, 167, 169).[9]

The models in Figure 8.4 point to two central results:

- Trust is a significant predictor of residential choice for whites, but not for African-Americans (or all respondents). The coefficient of trust on the neighbor closest factor is larger than I find for any other variable. Black stereotypes also matter strongly. Whites who believe that most people can be trusted and who have more positive views of African-Americans are more likely to favor greater residential integration. Neither trust nor any stereotypes shape African-Americans' preferences for neighborhood diversity. The findings for blacks should be taken with a note of caution because of the small sample size (N = 59) for African-Americans. The argument that more well-off and highly educated whites would find integrated neighborhoods more threatening is not supported: Neither whites' income nor their level of education shapes residential preferences. Nor do stereotypes of Asians or Hispanics.
- Residential choice is significant as a predictor of trust only for whites and even then only at $p < .10$. It is insignificant for blacks. This is not a function of the tiny sample. The zero-order correlation

[9] The models also include age, education, and income for residential choice. All three are insignificant for all respondents. Younger people are more likely to choose diverse neighborhoods among whites, and higher income respondents do so among blacks. The trust model includes education (always significant), age (significant for all respondents and whites), how happy you are (for all respondents and whites, marginally for blacks), whether you must be corrupt go get ahead in America (significant for all groups), whether you need to know the right people to get ahead (marginally significant only for all respondents), confidence in science (as a measure of optimism, see Uslaner, 2002, 99–101, marginally significant only for all respondents), and whether a desirable trait for children is to obey their parents rather than assert themselves (as part of a larger notion of authoritarianism, see Uslaner, 2002, 100, significant for all respondents and whites and marginally significant for African-Americans). Other exogenous variables included in the simultaneous equation model are whether the respondent was a fundamentalist at age 16, how important it is to work hard and to help others, satisfaction with one's financial situation, whether your financial situation is getting better or worse, and whether there are any people of a different race in your neighborhood.

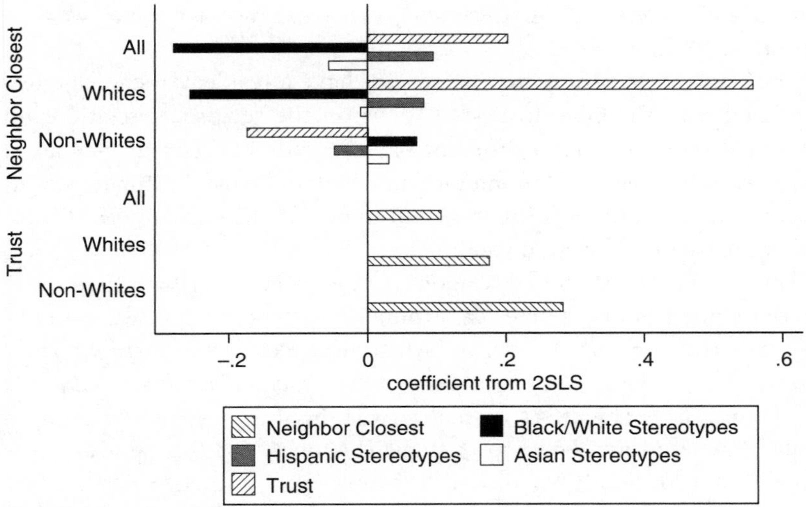

FIGURE 8.4. Reciprocal effects for trust and residential choice in US. General Social Survey 2000

between residential choice and trust for African-Americans is -.02 (N = 99).

Since I do not have the community codes for municipalities, I cannot test for the reciprocal effects of segregation (and having friends of a different race is not included in the 2000 GSS). So this is not a direct test of the reciprocal causation of Allport's optimal conditions and trust, as in the models of Chapter 3. But it taps the key underlying question of segregation: Why do people live where they do? And the results are not encouraging. Once I allow trust to shape residential preferences, the effects of preferred diversity on trust become very small. The far more powerful impact of trust on residential preference for whites is clear in Figure 8.4. These results strongly suggest that you can't simply build trust by changing the racial composition of neighborhoods because where people sit (live) depends upon where they stand (their levels of trust and racial tolerance).

Neighborhood Preferences in the United Kingdom

Britain is far less segregated than the United States. The effects of the optimal conditions on trust are substantially smaller (see Chapter 5).

Does allowing residential choice and trust to shape each other weaken this modest relationship?

The 2007 Citizenship Survey does not have a residential choice question similar to the GSS. Instead, I focus on the reciprocal relationship between having friends of different backgrounds living in diverse areas within walking distance (an interaction term) and trust. I estimate simultaneous equation models for these variables for the subsamples of race and ethnicity I employed in Chapters 5 and 7.[10]

The results for the United Kingdom are even more striking than those for the United States: For *every* group – all respondents, whites, nonwhites, Africans, South Asians, and Muslims – *trust is the most important predictor of living in integrated areas with diverse friendship networks* (see Figure 8.5). The effect is smallest for the most segregated group – whites – where the regression coefficient is one-third to one-fourth the value of that for South Asians and Muslims. For whites, other factors vie for influence on residential choice for the majority: respect for people of different backgrounds and mixing with people of different backgrounds while volunteering – neither of which is significant for other groups. The effects are most powerful for South Asians and Muslims, two of the least trusting groups. In Britain, the smaller share of minorities who trust strangers are considerably more likely to live in integrated areas and have diverse friendship networks.

Once I allow for trust and residential choice to shape each other, the optimal conditions no longer shape trust for most groups (see Figure 8.6).

[10] The equation for the interaction between diverse friends and neighborhood composition also includes an index of neighborhood problems (noise, teens hanging out, litter, vandalism, drugs, drunks, and abandoned cars), how long you have lived in your neighborhood, whether people in your neighborhood respect differences among groups, how safe is your neighborhood after dark, do local people get along well together, the importance of your ethnic identity to who you are, age, marital status, worried about being the victim of a racial attack, worried about crime, whether people mix with others of different backgrounds when doing volunteer work, satisfaction with local government, and the percentage of minority ethnic households in the ward. Detailed results are available upon request, but briefly respect for others, getting along together, neighborhood safety, and the importance of ethnic identity are *not* significant predictors for most groups. The trust equation also includes neighborhood problems, pride in your neighborhood, whether interests, nationality, or ethnicity determine your sense of who you are, whether everyone should speak English, trust in the police, worrying about racial attacks, worried about crime, age, income, and education. All variables are significant for the full set of respondents, the importance of ethnicity and country of origin and the expectation that everyone should speak English are generally insignificant. The equations also included the exogenous variables of gender, the importance of income to your sense of identity, and how well the government is protecting the rights of your group.

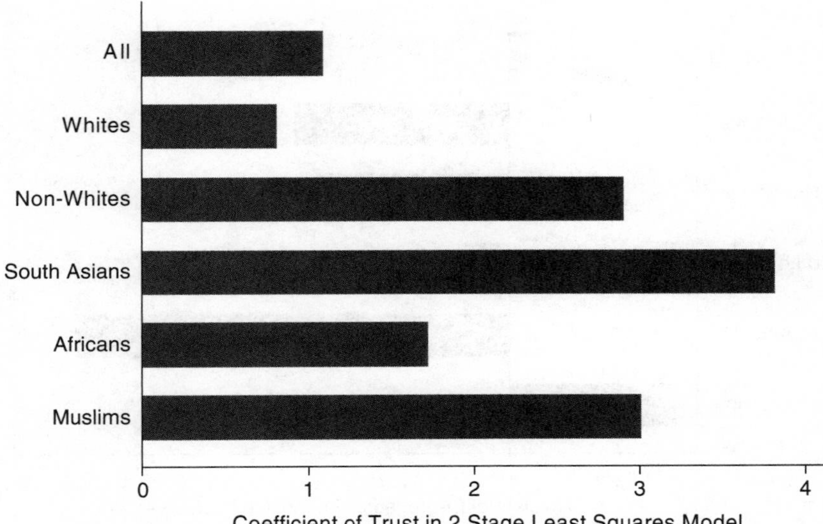

FIGURE 8.5. Effect of trust on segregation/friendship diversity in UK

The two exceptions are for nonwhites (where segregation/friendship is marginally significant, $p < .10$) and for Africans. People of African background, the least segregated *and* the least trusting of any race/ethnicity in the United Kingdom, appear to invest their housing choices based upon their faith in others but are also the only group that benefits from these optimal conditions. The effect for Africans are about the same as I found for them in a simple probit in Chapter 5 (about 8 percent). For Muslims, living among people of different backgrounds in an integrated neighborhood seems to drive trust down, but the effect is tiny and insignificant. The importance of the country of national origin is significant for Muslims (and South Asians more generally) – the only group for which it is significant.

Reprise

Trust seems to breed integration and diverse friendship networks in the United Kingdom more than the optimal conditions bring about trust. The pattern is even more pronounced than in the United States, where the link from trust to neighborhood choice is powerful only for whites. The comparisons are only tentative, since the questions are not the same. But they are similar enough to conclude that the most segregated groups seem to

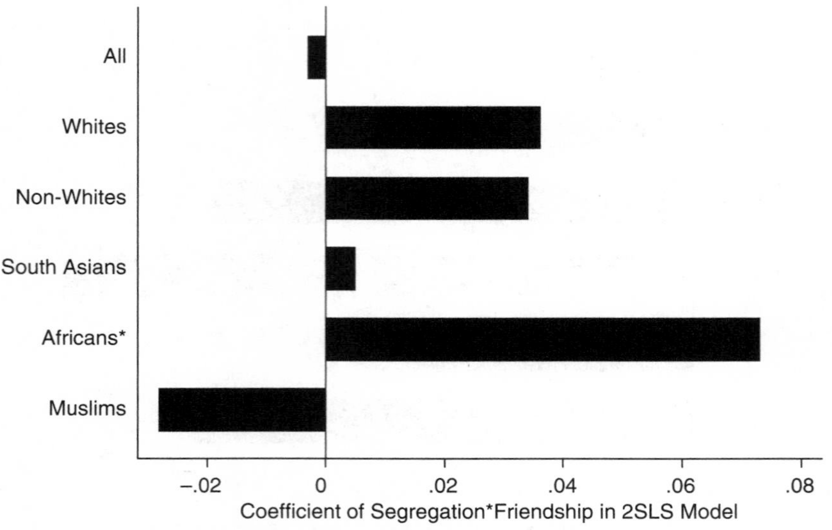

FIGURE 8.6. Effect of segregation/friendship diversity on trust in UK

benefit the least from the optimal conditions: African-Americans in the United States and whites and Muslims in the United Kingdom.

These results – for whites in the United States and all groups in the United Kingdom – show that trusting people are more likely to choose to live in racially integrated neighborhoods. The further gain from such surroundings – the "warm glow" – is generally far weaker or even nonexistent.

You can't build trust simply by reshuffling the ethnic or racial composition of neighborhoods. Neighborhood choice is self-selection. Or is it? The Pew data from the United States that I examined earlier in this chapter show that whites living in integrated and diverse communities hold fewer negative stereotypes about blacks. And both whites and especially African-Americans with heterogenous friendships in integrated and diverse neighborhoods are more satisfied with their communities. Can we "engineer" trust by changing neighborhoods? I discuss this in the final chapter.

9

The Farmer's Daughter and Intergroup Contact

"I started out as a child."

American comedian Bill Cosby[1]

If trust is the social glue that makes for a more cooperative and better functioning society, raising the level of trust should be a priority for each nation. Yet, it is not easy to convince us that others are part of our "moral community," especially when there are high levels of segregation and inequality. People of different backgrounds may not be ready to place their faith in each other. As societies become more diverse, finding commonalities becomes ever more important.

Contact with people of different backgrounds does lead to a reduction in racial prejudice (Pettigrew and Tropp, 2011). By itself, it does *not* lead to more trust. To get to trust, you need more than simple contact. Allport's "optimal conditions" demand more: a context favoring the development of deeper contacts (integrated neighborhoods) and equality (contacts between equals).

I review the findings of previous chapters and return to where I started: How does one build trust, especially as societies have become more diverse and especially as their publics increasingly come from countries with low levels of trust? Optimal contact may not do the job, largely because the majority's friendship networks are not sufficiently diverse – and especially because it is difficult to establish such ties when the social milieus are unequal. Whites across every society are far less likely to have friends of different backgrounds. We seek out people like ourselves as our

[1] http://www.amazon.com/I-Started-Out-As-Child/dp/B000062TH.

friends – and at least in the United States and the United Kingdom we prefer to live among people who look like ourselves. Even when segregation is low, minorities tend to live away from the majority population. The economic distance between majorities and minorities is often large, and even when it is not, feelings of discrimination may lead to a great social gap. After summarizing the evidence from previous chapters, I reconsider what might be done to build trust among people of different groups.

I have shown that simple contact with people of different backgrounds is insufficient to promote trust (Chapter 2). Friendships across racial, ethnic, and linguistic boundaries can build trust if they occur in integrated (and diverse) neighborhoods in the United States (Chapter 3), Canada (Chapter 4), the United Kingdom (Chapter 5), Australia, and Sweden (Chapter 6). People living in such neighborhoods are also more likely to give to charities and volunteer for causes that are secular rather than religious.

Although the data I have used are from different sources with varying questions and measures of segregation, there are several results that seem to hold:

- **Majorities are more trusting than minorities.**

This is a universal phenomenon. Minorities often face segregation, discrimination, and inequality. Nowhere is this as strong as in the United States. Ironically, for all of the debate over the negative consequences of immigration, the most segregated and unequal group in the United States is *not* composed of recent immigrants, but African-Americans who came to American shores centuries ago (and not voluntarily). Even where some minorities are highly trusting (in Australia and Sweden and Asians in Canada), they still have somewhat less faith in others than do majority white respondents.

- **Minorities have more contacts with people of different backgrounds.**

This result is partially due to simple math: If minorities are a small share of a country's population and if they have friends, their networks are simply more likely to be more diverse. But these results also point to a willingness by most minorities to develop ties among the majority white population and less of a willingness by the majority to have ties with people unlike themselves.

• Neither simple contact nor the diversity/integration of neighborhoods is sufficient to boost trust. You need both to approximate Allport's optimal conditions.

Having friends of different backgrounds doesn't create the kind of equality in contacts that Allport and Pettigrew held to be critical for greater tolerance. And one can live in an integrated neighborhood without establishing close bonds with people of different backgrounds.

• The impact of contact with people of different backgrounds in integrated neighborhoods is greater for majority groups than for minorities in most cases.

The impact of optimal conditions is greater for the majority white population in the United States, Canada, and Australia. In Canada and Australia, minorities do *not* become more trusting if they live in integrated communities and have diverse friendship networks. Immigrants to Canada and Australia must qualify on "points" based upon their education, financial status, language ability, and guarantee of employment. The new Canadians and Australians thus come from elite strata of their home countries and are likely to have high levels of trust (as they do). They appear to get no extra boost from contact with the white majority even if they live in integrated communities. Minorities *do* gain from such optimal contact when they either live in segregated neighborhoods – especially African-Americans, Canadian blacks, and to a lesser extent minorities in the United Kingdom – and face discrimination by the white majority. They also become *substantially more trusting* through such contact when the state makes positive efforts to improve their socioeconomic status, as in Sweden.

• Multiculturalism does *not* lead to increases in generalized trust. It may promote stronger in-group trust at the expense of generalized faith in others.

Multiculturalism does *not* build trust. In the two countries where multiculturalism still reigns as official public policy – Canada and the United Kingdom, minorities often have stronger senses of in-group identity than generalized trust. The exception – Asian Canadians – are high trusting largely because they are highly educated and professionalized. Like their Australian counterparts, they do not become more trusting when they have friends of different races in integrated communities. Australia has largely jettisoned multiculturalism – and, coincidentally (?) generalized trust seems to have risen. Nevertheless, *assimilationist policies don't necessarily lead to high levels of trust either.*

The United States seems to have the "right" policy on identity (assimilationism) for generating trust among both majority and minority groups. But the high levels of segregation and inequality lead people of different backgrounds to have *less* trust in each other, not more. Sweden seems to be best able to build trust among diverse groups: It does not restrict immigrants to highly educated professionals who come with bank accounts and a good knowledge of the language of their new country. Sweden has downplayed multiculturalism because it conflicts with the idea of universalism in social welfare policy, which seems to have led to far more trusting minorities than we are likely to find elsewhere.

- **Integrated neighborhoods don't just happen. They are the result of people's choices of where they want to live and among whom they wish to reside. People with negative racial stereotypes and *lower levels of trust* will be less likely to prefer living in more diverse and integrated neighborhoods.**

When I account for the mutual dependence of trust and residential racial preferences, the effect of living in integrated neighborhoods with diverse friendship networks either vanishes or declines substantially. Not only do majorities (whites) not want to live among minorities, they also have relatively few close friends among minorities.

Contacts and residential choice point to a preference for what sociologists call "*homophily*." More simply put, we live among and hang out with people very much like ourselves. So it should not be surprising that trust does *not* reflect our life experiences. If we don't have extensive contacts with people who are different from ourselves and don't live among them, we are unlikely to develop the deep ties needed to build trust. Our faith in others will thus reflect other, earlier experiences – such as parental influence – or our cultural background from our ethnic heritage.

In one sense, then, diversity *is* the problem and Putnam (2007) is correct. More diverse communities have lower levels of trust because minorities are less trusting. They face discrimination and thus have little reason to believe that the majority whites are part of their "moral community." Yet, majorities don't want to accommodate, much less live among or become friends with, minorities. To a considerable extent, putting the onus on immigrants and minorities is blaming the victim. Some minorities *don't* want to blend in. Yet most minorities have more diverse friendship networks than do the majority populations – and few prefer to live in segregated communities. Allport's optimal conditions require social contacts on the basis of equality – but as long as there are large gaps in income, education, and social status and as long as minorities widely perceive discrimination, such contacts will be difficult to attain.

What Can Public Policy Accomplish?

Can we engineer trust through public policy? Governments in many parts of the world recognize a responsibility to foster social values. The government of Bhutan was among the first to develop a program of "gross national happiness." The Organization for Economic Cooperation and Development and the new Conservative government in Britain have also sought to raise the levels of happiness. Australians can now trace their happiness (and that of their fellow citizens) on a television program designed to apply social science research to social engineering.[2]

What makes me happy may not make you happy (Blastland, 2010). Happiness may be ephemeral. There is little evidence that simple satisfaction can reduce intergroup tensions. Indeed, the new emphasis on happiness may reflect a frustration that more bridging initiatives have not been sufficient to resolve social problems. The United Kingdom established commissions on social cohesion (see Chapter 5). Governments in many countries – notably Canada, the United Kingdom, Sweden, and Australia – wrote multiculturalism into their national policy agendas.

The goals have either sometimes been too broad – "social cohesion" is a slippery concept that defies easy comprehension, much less measurement. Or they have little relationship to intergroup tensions–as in happiness. Or they may actually insulate people from each other, as in multiculturalism. Trust may not be easy to develop, but it is a more likely route to better governance than multiculturalism or happiness.

There seem to be four possible routes to increasing trust:

- Generating a more trusting minority population by limiting who can immigrate to a country.

[2] See http://www.grossnationalhappiness.com/ on Bhutan, http://www.oecdbetterlifeindex.org/topics/life-satisfaction/ for the OECD (life satisfaction and happiness are generally used interchangeably), http://www.ons.gov.uk/well-being on the United Kingdom, and http://makingaustraliahappy.abc.net.au/theshow.php on Australia.

- Government intervention in housing markets to create more integrated neighborhoods and thus more trust among majorities and minorities.
- Creating more bridging between majorities and minorities by pursuing policies that make minorities more equal.
- Focusing on those who do become more trusting in an integrated environment with diverse friendship networks but who don't recoil from living in diverse communities – children.

Limiting immigration is becoming increasingly popular in the West. Only in Canada among the countries I examine is there no movement to limit immigration (Kymlicka, 2010b, 7). Opposition to immigration seems louder than it may actually be. In the European Social Survey for 2008 (the latest wave), in 10 of 28 countries a majority of respondents who gave a strong opinion said that immigrants made their country a better place – and almost all Western European countries (except for Britain and France) either had majorities or near-majorities taking this position, ranging from 53 percent of Danes to 78 percent of Swedes.[3] In 16 countries, majorities (ranging from 51 percent in Britain to 87 percent in Sweden) favored allowing people from ethnic groups other than the majority to immigrate there. Majorities in 12 countries (from half in France to 87 percent in Sweden) favored immigration of people living in poor countries outside Europe. Three-quarters of Swedes believe that national life is enriched by immigrants from diverse backgrounds, compared to just 39 percent of British respondents. The 2007 Citizenship survey in the United Kingdom presented a more gloomy picture than the European Social Survey: 73 percent of whites – and 53 percent of BMEs ("blacks and ethnic minorities") favored restricting immigration.

Forty-three percent of Canadians favor restricting immigration; about the same share say that immigrants don't want to fit into Canadian society (from the Equality Security Community Survey).[4] In Australia, 59 percent of whites and 63 percent of minorities believe that immigration on balance is good for the society and just 38 percent of whites and 32 percent of minorities say that immigration is too high.

[3] Strong positions mean not giving a "5" on a 0–10 scale. Belgians and Spaniards gave positive responses of 49 and 47 percent, respectively.

[4] The positive and negative groups largely overlap (though hardly completely): 56 percent of those who say that immigrants don't want to blend in favor restricting immigration, while 63 percent who say that immigrants do want to fit into Canadian society favor admitting more immigrants (tau-c = .337).

In the United States (in the 2008 American National Election Study) 57 percent of respondents said that immigration levels should be increased (only 15 percent) or kept at present levels. Despite the high levels of segregation and inequality in the United States, the sense of national identity is strong: In the 2002 General Social Survey only 20 percent of respondents said that it was not important for minorities to adapt to the common culture. African-Americans are somewhat more likely to say that adaption is not essential (by 32 percent compared to 18 percent for others). Yet Hispanics – who comprise the largest number of recent immigrants and who some say constitute a threat to the common culture (Huntington, 1998) – are no more likely to say that adaptation should be optional (19 percent compared to 20 percent of non-Hispanics).

Ninety percent of Americans – two-thirds of blacks and 80 percent of Latinos – considered themselves to be "just an American" rather than having any dual identity.[5] Harris and McKenzie (2011) report that about half of blacks see themselves as Americans first: African-Americans who report facing discrimination were 16 percent less likely to see themselves primarily as Americans, while those living in the most segregated neighborhoods were 7 percent less likely to identify with the larger culture.

A very large survey (with over 8300 respondents) of Hispanics in 2006 – the Latino National Survey (Fraga et al., 2006) shows that 68 percent of Latinos do identify as Americans either somewhat or very strongly. While 87 percent identify with their country of origin and 90 percent as Latinos, in-group identification is *not* a substitute for connections to the larger society. The most common patterns are for strong identification with *both* the home country and as an American (26 percent) and as a Latin American and an American (29 percent). Ethnic identification is largely unrelated to connections to the American culture (tau-c = -.046 for country of origin, .073 for Latin American identity with American identity).

As with African-Americans, Hispanics who say that they have faced discrimination (in employment, by the police, in housing, or in restaurants or stores) are less likely to identify as Americans – but these relationships are small (tau-c = .02, .08, .02, and .11, respectively). Relatively few Hispanics report such discrimination (ranging from 6 percent in housing to 18 percent in employment) – and because 95 percent say that if they work hard in America, they can get ahead in the United States. For

[5] There are 369 African-Americans but only 69 Hispanics in this analysis, so the results for both samples should be taken with caution, but especially for Hispanics.

Hispanics, dual identity is more of a sense of ethnic pride than withdrawal from the larger society. For African-Americans, it reflects a long-standing "duality" of identity for a people who for much of American history were excluded from the rights and freedoms of white society (Harris and McKenzie, 2011, 6–7). The General Social Survey results address the larger point that both African-Americans and Hispanics feel connected to the larger society – as much or more so than immigrants in the other countries I have examined.

The calls for restrictions on immigration are not based on popular demands as one might suppose. And for many countries, it is simply too late to shut the borders. Immigrants are among us. In 2008, the foreign born stock represented 25.4 percent of Australians, 20.2 percent of Canadians, 13.9 percent of Swedes, 13.7 percent of Americans, and 10.8 percent of the British – in most cases up substantially over a decade and a half.[6]

Even if no more immigrants come – or no more come who don't meet a points system – the problem of the minority and majority populations adapting to each other will not go away. In the United States, the biggest problem of intergroup relations is not between immigrants and the majority white population, but between African-Americans and whites. African-Americans are not strangers to the land (and indeed are slightly more supportive of restricting immigration than are whites).[7]

Across the five countries I have examined, support for immigration is strongest in Sweden and weakest in the United Kingdom.[8] The larger story is that the majority group and immigrants are most comfortable *with each other* when the levels of segregation and inequality are low and trust is high and where there is an attempt to shape a common culture. A common culture helps bridge some gaps in the United States – especially over national identity, but it cannot "go all the way" to build trust when segregation and

[6] The data come from http://www.oecd.org/dataoecd/7/40/45594799.xls. In 1995 the share of foreign-born stock in Australia was 23.0 percent, in Sweden 10.5 percent, in the United States 9.0 percent. No data are reported for 1995 for Canada or the United Kingdom, but their 1999 shares are 10.0 and 7.8 percent, respectively. Most European countries average about 7–8 percent foreign stock.

[7] Fifty percent of African-Americans are opposed to admitting more immigrants compared to 43 percent of whites.

[8] Dag Wollebæk has asked (personal communication) why other high-trusting Nordic countries have had greater conflicts over immigration. While I cannot trace the varying attitudes on immigration to trust, Swedes are more favorable across all of the immigration questions in the 2008 European Social Survey by more than 10 percent compared to other Nordic countries.

inequality are both strong – and especially if they are linked so tightly to each other. Canada and Britain, with moderate segregation and inequality and powerful commitments to multiculturalism, have failed to bridge the gaps in national identity among majorities and minorities. Canada has fared better in building trust among minorities even with multiculturalism – but largely by restricting who could immigrate there.

It would be too facile to claim that the shift toward a more assimilationist model has led to the high levels of trust among immigrants in Sweden and Australia. But both countries have committed themselves to forging a greater sense of identity among minorities. Multiculturalism does seem to promote in-group identity and reduce trust among minorities except where immigrants are selected on the basis of points. But an assimilationist policy does not guarantee a high level of trust by itself. Hispanics, who face far less segregation than African-Americans (see Chapter 3; de Souza Briggs, 2005, 25; Massey and Denton, 1993, 74), are barely more trusting. Multiculturalism, inequality, and segregation all disrupt social cohesion.

Segregation and inequality may not be inevitable. But is multiculturalism inescapable in an increasingly diverse society with a culture defined by racial identity? Might new groups threaten racial people's conception of their national identity, as some in the United Kingdom and elsewhere claim (Bowyer, 2009, 564)? Minorities such as Muslims who are economically deprived (Change Institute, 2009, 25), highly segregated (Modood, 2008, 133), and stand outside the dominant white Christian culture may be seen as the source of the problem of waning social cohesion (Mirza, Senthilkumaran and Ja'far, 2007, 90). Women who wear the veil are seen as protesting the dominant culture and rebuked even by (former) Prime Minister Tony Blair (Cowell, 2006).

Their segregation is perceived as a desire for isolation (Mirza, Senthilkumaran and Ja'far, 2007, 39) and terrorist attacks by a small number of radicals launched a national debate over extremism among Muslims in 2006 (Lyall, 2006). Across eight European nations,[9] the British were the most likely to agree that "I sometimes feel like a stranger in my country because of immigrants" (46 percent), second in holding that immigrants are a strain on the welfare system (60 percent) and that the majority of Muslims find terrorism justifiable (26 percent) (Zick, Kupper, and Hovermann, 2011, 54, 61).

[9] The other countries surveyed were Germany, France, the Netherlands, Italy, Portugal, Poland, and Hungary.

The British are hardly unique in such concerns: They are widespread throughout Europe. As with any stereotype, there is some truth in them. But there is also more fear than reality in these arguments. Britain – and other European countries – are hardly being overrun by Muslim immigrants. In 2009, Muslims comprised less than 3 percent of the British population – not much larger than in Sweden (Pew Forum on Religion in Public Life, 2009, 31). What worries many is not the absolute size, but the increasing rate of Muslim immigration: Muslims are projected to be 8.2 percent of the British population by 2030, and 28 percent of all immigrants to the United Kingdom in 2010 were Muslims (Pew Forum on Religion and Public Life, 2011). Negative views of Muslims have little to do with specific "objections" to who Muslims are, what they wear, or how they pray. Anti-Muslim sentiments in the United States and Europe (where they are more negative) reflect a more general intolerance of minorities, including those who are presumably more acceptable in Western society, notably Jews, blacks, and gays – as well as immigrants more generally (Gallup, 2009; Kalkan, Layman, and Uslaner, 2009; Zick, Kupper, and Hovermann, 2011, 67–72).

If Putnam (2007) is right that increasing immigration leads to problems, it is because many in Western societies don't like minorities, especially people who don't look like they do or dress like they do. One way to ensure that minorities remain distinct is for the majority to avoid social contact with them and to choose to live apart from them. This ensures that minorities will have fewer opportunities for economic advancement and little reason to believe that "most people can be trusted." And the people who don't like them also are less likely to have faith in their fellow citizens (Uslaner, 2002, 196; Zick, Kupper, and Hovermann, 2011, 136).

When minorities live apart from majority groups, we often presume that they prefer to live among their own kind – even as data show that minorities often avoid integrated neighborhoods because they fear discrimination (see Chapter 8). There is little evidence that minorities choose to live in segregated neighborhoods because they reject mainstream society. Even as some Muslim leaders espouse radical ideology and theology, most Muslims are "mainstream" citizens identifying as British (Manning and Roy, 2007, 4–5) and hardly socially isolated from the larger society (Maxwell, 2006, 745). And this is true elsewhere as well: In Canada, 57 percent of Muslims want to adopt Canadian customs and less than a quarter believe that their fellow believers want to remain distinct from Canadian society (Adams with Langstaff, 2007, 93). American Muslims are the most moderate of all (Pew Research Center, 2007) – in part because of their higher level of education but also because integration is easier in a more diverse society.

This is not just a story about Muslims. It is a cautionary note about why we hear so much about problems of diversity. Some people – more in some countries than in others – dislike people who are different from themselves. Intolerant jeers are louder than tolerant cheers. If we perceive a clash of cultures, we naturally think that ours (whomever it might belong to) is superior, or at least more defensible. Faced with such perceptions of conflict, it is understandable that some burrow into their shells as a turtle does. The more we tell people that it is acceptable to be distinct, the more likely we are to believe that they don't have much in common with us. If we deny a common national identity and believe that only some citizens are "entitled" to the country's resources, it should not seem so strange if immigrants wonder where they fit in.

From this perspective, multiculturalism appears to be as much the effect of low trust among different groups as the cause. Multiculturalism – live and let live among different groups – may be the best solution in a society where groups either contest their heritage (Canada) or there is no superordinate identity that is inclusive (the United Kingdom). But multiculturalism as public policy may reinforce strong in-group ties at the expense of bridging networks. When a country can limit who may enter, it can mitigate the negative effects of the policy. When it cannot (former colonial powers) or chooses not to do so (needing guest workers), multiculturalism may be a safety valve against claims that minorities don't really fit into the dominant culture. Or it may be blamed for minorities' failure to assimilate, as in Britain (Kirkup, 2011), Germany (Brown, 2010), and elsewhere.

Is Housing the Solution?

Segregation stems to a considerable degree from whites' refusal to live among minorities and minorities' fear of discrimination should they move into mostly white neighborhoods. Yet other factors are at work that reflect discrimination in a variety of ways: higher mortgage rates for minorities, bias among real estate agents, restricted zoning, and weak laws and even more anemic enforcement against racial favoritism (see especially Chapter 3).

Overt bias has been reduced in the United States in recent decades. Segregation has declined, but it persists at high levels and has become even more strongly linked to poverty and economic inequality. Can government do more?

Elsewhere it has – in Canada and Sweden. Government policies in these countries are linked to lower levels of segregation. Governments have both subsidized rentals and built houses for immigrants and have actively pursued policies designed to produce a racial mix (Fong and Shibuya, 2005, 455; Joseph, 2007, 15–16; Musterd, 2003, 628; Nesslein, 2003). The Swedish housing policy of promoting ethnic diversity and reducing segregation is part of the larger commitment to universalism and greater equality that underlies social policy in Sweden (Phillips, 2010, 213). Can this serve as a more general model for increasing trust among majority whites and especially minorities – who are more negatively affected by segregation?

Housing policy is not a panacea for segregation and inequality. After building a "million homes," Sweden found that the supply of housing was outpacing demand. So it moved away from public housing and toward privatization – giving immigrants the right to choose where to live (Holmquist, 2009; Joseph, 2007). Segregation increased, though not to levels found elsewhere (Nesslein, 2003, 1274–5).

The British story leads to even less optimism. Britain long has developed public housing for the working class. However, even in such "council housing," there has been widespread discrimination against ethnic minorities, notably including policies that excluded many immigrants by requiring residence of up to five years in the local area (Peach, 1998, 1670). Two experimental programs in the United Kingdom had mixed results. The New Towns Act of 1946 was designed to create diverse neighborhoods – although Britain was not very heterogenous then. The program ultimately led to what we see today: an area that is mixed, but comprised of a multiplicity of segregated neighborhoods (Feitosa and Wissman, 2006, 15–16). An experiment in the London borough of Tower Hamlets in the mid-1980s was also designed to integrate council housing. The plan foundered when the ethnic community targeted – the highly segregated Bengalis – hesitated to move in because of fear of racial harassment (Phillips, 1998, 1693–4).

As in Sweden, the United Kingdom opted out of the housing market. Renters were encouraged to buy, making the housing market more like that in the United States (Feitosa and Wissman, 2006, 16–17; Phillips and Karn, 1991, 87). Canada was more reluctant to privatize housing, but some conversion has already occurred (Loomis, 2006) and Conservative office holders in Toronto and the province of Ontario have proposed selling off government housing (Co-Operative Housing Confederation of Canada, 2011; Dale, 2011).

The American housing experiments have been a mixed success. Following a lawsuit against the Chicago Housing Authority and the federal Department of Housing and Urban Development (HUD) in 1966, the United States Supreme Court issued a ruling a decade later leading to what became known as the Gatreaux program. The initiative provided vouchers to residents of public housing who could choose to move into other neighborhoods in the city or in the suburbs. A small sample of Gatreaux program participants were interviewed. The survey showed dramatic improvements in job opportunities and social ties with their neighbors among those who moved to the suburbs compared to poor people who remained in the city. A companion survey of young people found that those whose families moved to the suburbs attained much higher scores on standardized tests, high school graduation rates, attendance at colleges and universities, especially four-year institutions, were more likely to be employed, and had jobs that paid more with better benefits (Rosenbaum, 1991, 1190–1201; Rosenbaum et al., 1991, 451).

Participants who moved within the cities stayed in highly segregated neighborhoods, while those who chose suburbs lived in overwhelmingly white areas. People who moved to white suburbs quite naturally had more white friends, but a majority reported initial harassment. Over time the share reporting provocations fell to 25 percent. Overall, Rosenbaum et al. (1991, 451–459, quoted at 459) argued: "The success of the Gatreaux families in becoming socially integrated suggest that housing vouchers may provide a workable alternative to traditional programs aimed at ameliorating the problems of the urban underclass" (1991, 451–9, quoted at 459).

A much more widespread program beginning in 1992, Moving to Opportunity (MTO), was not perceived as so successful. The program covered five cities – Baltimore, Boston, Chicago, Los Angeles, and New York.[10] Over 4,600 families participated and HUD contacted 8,900 adults and children a decade after the program began. The families who received vouchers and moved reported greater satisfaction with neighborhoods: less litter, graffiti, abandoned buildings, and loitering. They also said that the police were more responsive and, as in Gatreaux, they were more likely to have friends who were college educated and earning middle-class salaries. Nevertheless, a substantial minority still complained that the police did not respond to their calls and barely more than half

[10] This discussion on MTO summarizes the work of Orr et al. (2003).

said that they felt safe in their neighborhoods at night. A third were not satisfied with their neighborhoods.

On some more concrete measures – school performance, pupil–teacher ratios, employment rates, and welfare dependency – there was no appreciable improvement for people who moved. Neither adults nor young people received a boost in their opportunities for employment or in how much they earned.

MTO was hardly a failure. Orr et al. (2003, 160) argue that "MTO had real effects on the lives of participating families in the domain of housing conditions and assistance and on the characteristics of the schools attended by their children … many [effects] are quite large." But others aren't and this may be attributed to where participants moved: 60 percent migrated to heavily segregated minority communities and both people who moved and a control group for the survey resided in areas that were more than 80 percent minority (Orr et al., 2003, 46).

The two major housing experiments in the United States did improve the lives of the minorities who moved, especially to suburban areas. However, the effects seems to be mixed and it is difficult to extrapolate too much from the Gatreaux project: Not only was the sample size small, but the survey did not consider whether the families who chose the suburbs over the city might have been more advantaged in the first place (Orr et al., 2003, v). Neither survey tells us anything about the extensiveness of contacts between whites and minorities – which are likely to be small in the MTO experiment because so few minorities moved into integrated neighborhoods. We also have no information on whether white neighbors interacted with the minorities who moved into their communities and whether this changed their racial attitudes, much less trust. Most critically, such modest-scale experiments are unlikely to make a significant change in the level of segregation in American municipalities. Simply moving people from one neighborhood to another may not accomplish that much. As Allport (1958, 260) argued, "We must not assume that integrated housing automatically solves the problem of prejudice. At most we can say that it creates a condition where friendly contacts and accurate social perceptions can occur."

Back to Equality, Back to Children

Allport's (1958, 263) optimal conditions are based upon sustained relationships based upon *equal status*. Trust also depends upon, more than anything else, the level of economic equality in a society.

Minorities – immigrants and groups that have been in a country for centuries such as African-Americans – are mostly *not* equal to the majority white population. They also perceive considerable discrimination from whites. It is thus not surprising that minorities are generally lower trusting. I have, however, noted two counter-examples: Asians in Canada and Australia (as well as the United States) and minorities more generally in Sweden. Asians come to their new homes with higher levels of education and professional opportunities. They are "more equal" than most immigrants. Sweden admits people who are not high status – but pursues policies that promote greater equality.

The story is largely one of equality – since across nations and American communities, segregation leads to greater disparities of wealth among ethnic groups and races. At a time when inequality is increasing in most countries and when fiscal crises portend huge cuts in social spending, the outlook for reducing inequality seems glum.

There is one ray of hope – but also some caution as well. Housing preferences are a key reason why people of different backgrounds don't develop strong ties. Yet there is one group within the majority population whose trust and racial views *don't* shape their preferences for where they live and who seem to be more positive toward people of different backgrounds: young people. Children aren't asked where they want to live, nor do they have much choice.

The farmer's daughter who didn't recall the race of her new friend at school (Chapter 1) may be an extreme case of color-blindness. But young people seem to be far more tolerant and welcoming of people of different backgrounds. In Canada and most European countries young people (under 30) are more welcoming of immigrants from different backgrounds than are older people. Sixty-one percent of younger Canadians, compared to 41 percent of those over 30, believe that immigrants want to blend into the larger society. In the United States the under 30s are more willing to let in more immigrants and are (slightly) less willing to say that immigrants have gone too far in pushing for their rights.[11]

The farmer's daughter is hardly unique: In each of the five countries I examine young people (under 30) from the majority are considerably more likely to have friends of other races, ethnicities (Canada), or who

[11] The Canadian data come from the Equality, Security, Community survey; the European data from the fourth wave (2008) of the European Social Survey; and the American data from the 2008 and 2010 General Social Survey. In Sweden, Norway, the Netherlands, Germany, and Switzerland, there are no cohort differences in attitudes on immigration.

speak other languages (Sweden) than are their elders.[12] Dinesen (2011) shows that native Danish elementary students develop more out-group trust if their school populations are *more* diverse.[13] Stolle and Harrell (2009) show that young Canadians whose social networks are more racially and ethnically heterogenous *in diverse neighborhoods* have higher levels of trust, even as older people become *less* trusting when they live among people who are different from themselves. I have elsewhere shown that people who had friends of a different race in secondary school were less likely to trust only their own in-groups as adults and became more trusting in general over the course of their lives (Uslaner, 2002, 105, 169–71). Optimal contact may not boost trust substantially in some contexts – though differences in measurement call for caution in such summaries – the opportunity for building trust may be much higher for young people. They can't choose where they live and are more likely to be color-blind when choosing their friends.

The low level of school segregation – with greater opportunities for developing friendships across racial, ethnic, linguistic, and class lines – makes Sweden stand out (see Chapter 6). In the United States, both overall residential segregation and school segregation are high. While residential segregation has declined, albeit slowly, over time, school segregation has either increased (Orfield, 2009, 6) or remained essentially stable, perhaps trending a bit lower.[14] White, African-American, and Hispanic students remain largely isolated from each other.

School segregation, as much as residential segregation, leads to greater inequality. In Tables 9.1 and 9.2, I examine how well minorities fare economically in American communities compared to whites. The

[12] In the Social Capital Benchmark Survey, an implausibly high 79 percent of whites under 30 say that they have friends of a different race (compared to 61 percent of older people, also too high). In the United Kingdom, the figures are 25 percent and 15 percent; for Canada, 82 percent of younger respondents and 73 percent of older people have friends of different ethnicities (a less demanding criterion). In Sweden, 53 percent of younger respondents have a friend who speaks a different language, compared to 43 percent of older people. In Australia, 47 percent of younger people visit friends of different ethnic groups compared to 33 percent of older people (the age ranges are 18–34 for Australia since the exact age is not available).

[13] There is, surprisingly, only an increase in out-group trust, not generalized trust.

[14] The data from the American Communities Project at Brown University are available at http://www.s4.brown.edu/cen2000/SchoolPop/SPDownload.html. They show virtually no change in the segregation of whites and African-Americans across 329 metropolitan areas from 1989 to 1999: The mean levels of black-white dissimilarity were .540 and .535, respectively. Hispanic-white segregation dropped from .510 to .480. Group isolation were constant for blacks but dropped slightly for Hispanics: Their isolation (P*) from whites were, respectively, .096 and .101 for blacks and .066 and 099 for Hispanics.

TABLE 9.1 *Minority/white income ratio and black-white contact in schools*

Variable	Coefficient	Standard Error	t ratio
Black-white contact in schools	.001**	.0005	2.30
Segregation	–.420****	.078	–5.37
Constant	.766****	.036	21.54

RMSE = .089 R^2 = .292 N = 321
* p < .10 ** p < .05 *** p < .01 **** p < .0001 (all tests one tailed except for constant)

TABLE 9.2 *Minority/white income ratio and African-American Isolation in Schools*

Variable	Coefficient	Standard Error	t ratio
African-American isolation in schools	–.002****	.0003	–5.40
Segregation	–.271****	.073	–3.71
Constant	.844	.012	67.59

RMSE = .087 R^2 = .324 N = 321
* p < .10 ** p < .05 *** p < .01 **** p < .0001 (all tests one tailed except for constant)

minorities–white income ratio is the measure of economic well-being.[15] Across 321 American metropolitan statistical areas, communities with a higher level of contact between African-American and white students in elementary schools (measured by the P* isolation index) have higher minority–white income ratios, even controlling for the overall level of residential segregation. And communities where black students are isolated from other groups have substantially lower minority/white income ratios – with a coefficient more strongly significant than overall residential segregation.[16]

The studies I have used employed different measures. While some of my inferences might reflect the available data,[17] the overall picture makes

[15] This measure comes from data supplied by Rodney Hero.

[16] The minority/white income ratio and overall segregation (multigroup entropy) measures are discussed in Chapter 2.

[17] The most likely "misfires," if any, are for the United States and Sweden. The cross-racial friendship estimates in the SCBS (as with the trust estimates) seem way too high and the differences between the best and worst connected may be overestimated. The Swedish survey only asks about having friends of different religions or who speak different languages. In a country where many immigrants are Muslims, having friends of a different religion may mean having Muslim friends, but this could exclude other immigrants. Having friends who speak different languages might also include Finnish Swedes but this would overestimate how diverse a network is.

sense. Contact matters most where segregation and inequality are highest. Optimal contact can make a difference when it is most needed. But contact will be less common when neighborhoods are segregated. The issue is not who lives there, but who lives *where*. Diversity is not at the heart of the problem, except as people want to live apart from each other. Living apart from people who are different from yourself makes it difficult to build trust across groups.

Contact among children may be a partial key to building trust. While social relations among white and minority adults may reflect the overall social distance between races and ethnic groups, kids are more likely to view their friends as equals and to develop the sort of contacts of which Allport wrote six decades ago.

Yet, contact is just part of the story. Context matters mightily. Kids won't develop the sort of bridging ties that build trust if they don't interact with each other. Their opportunities to meet are critical. If their parents won't select an integrated neighborhood, finding ways for kids of different backgrounds to interact with each other should become an issue for public policy.

On the one hand, it is important to realize that optimal contact depends upon opportunities for people to interact on an equal footing where groups are cooperative with each other rather than isolated or competitive (Pettigrew, 1998, 66). We cannot readily create tolerance between or among groups. When members of different groups don't see a greater (superordinate) identity, governments try to "solve" the problem through multiculturalism as public policy. Multiculturalism acknowledges group difference, it does not try to resolve them. Segregation leads to less trust, but it has proven difficult to eradicate. To build trust, one must overcome the inequalities of income and social status and to make immigrants feel that they are an integral part of their new country. Especially in an era when initiatives to reduce inequality are out of fashion in much of the world, the best place to start is at the beginning, with children.

References

Adams, Michael with Amy Langstaff. 2007. *Unlikely Utopia: The Surprising Triumph of Canadian Pluralism*. Toronto: Viking Canada.

Ai, Chunrong and Edward C. Norton. 2003. "Interaction Effects in Probit and Logit Models," *Economics Letters*, 80:123–9.

Alesina, Alberto, Reza Baqir, and William Easterly. 1999. "Public Goods and Ethnic Divisions," *Quarterly Journal of Economics*, 114:1243–84.

Alesina, Alberto, Arnaud Devleeschauwer, William Easterly, Sergio Kurlat, and Romain Wacziarg. 2003. "Fractionalization," *Journal of Economic Growth*, 8:155–94.

Alesina, Alberto and Eliana LaFerrara. 2000. "The Determinants of Trust." National Bureau of Economic Research Working Paper 7621.

2004. "Ethnic Diversity and Economic Performance." NBER Working Paper 10313, available at http://www.nber.org/papers/w10313.

Alesina, Alberto and Ekaterina Zhuravskaya. In press. "Segregation and the Quality of Government in a Cross-section of Countries," *American Economic Review*.

Algan, Yann and Pierre Cahuc. 2010. "Inherited Trust and Growth," *American Economic Review*, 1000:2060–92.

Allport, Gordon W. 1958. *The Nature of Prejudice (Abridged)*. Garden City, NY: Doubleday Anchor. Originally published in 1954.

Anant, Elizabeth Oltmans and Ebonya Washington. 2009. "Segregation and Black Political Efficacy," *Journal of Public Economics*, 93:807–22.

Anderson, Christopher J. and Aida Paskeviciute. 2006. "How Ethnic and Linguistic Heterogeneity Influence the Prospects for Civil Society: A Comparative Study of Citizenship Behavior," *Journal of Politics*, 68:783–802.

Anderson, Elijah. 2011. *The Cosmopolitan Canopy: Race and Civility in Everyday Life*. New York: W.W. Norton.

Anderson, Elizabeth. 2010. *The Imperative of Integration*. Princeton: Princeton University Press.

Andersson, Roger. 2007. "Ethnic Residential Segregation and Integration Processes in Sweden." In Karen Schönwälder, ed., *Residential Segregation and the Integration of Immigrants: Britain, the Netherlands and Sweden.* Wissenschaftszentrum Berlin für Sozialforschung, Discussion Paper SP IV 2007–62.

2008. "Clustered, Trapped and Excluded? Exploring Immigrants' Social and Geographical Trajectories in Sweden 1990–2006." *Presented at the NSBB conference on Urban Transformation*, Governance Cultures and Housing Policies. Arranged by YTK – Centre for Urban and Regional Studies/Helsinki University of Technology. September, Hanasaari, Espoo, Finland.

Andreoni, James. 1989. "Giving with Impure Altruism: Applications to Charity and Ricardian Ambivalence," *Journal of Political Economy*, **97**:1447–58.

Australian Government Department of Immigration and Citizenship. 2010. *Report on Migration Program 2009–10: Program Year to 30 June 2010*, available at http://www.immi.gov.au/media/statistics/pdf/report-on-migration-program-2009–10.pdf.

Australian Multicultural Advisory Council. 2010. *The People of Australia: Australia's Multiculturalism Policy*, available at http://www.immi.gov.au/media/publications/multicultural/pdf_doc/people-of-australia-multicultural-policy-booklet.pdf.

Baker, P. E. 1934. *Negro-White Adjustment.* New York: Association Press.

Balakrishnan, T. R. and Stephen Gyimah. 2003. "Spatial Residential Patterns of Selected Ethnic Groups: Significance and Policy Implications," *Canadian Ethnic Studies Journal*, 35:113–34.

Baldwin, James. 1961. *Nobody Knows My Name: More Notes of a Native Son.* New York: Dell, originally published in 1954.

Baldwin, Kate and John D. Huber. 2010. "Economic versus Cultural Differences: Forms of Ethnic Diversity," *American Political Science Review*, 104:644–62.

Banting, Keith G. 2010. "Is There a Progressive's Dilemma in Canada? Immigration, Multiculturalism and the Welfare State," *Canadian Journal of Political Science*, 43:797–820.

Bay, Ann-Helen, Ottar Hellevik, and Tale Hellevik. 2009. "Does Immigration Undermine Welfare State Support?" Presented at the Workshop on Diversity and Democratic Politics: Canada in Comparative Perspective, Queens University, Kingston, Ontario, Canada, May 7–8.

Bean, Clive. 2005. "Is There a Crisis of Trust in Australia?" In Shaun Wilson, Gabrielle Meagher, Rachel Gibson, David Denemark, and Mark Western, eds., *Australian Social Attitudes: The First Report.* Sydney: University of New South Wales Press.

Bécares, Laia, Mai Stafford, James Laurence and James Nazroo. 2011. "Composition, Concentration and Deprivation: Exploring their Association with Social Cohesion among Different Ethnic Groups in the UK," *Urban Studies*, **DOI**: 10.1177/0042098010391295.

Bennhold, Katrin. 2005. "'We're French,' but not 'real' French," *International Herald Tribune* (November 5–6), 1–4, available at http://www.nytimes.com/2005/11/04/world/europe/04iht-france.html.

Bennich-Björkman, Li. 2007. *Political Culture Under Institutional Pressure*. Hampshire, UK: Palgrave Macmillan.

Bergqvist, Christina and Anders Lindbom. 2003. "The Swedish Welfare State: Neo-liberal Challenge and Welfare State Resilience," *OZP*, 32:389–401, available at www.oezp.at/pdfs/2003-4-02.pdf.

Bhattacharya, Surya, Ashifa Kassam, and Simona Siad. 2007. "When Identity Is Mix-and- Match," Toronto *Star* (June 30), available at http://www.thestar.com/article/231161.

Birrell, Bob. 2003. "Immigration and Social Capital in Australia." In Leonie Kramer, ed., *The Multicultural Experiment: Immigrants, Refugees, and National Identity*. Sydney: Macleay Press.

Bissoondath, Neil. 1998. "Multiculturalism," *New Internationalist*, 305, available at http://www.newint.org/features/1998/09/05/multiculturalism/.

Blalock, Hubert M., Jr. 1982. *Race and Ethnic Relations*. Englewood Cliffs, NJ: Prentice-Hall.

Blastland, Michael. 2010. "Why It's Hard to Measure Happiness," available at http://www.bbc.co.uk/news/magazine-11765401.

Bobo, Lawrence and James R. Kluegel. 1993. "Opposition to Race-Targeting: Self-Interest, Stratification Ideology, or Racial Attitudes?" *American Sociological Review* 58:443–64.

Bobo, Lawrence and Camille L. Zubrinsky. 1996. "Attitudes on Residential Integration: Perceived Status Differences, Mere In-Group Preference, or Racial Prejudice?" *Social Forces*, 74:883–909.

Bobo, Lawrence D. and Michael P. Massagali. 2001. "Stereotyping and Urban Inequality." In Alice O'Connor, Chris Tilly, and Lawrence D. Bobo, eds., *Urban Inequality*. New York: Russell Sage Foundation.

Bok, Sissela. 1978. *Lying*. New York: Pantheon.

Borevi, Karin. 2010. "Dimensions of Citizenship, European Integration Policies from a Scandinavian Perspective." Presented at the Swedish Political Science Association Annual Meeting, September/October, available at www.pol.gu.se/digitalAssets/1315/1315853_boreviswepsa.pdf.

Bowles, Samuel, Glenn C. Loury, and Rajiv Sethi. 2009. "Group Inequality." Unpublished paper, Santa Fe Institute.

Bowyer, Benjamin. 2009. "The Contextual Determinants of Whites' Racial Attitudes in England," *British Journal of Political Science*, 39:559–86.

Bradburn, Norman M., Seymour Sudman, and Galen L. Gockel with the assistance of Joseph R. Noel. 1970. *Racial Integration in American Neighborhoods: A Comparative Survey*. Chicago: National Opinion Research Corporation.

Brambor, Thomas, William Roberts Clark, and Matt Golder. 2006. "Understanding Interaction Models: Improving Empirical Analyses," *Political Analysis*, 14:63–82.

Brännström, Lars. 2006. "The Corrosion of Trust: The Impacts of Disadvantaged Neighbourhood Conditions, Fear of Victimisation, Powerlessness, and Precarious Labour Market Positions." In Lars Brännström, *Phantom of the Neighbourhood: Longitudinal Studies on Area-Based Conditions and Individual Outcomes*. Unpublished PhD dissertation, Swedish Institute for Social Research, University of Stockholm.

Brehm, John and Wendy Rahn. 1997. "Individual Level Evidence for the Causes and Consequences of Social Capital," *American Journal of Political Science*, 41:888–1023.

Breton, Raymond, Norbert J. Hartmann, Jos L. Lennards, and Paul Reed. 2004. *A Fragile Social Fabric? Fairness, Trust, and Commitment in Canada*. Montreal: McGill-Queens University Press.

Brewer, Marilynn B. 1979. "In-Group Bias in the Minimal Intergroup Situation: A Cognitive-Motivational Analysis," *Psychological Bulletin*, 86:307–24.

Bros, Catherine. 2010. "Social Fragmentation and Public Goods: Polarization, Inequality and Patronage in Uttar Pradesh and Bihar." Working Paper 2010.26, Centre d'Economie de la Sorbonne, available at http://ideas.repec.org/p/mse/cesdoc/10026.html.

Brown, Gordon (Prime Minister). 2006. "The Future of Britishness," available at http://www.fabians.org.uk/events/speeches/the-future-of-britishness.

Brown, Stephen. 2010. "German Muslims Must Obey Law, Not Sharia: Merkel," *Reuters*, October 6, available at http://www.reuters.com/article/2010/10/06/us-germany-muslims-idUSTRE69552W20101006.

Bryce, James. 1916. *The American Commonwealth*. New York: Macmillan, volume 2.

Burnley, Ian, Peter Murphy, and Robert. Fagan. 1997. *Immigration and Australian Cities*, Sydney: Federation Press.

Burns, John F. 2010. "On the Sceptred Isle, an Issue Fit for Whispers," *New York Times Week in Review* (April 25), WK4, available at http://www.nytimes.com/2010/04/25/weekinreview/25burns.html?sq=On%20the%20Sceptered%20Isle,%20An%20%20Issue%20Fit&st=cse&scp=1&pagewanted=print.

2011. "Prime Minister Criticizes British 'Multiculturalism' as Allowing Extremism," New York *Times* (February 6):A6, available at http://www.nytimes.com/2011/02/06/world/europe/06britain.html?_r=1&ref=world.

Burt, Ronald S. 2000. "Structural Holes versus Network Closure as Social Capital," in Nan Lin, C. S. Cook, and Ronald.S. Burt, eds, *Social Capital: Theory and Research*. New York: Aldine de Gruyter.

Calma, Tom (Acting Race Discrimination Commissioner). 2007. *Multiculturalism*, available at http://www.hreoc.gov.au/racial_discrimination/multiculturalism/index.html.

Campbell, Angus, Philip E. Converse, and Willard L. Rodgers. 1976. *The Quality of American Life*. New York: Russell Sage Foundation.

Cantle, Ted. 2001. *The Cantle Report – Community Cohesion: A Report of the Independent Review Team*. London: Home Office, available at http://resources.cohesioninstitute.org.uk/Publications/Documents/Document/Default.aspx?recordId=96.

Card, David and Jesse Rothstein. 2007. "Racial Segregation and the Black White Test Score Gap," *Journal of Public Economics*, 91:2158–84.

Carrington, Kerry and Ron Reavell. 2007. "Toowomba." In Kerry Carrington, Alison McIntosh, and Jim Walmsley, eds., *The Social Costs and Benefits of Migration into Australia*. Armidale, NSW, Australia: Centre for Applied

Research in Social Science, available at http://www.immi.gov.au/media/publications/research/social-costs-benefits/.

Carter, William H., Michael H. Schill, and Susan M. Wachter. 1998. "Polarisation, Public Housing and Racial Minorities in US Cities," *Urban Studies*, 35:1889–1911.

Castles, Stephen, Bill Cope, Mary Kalanztis, and Michael Morrissey. 1988. *Mistaken Identity: Multiculturalism and the Demise of Nationalism in Australia*. Sydney: Pluto Press.

Change Institute. 2009. *Understanding Muslim Ethnic Communities*. London: Communities and Local Government, available at www.communities.gov.uk/documents/communities/pdf/1203896.pdf.

Charles, Camille Zubrinsky. 2003. "The Dynamics of Racial Residential Segregation," *Annual Review of Sociology*, 29:167–207.

2006. *Won't You Be My Neighbor? Race, Class and Residence in Los Angeles*. New York: Russell Sage Foundation.

2007. "Can We Live Together? Racial Preferences and Neighborhood Outcomes." In Xavier de Souza Briggs, ed., *The Geography of Opportunity*. Washington: Brookings Institution Press.

Citizenship and Immigration Canada. N.d. (a). "Skilled Workers and Professionals: Who Can Apply – Six Selection Factors and Pass Mark," available at http://www.cic.gc.ca/english/immigrate/skilled/apply-factors.asp.

N.d. (b). "Skilled Workers and Professionals: Who Can Apply – Selection Factors," available at http://www.cic.gc.ca/english/immigrate/skilled/factor-adaptability.asp.

Claiborn, M. P. and Martin, P. S. 2002. "Trusting and Joining? An Empirical Test of the Reciprocal Nature of Social Capital," *Political Psychology*, 22, 267–91.

Clark, Jeremy and Bonggeun Kim. 2009. "The effect of Neighbourhood Diversity on Volunteering: Evidence from New Zealand." Department of Economics and Finance, College of Business and Economics, University of Canterbury, Christchurch, NZ, available at www.aeaweb.org/aea/conference/program/retrieve.php?pdfid=194.

Clark, Tom, Robert D. Putnam, and Edward Fieldhouse. 2010. *The Age of Obama: The Changing Place of Minorities in British and American Society*. Manchester: Manchester University Press.

Cnaan, Ram, Amy Kasternakis, and Robert J. Wineburg. 1993. "Religious People, Religious Congregations, and Volunteerism in Human Services: Is There a Link?" *Nonprofit and Voluntary Sector Quarterly*, 22:33–51.

Collier, Paul, Patrick Honahan, and Karl Ove Moene. 2001. "Implications of Ethnic Diversity," *Economic Policy*, 16:129–66.

Commager, Henry Steele. 1950. *The American Mind*. New Haven: Yale University Press.

Commission for Racial Equality. 1998. *Stereotyping and Racism: Findings from Two Surveys*. London, available at http://www.cre.gov.uk/pdfs/stereotype.pdf.

Committee to Advise on Australia's Immigration Policies. 1988. *Immigration: A Commitment to Australia*. Canberra: Australian Government Printing Service.

Community Cohesion Panel (UK). 2004. *The End of Parallel Lives?* Available at http://www.communities.gov.uk/archived/publications/communities/endparallellives.

Condor, Sujsan, Stephen Gibson, and Jackie Abell. 2006. "English Identity and Ethnic Diversity in the Context of UK Constitutional Change," *Ethnicities*, 6:123–58.

Co-Operative Housing Confederation of Canada. 2011. "Recent News from the Ontario Region: Bill 140 Moves To Third Reading," available at http://www.chfcanada.coop/eng/pages2007/ontnews.asp?id=818.

Coulibaly, Modibo, Rodney D. Green, and David M. Jones. 1998. *Segregation in Federally Subsidized Low-Income Housing in the United States*. Westport, CT: Praeger.

Cowell, Alan. 2005. "News Analysis: Britain's Multicultural Experiment Goes On," *International Herald Tribune* (November 19–20), 2, available at http://www.nytimes.com/2005/11/18/world/europe/18iht-brixton.html.

2006. "Blair Criticizes Full Islamic Veils as 'Mark of Separation'," *New York Times* (October 18), available at http://www.nytimes.com/2006/10/18/world/europe/18britain.html?_r.

Crepaz, Markus M. L. 2008. *Trust Beyond Borders: Immigration, the Welfare State, and Identity in Modern Societies*. Ann Arbor: University of Michigan Press.

Croly, Herbert. 1965. *The Promise of American Life*. Edited by Arthur M. Schlesinger, Jr. Cambridge: Belknap.

Cutler, David M. and Edward L. Glaeser. 1997. "Are Ghettos Good or Bad?" *Quarterly Journal of Economics*, 112:827–72.

Cutler, David M., Edward L. Glaeser, and Jacob L. Vigdor. 1997. "The Rise and Decline of the American Ghetto," *Journal of Political Economy*, 107:455–506.

2005. "Ghettos and the Transmission of Ethnic Capital." In Glenn C. Loury, Tariq Modood, and Steven M. Teles, eds., *Ethnicity, Social Mobility, and Public Policy: Comparing the US and UK*. New York: Cambridge University Press.

2008. "When Are Ghettos Bad? Lessons from Immigrant Segregation in the United States." *Journal of Urban Economics*, 63:759–74.

Dahlström, Carl. 2004. "Rhetoric, Practice and the Dynamics of Institutional Change: Immigrant Policy in Sweden, 1964–2000," *Scandinavian Political Studies*, 27: 287–310.

Dale, Daniel. 2011. "Ford 'Absolutely' Wants to Try to Privatize TCHC," *The Star* (March 2), available at http://www.thestar.com/news/article/947237 – ford-absolutely-wants-to-try-to-privatize-tchc.

Daley, Patricia O. 1998. "Black Africans in Great Britain: Spatial Concentration and Segregation," *Urban Studies*, 35:1703–24.

Daley, Suzanne. 2011. "Swedes Begin to Question Liberal Migration Tenets," New York *Times* (February 27):A6.

Dasgupta, Partha. 1988. "Trust as a Commodity." In Diego Gambetta, ed., *Trust* Oxford: Basil Blackwell.

Davis, Lanny. 2007. *Scandal: How "Gotcha" Politics Is Destroying America*. New York: Palgrave Macmillan.

de la Garza, Rodolfo, Angelo Falcon, F. Chris Garcia, and John A. Garcia. 1998. *Latino National Political Survey, 1989–1990* [Computer file]. ICPSR06841-v3. Ann Arbor, MI: Inter-university Consortium for Political and Social Research [distributor]. doi:10.3886/ICPSR06841.

Deininger, Klaus and Lyn Squire. 1996. "A New Data Set: Measuring Economic Income Inequality," *World Bank Economic Review*, 10:565–92.

Delhey, Jan and Kenneth Newton. 2004. "Social Trust: Global Pattern or Nordic Exceptionalism?" Wissenschaftszentrum Berlin für Sozialforschung Working Paper SP I 2004–202, available at bibliothek.wz-berlin.de/pdf.

Demker, Marie. 2007. "Attitudes Toward Immigrants and Refugees, Swedish Trends with Some Comparisons." Presented at the International Studies Association Annual Convention, February/March, Chicago, available at http://www.mim.org.gu.se/pdf/Attitudes%20toward%20immigrants%20and%20refugees.%20ISA%202007.pdf.

Denham, John. 2001. *Building Cohesive Communities: A Report of the Ministerial Group on Public Order and Community Cohesion*. London: Home Office, available at http://www.communities.gov.uk/archived/publications/communities/publicordercohesion.

DeParle, Jason. 2010. "Defying Trend, Canada Lures More Migrants," New York *Times* (November 13), available at http://www.nytimes.com/2010/11/13/world/americas/13immig.html?_r.

Department of Immigration and Citizenship, Government of Australia. n.d. (a) "What is Multiculturalism?" available at http://www.immi.gov.au/media/publications/multicultural/agenda/agenda89/whatismu.htm.

n.d. (b) "Basic Rights," available at http://www.immi.gov.au/media/publications/multicultural/agenda/agenda89/basicrig.htm.

de Souza Briggs, Xavier. 2005. "More *Pluribus*, Less *Unum*? The Changing Geography of Race and Opportunity." In Xavier de Souza Briggs, ed., *The Geography of Opportunity*. Washington: Brookings Institution Press.

Deutsch, Morton and Mary Evans Collins. 1951. *Interracial Housing: A Psychological Evaluation of a Social Experiment*. Minneapolis: University of Minnesota Press.

Dincer, Oguzhan. In press. "Ethnic Diversity and Trust," *Contemporary Economic Policy*.

Dinesen, Peter Thisted. 2011a. *When in Rome, Do as the Romans Do? An Analysis of the Acculturation of Generalized Trust of non-Western Immigrants in Western Europe*, unpublished PhD dissertation, University of Aarhus (Denmark).

2011b. "Me and Jasmina Down by the Schoolyard: An Analysis of the Impact of Ethnic Diversity in School on P:upils' Trust," *Social Science Research*, 40:572–85.

Dinesen, Peter Thisted, and Kim Mannemar Sonderskov. 2011. "Becoming Diverse: Ethnic Heterogeneity and Social Trust from 1980 Until Today." Presented at the Annual Meeting of the Midwest Political Science Association, April, Chicago.

Dixon, Jeffrey C. 2006. "The Ties That Bind and Those That Don't: Toward Reconciling Group Threat and Contact Theories of Prejudice," *Social Forces*, 84:2179–804.

Dixon, John, Kevin Durrheim, and Colin Tredoux. 2005. "Beyond the Optimal Contact Strategy: A Reality Check for the Contact Hypothesis," *American Psychologist*, 60:697–711.

Easterly, William and Ross Levine. 1997 "Africa's Growth Tragedy: Policies and Ethnic Divisions," *Quarterly Journal of Economics*, 112:1203–50.

Echenique, Federico and Roland G. Fryer, Jr. 2007. "A Measure of Segregation Based on Social Interactions," *Quarterly Journal of Economics*, 122:44–485.

Economist. 1987. "Whatever Happened?" September 12, 11–12.

(The) Economist. 1990. *The Economist Book of Vital World Statistics*. New York: Times Books.

Edin, Per-Anders, Peter Fredriksson, and Olof Åslund. 2000. "Ethnic Enclaves and the Economic Success of Immigrants – Evidence from a Natural Experiment." IFAU – Office of Labour Market Policy Evaluation Working Paper 2000:9, available at http://ideas.repec.org/p/hhs/ifauwp/2000_009.html.

Ekman, Ivar. 2006. "Sweden Ethnic Harmony: Darin Zanyar Won the "Best Song" Award," *Kurdnet* (February 17), available at http://www.ekurd.net/mismas/articles/misc2006/2/kurdsworldwide51.htm.

Ellen, Ingrid Gould. 2000. *Sharing America's Neighborhoods: The Prospects for Stable Racial Integration*. Cambridge: Harvard University Press.

Ellison, Ralph. 1952. *Invisible Man*. New York: Signet Books, originally published in 1947.

Emerson, Michael, Karen J. Chai, and George Yancey. 2001. "Does Race Matter in Residential Segregation? Exploring the Preferences of White Americans?" *American Sociological Review*, 66:922–35.

Ersanilli, Evelyn and Ruud Koopmans. 2009. "Ethnic Retention and Host Culture Adoption among Turkish Immigrants in Germany, France and the Netherlands: A Controlled Comparison." WZB Discussion Paper SP IV 2009–701 Berlin:Wissenschaftszentrum Berlin für Sozialforschung, available at http://bibliothek.wzb.eu/pdf/2009/iv09–701.pdf.

ETHNOS Research and Consultancy. 2006. *The Decline of Britishness: A Research Study*. London: Commission for Racial Equality, available at www.ethnos.co.uk/decline_of_britishness.pdf.

Farley, Reynolds, Howard Schuman, Suzanne Bianchi, Diane Colastano, and Shirley Hatchett. 1978. "'Chocolate City, Vanilla Suburbs': Will the Trend toward Racially Separate Communities Continue?" *Social Science Research*, 7:319–44.

Farley, Reynolds and Alma F. Tauber. 1974. "Racial Segregation in the Public Schools," *American Journal of Sociology*, 79:888–905.

Fearon, James D. 2003. "Ethnic and Cultural Diversity by Country," *Journal of Economic Growth*, 8:195–222. Article and data available at http://www.stanford.edu/~jfearon/.

Feitosa, Flávia da Fonseca and Anna Wissman. 2006. "Social-Mix Policy Approaches to Urban Segregation in Europe and the United States," Interdisciplinary Term Paper, International Doctoral Studies Programme, Zentrum für Entwicklungsforschung, Center for Development Research, Universität Bonn (Germany).

Fetzer, Joel S. 2001. *Public Attitudes toward Immigration in the United States, France, and Germany*. New York: Cambridge University Press.

Fieldhouse, Edward and David Cutts. 2010. "Does Diversity Damage Social Capital? Comparative Study of Neighbourhood Diversity and Social Capital in the US and Britain," *Canadian Journal of Political Science*, 43:289–319.

Finney, Nissa and Ludi Simpson. 2009. *Sleepwalking to Segregation? Challenging Myths About Race and Migration*. Bristol, UK: Policy Press.

Finseraas, Henning. 2009. "Xenophobic Attitudes, Preferences for Redistribution, and Partisan Alignments in Europe." Presented at the Workshop on Diversity and Democratic Politics: Canada in Comparative Perspective, Queens University, Kingston, Ontario, Canada, May 7–8.

Fischer, Mary J. 2003. "The Relative Importance of Income and Race in Determining Residential Outcomes in U.S. Urban Areas," *Urban Affairs Review*, 38:669–96.

Fischer, Mary J. and Douglas S. Massey. 2000. "Residential Segregation and Ethnic Enterprise in U.S. Metropolitan Areas," *Social Problems*, 47:408–24.

Florida, Richard, Charlotta Mellander, and Peter J. Rentfrow. 2009. "Happy States of America: A State-level Analysis of Psychological, Economic, and Social Well-being," Martin Prosperity Institute Working Paper 003, available at http://research.martinprosperity.org.

Fong, Eric. 1996. "A Comparative Perspective on Racial Residential Segregation: American and Canadian Experiences," *Sociological Quarterly*, 37:199–226.

Fong, Eric and Kumiko Shibuya. 2005. "Multiethnic Cities in North America," *Annual Review of Sociology*, 31:285–304.

Fong, Eric and Rima Wilkes. 2003. "Racial and Residential Segregation Patterns in Canada," *Sociological Forum*. 18:577–602.

Forbes, Hugh Donald. 1993. "Canada: From Bilingualism to Multiculturalism," *Journal of Democracy*, 4:69–84.

1997. *Ethnic Conflict: Commerce, Culture, and the Contact Hypothesis*. New Haven: Yale University Press.

Fossett, Mark A. and K. Jill Kielcolt. 1989. "The Relative Size of Minority Populations and White Racial Attitudes," *Social Science Quarterly*, 70:820–35.

Foster, Clive. 1995. *Australian Cities: Continuity and Change*. Melbourne: Oxford University Press.

Foster, Lois and Anne Seitz. 1990. "The OMA Survey on Issues in Multicultural Australia," *The Australian Quarterly*, 62:277–92.

Fraga, Luis, John A. Garcia, Rodney Hero, Michael Jones-Correa, Valerie Martinez-Ebers, and Gary M. Segura. 2006. *Latino National Survey (LNS), 2006*. Computer file]. ICPSR20862-v1. Miami, FL: Geoscape International [producer], 2006. Ann Arbor, MI: Inter-university Consortium for Political and Social Research [distributor], 2008–05–27. doi:10.3886/ICPSR20862.

Frey, William H. 1979. "Central City White Flight: Racial and Nonracial Causes," *American Sociological Review*, 44:425–48.

Fry, Earl. 1992. *Canada's Unity Crisis: Implications for U.S.-Canadian Economic Relations*. New York: Twentieth Century Foundation.

Galligan, Brian and Winsome Roberts. 2003. "Australian Multiculturalism: Its Rise and Decline." Presented at the Australasian Political Science Association, University of Tasmania, Hobart, September/October, available at www.utas.edu.au/government/APSA/GalliganRoberts.pdf.

Gallup/The Coexist Foundation. 2009. *Religious Perceptions in America: With an In-Depth Analysis of U.S. Attitudes Toward Muslims and Islam*. Washington: Gallup Inc.

Gambetta, Diego. 1988. "Can We Trust Trust?" In Diego Gambetta, ed., *Trust*. Oxford: Basil Blackwell.

Garcia-Montalvo, Jose and Marta Reynal-Querol. 2005. "Ethnic Polarization and the Duration of Civil Wars," available at http://www.econ.upf.es/~reynal/war_duration_polarV4.pdf.

Georgiou, Petro. 2008. "The New Australian Citizenship Test–A Template for National Identity," available at http://www.manningclark.org.au/html/Paper-Georgiou_Petro-The_new_Australian_citizenship_test.html.

Gerard, David. 1985. "What Makes a Volunteer?" *New Society* (November 8):236–8.

German Marshall Fund of the United States. 2008. *Transatlantic Trends: Immigration Topline Data 2008*, available at http://www.gmfus.org/trends/immigration/index.html.

Gesthuizen, Maurice, Tom van der Meer, and Peer Scheepers. 2009. "Ethnic Diversity and Social Capital in Europe: Tests of Putnam's Thesis in European Countries," *Scandinavian Political Studies*, 32:121–42.

Gibbon, John Murray. 1938. *Canadian Mosaic*. Toronto: McClelland and Stewart.

Gidengil, Elisabeth, Jason Roy, and Andrea Lawlor. 2009. "The Impact of Ethno-Racial Diversity and Immigration on Political Engagement." *Presented at the Annual Meeting of the American Political Science Association*, Toronto, September.

Gijsberts, Me´rove, Tom van der Meer, and Jaco Dagevos. 2011. "'Hunkering Down' in Multi-Ethnic Neighbourhoods? The Effects of Ethnic Diversity on Dimensions of Social Cohesion," *European Sociological Review*, DOI:10.1093/esr/jcr022, available at www.esr.oxfordjournals.org.

Gilroy, Paul. 1991. *There Ain't No Black in the Union Jack*. Chicago: University of Chicago Press.

Goldin, Claudia and Lawrence F. Katz. 1999. "Human Capital and Social Capital: The Rise of Secondary Schooling in America, 1910–1940," *Journal of Interdisciplinary History*, 29:683–723.

Goldstein, Eric L. 2006. *The Price of Whiteness: Jews, Race, and American Identity*. Princeton: Princeton University Press.

Goodhart, David. 2004. "Too Diverse?" *Prospect* (February 20), available at http://www.prospectmagazine.co.uk/2004/02/too-diverse-david-goodhart-multiculturalism-britain-immigration-globalisation/.

Goot, Murray and Ian Watson. 2005. "Immigration, Multiculturalism, and National Identity." In Shaun Wilson, Gabrielle Meagher, Rachel Gibson, David Denemark, and Mark Western, eds., *Australian Social Attitudes: The First Report*. Sydney: University of New South Wales Press.

Granovetter, Mark S. 1973. "The Strength of Weak Ties." *American Journal of Sociology*, 78: 1360–80.

Greeley, Andrew. 1996. "Reading to Someone Else: The Strange Reappearance of Civic America." Unpublished manuscript, *National Opinion Research Center*, University of Chicago.

Greenberg, Anna. 1999. "Doing God's Work? The Political Significance of Faith-Based Social Service Delivery." *Presented at the Annual Meeting of the Midwest Political Science Association*, April, Chicago.

Gregg, Allan. 2006. "Identity Crisis: Multiculturalism: A Twentieth-century Dream Becomes a Twenty-first-century Conundrum," *The Walrus* (March), available at http://www.walrusmagazine.com/articles/2006.03-society-canada-multiculturism/.

Greif, Avner. 1993. "Contract Enforceability and Economic Institutions in Early Trade: The Maghribi Traders' Coalition," *American Economic Review*, 83:525–48.

Grimes, Seamus. 1993. "Residential Segregation in Australian Cities: A Literature Review," *International Migration Review*, 27:103–20.

Guest, Avery M., Charis E. Kubrin, and Jane K. Cover. 2008. "Heterogeneity and Harmony: Neighbouring Relationships among Whites in Ethnically Diverse Neighbourhoods in Seattle," *Urban Studies*, 45:501–26.

Gurin, Patricia, Biren (Ratnesh) A. Nagda, and Gretchen E. Lopez. 2004. "The Benefits of Diversity in Education for Democratic Citizenship," *Journal of Social Issues*, 60:17–34.

Habyarimana, James, Macartan Humphreys, Daniel N. Posner, and Jeremy N. Weinstein. 2009. *Coethnicity: Diversity and the Dilemmas of Collective Action*. New York: Russell Sage Foundation.

Hall, Peter. 1999. "Social Capital in Britain," *British Journal of Political Science*, 29 417–61.

Hällsten, Martin and Ryszard Szulkin. 2009. "Families, Neighborhoods, and the Future: the Transition to Adulthood of Children of Native and Immigrant Origin in Sweden." Working Paper 2009:9, Stockholm University Linnaeus Center for Integration Studies, available at http://ideas.repec.org/p/hhs/sulcis/2009_009.html.

Hamilton, David L., Sandra Carpenter, and George D. Bishop. 1984. "Desegregation in Suburban Neighborhoods." In Norman Miller and Marilyn B. Brewer, eds., *Groups in Contact: The Psychology of Desegregation*. Orlando: Academic Press

Hamilton, W. D. 1964. "The Genetical Evolution of Social Behavior, II," *Journal of Theoretical Biology*, 7:17–52.

Hardin, Russell. 2004. *Trust and Trustworthiness*. New York: Russell Sage Foundation.

Harrell, Allison. 2009. "Changing Realities: The Rights Regime and the Adoption of Multicultural Values." Presented at the Workshop on Diversity and Democratic Politics: Canada in Comparative Perspective, Queens University, Kingston, Ontario, Canada, May 7–8.

Harris, Frederick C. 1994. "Something Within: Religion as a Mobilizer of African-American Political Activism," *Journal of Politics*, 56:42–68.

Harris, Frederick C. and Brian D. McKenzie. 2011. "Still Waters Run Deep: The Complexities of African-American Identities and Political Attitudes." Presented at the American Politics Workshop, Department of Government and Politics, University of Maryland, September 23, available at http://www.bsos.umd.edu/gvpt/apworkshop/papers_fall11/Harris%20and%20McKenzie%2009-2011.pdf.

Harsman, Bjorn. 2006. "Ethnic Diversity and Spatial Segregation in the Stockholm Region," *Urban Studies*, 43:1341–64.

Healy, Ernest. 2007. "Ethnic Diversity and Social Cohesion in Melbourne," *People and Place*, 15:49–64.

Higham, John. 1951 *Strangers in the Land: Patterns of American Nativism, 1860–1925*. New York: Atheneum.

Herring, Cedric. 2006. "*Does Diversity Pay? Racial Composition of Firms and the Business Case for Diversity*." Unpublished paper, University of Illinois at Chicago.

Hewstone, Miles. 2009. "Living Apart, Living Together? The Role of Intergroup Contact in Social Integration," *Proceedings of the British Academy*, 162:243–300.

Hodgkinson, Virginia A., Murray S. Weitzman, and Arthur D. Kirsch. 1990. "From Commitment to Action: How Religious Involvement Affects Giving and Volunteering." In Robert Wuthnow, Virginia Hodgkinson, and Associates, *Faith and Philanthropy in America*. San Francisco: Jossey-Bass.

Hodgkinson, Virginia A., Murray B. Weitzman, and Associates. 1992. *Giving and Volunteering in the United States: Findings from a National Survey*. Washington: INDEPENDENT SECTOR.

Holmberg, Soren and Lennart Weibull, eds. 2009. *Swedish Trends 1986–2009*, unpublished document from the SOM Institute, University of Gothenburg.

Holmquist, Emma. 2009. "Policy and Planning for Social and Housing Mix And Decreased Housing Segregation." Summary of PhD dissertation, *Department of Social and Economic Geography*, Uppsala University, Uppsala, Sweden.

Home Office of the United Kingdom. 2004a. *Strength in Diversity: Towards a Community Cohesion and Race Equality Strategy*. London: Home Office Communication Directorate.

2004b. *2003 Home Office Citizenship Survey: People, Families and Communities*. London: Home Office Research, Development and Statistics Directorate, available at rds.homeoffice.gov.uk/rds/pdfs04.

Home Office Research. 2004. *2003 Home Office Citizenship Survey: People, Families and Communities*. London: Home Office Research, Development and Statistics Directorate, available at *w*ww.homeoffice.gov.uk/rds/pdfs04/hors289.pdf.

Hooghe, Marc. 2007. "Social Capital and Diversity: Generalized Trust, Social Cohesion, and Regimes of Diversity," *Canadian Journal of Political Science*, 40:709–32.

Hooghe, Marc, Tim Reeskens, Dietlind Stolle, and Ann Trappers. 2009. "Ethnic Diversity and Generalized Trust in Europe: A Cross-National Multilevel Study," *Comparative Political Studies*, 42:198–223.

Horin, Adele. 2010. "Young Take on the Monoculture," Sydney *Morning Herald* (November 13): 26, available at http://www.smh.com.au/opinion/society-and-culture/young-take-on-the-monoculture-20101112–17r3d.html.

Hou, Feng. 2004. "Recent Immigration and the Formation of Visible Minority Neighbourhoods in Canada's Largest Cities." Ottawa: Statistics Canada, available at http://www.statcan.gc.ca/pub/11f0019m/11f0019m2004221-eng.pdf.

2006. "Spatial Assimilation of Racial Minorities in Canada's Immigrant Gateway Cities," *Urban Studies*, 43:1191–1213.

Hou, Feng and Garnett Picot. 2004. "Visible Minority Neighbourhoods in Toronto, Montreal, and Vancouver," *Canadian Social Trends*, Spring. Ottawa: Statistics Canada.

Hou, Feng and Zheng Wu. 2009. "Racial Diversity, Minority Concentration, and Trust in Canadian Urban Neighborhoods," *Social Science Research*, 38:693–716.

Hudson, Maria, Joan Phillips, Kathryn Ray, and Helen Barnes. 2007. *Social Cohesion in Diverse Communities*. York, UK: Joseph Roundtree Foundation.

Hunt, Chester L. 1959–60. "Private Integrated Housing in a Medium Size Northern City," *Social Problems*, 7:196–209.

Huntington, Samuel P. 1998. *The Clash of Civilizations and the Remaking of World Order*. New York: Simon and Shuster.

Iceland, John. 2004. "The Multigroup Entropy Index (Also Known as Theil's H or the Information Theory Index)." Unpublished manuscript, University of Maryland, College Park, available at http://www.wwwcensusgov.zuom.info/hhes/www/housing/housing_patterns/multi-group.html.

2009. *Where We Live Now: Immigration and Race in the United States*. Berkeley: University of California Press.

Iceland, John and Melissa Scopilliti. 2008. "Immigrant Residential Segregation in U.S. Metropolitan Areas, 1990–2000," *Demography*, 79–94.

Iceland, John and Daniel H. Weinberg with Erika Steinmetz. 2002. *Racial and Ethnic Residential Segregation in the United States: 1980–2000*. Washington: U.S. Department of Commerce Economics and Statistics Administration, U.S. Census Bureau, available at www.census.gov/hhes/www/housing/resseg/pdf/paa_paper.pdf.

Ihlanfeldt, Keith R. and Benjamin P. Scafaldi. 2002. "The Neighbourhood Contact Hypothesis: Evidence from the Multicity Study of Urban Inequality," *Urban Studies*, 39:619–41.

Ivarsflaten, Elisabeth and Kristin Strømsnes. 2010. "Inequality, Diversity and Social Trust in Norwegian Communities." *Presented at the National Norwegian Conference in Political Science*, Kristiansand, January.

Jantzen, Loma. 2005. "The Advantages of Analyzing Ethnic Attitudes Across Generations – results from the Ethnic Diversity Survey." In Margaret Adsett, Margaret, Caroline Mallandain, and Shannon Stettner, eds., *Canadian and French Perspectives on Diversity*. Ottawa: Minister of Public Works and Government Services Canada, available at http://dsp-psd.pwgsc.gc.ca/Collection/CH36-4-1-2004E.pdf.

Jargowsky, Paul A. 1996. "Take the Money and Run: Economic Segregation in U.S. Metropolitan Areas," *American Sociological Review* 61:984–98.

Jayasuriya, Laksiri and Kee Pookong. 1999. *The Asianisation of Australia: Some Facts About the Myths*. Melbourne: Melbourne University Press.

Jiminez, Marina. 2007. "How Canadian Are You? Visible-minority Immigrants and Their Children Identify Less and Less with the Country, Report Says," *Globe and Mail* (January 27), A1, available at www.crr.ca/index2.php?option=com_content&do_pdf=1&id=511.

Johnston, Barry V. 1991. "Housing Segregation in the Urban Black Population of the Midwest." In Edward D. Huttman, ed., and Wim Blauw and Juliet Saltman, co-editors, *Urban Housing Segregation of Minorities in Western Europe and the United States*. Durham: Duke University Press.

Johnston, Richard, Keith Banting, Will Kymlicka, and Stuart Soroka. 2010. "National Identity and Support for the Welfare State," *Canadian Journal of Political Science*, 43:349–77.

Johnston, Ron, James Forrest, and Michael Poulsen. 2002. "Are There Ethnic Enclaves/Ghettos in English Cities?" *Urban Studies*, 39:591–618.

2005. "On the Measurement and Meaning of Residential Segregation: A Response to Simpson," *Urban Studies*, 42:1221–7.

2007. "The Geography of Residential Segregation: A Comparative Study of Five Countries," *Annals of the Association of American Geographers*, 97:713–38.

Jones, Dale E., Sherri Doty, Clifford Grammich, James E. Horsch, Richard Houseal, Mac Lynn, John P. Marcum, Kenneth M. Sanchagrin, and Richard H. Taylor, *Religious Congregations and Membership in the United States*. Nashville, TN: Glenmary Research Center.

Joppke, Christian. 2007. "Beyond National Models: Civic Integration Policies for Immigrants in Western Europe," *Western European Politics*, 30:1–22.

Jordan, Mary. 2008. "Iraqi Refugees Find Sweden's Doors Closing: Immigrants Overtax System, Critics Say," *Washington Post* (April 10), A1, A10, available at http://www.washingtonpost.com/wp-dyn/content/article/2008/04/09/AR2008040904319_pf.html.

Joseph, Makawaya Shija. 2007. *Housing Policy and Segregation in Sweden*. Master of Science Thesis, Department of Urban Planning and Environment, Division of Urban and Regional Studies, Kungliga Tekniska Högskolan, Stockholm, available at http://www.infra.kth.se/bba/MASTER%20THESISES/master_thesis.htm.

Jupp, James. 2002. *From White Australia to Woomera: The Story of Australian Immigration*. Cambridge: Cambridge University Press.

2008. "A Pragmatic Response to a Novel Situation: Australian Multiculturalism." In Geoffrey Brahm Levey, ed., *Political Theory and Australian Multiculturalism*. New York: Berghahn Books.

Kalkan, Ozan Kerem, Geoff Layman, and Eric M. Uslaner. 2009. "A 'Band of Others'? Attitudes toward Muslims in Contemporary American Society," *Journal of Politics*, 71:847–62.

Key, V.O., Jr. 1949. *Southern Politics in State and Nation*. New York: Vintage Books.

Kirkup, James. 2011. "Muslims must Embrace Our British Values, David Cameron Says," *The Telegraph*, February 5, available at http://www.telegraph.co.uk/news/politics/david-cameron/8305346/Muslims-must-embrace-our-British-values-David-Cameron-says.html.

Koopmans, Ruud. 2008. "Tradeoffs between Equality and Difference: Immigrant Integration, Multiculturalism, and the Welfare State in Cross-National Perspective," Berlin: Wissenschaftszentrum Berlin für Sozialforschung, available at socsci.colorado.edu/~smithms/Koopmans.doc.

2010. "Trade-Offs Between Equality and Difference: Immigrant Integration, Multiculturalism and the Welfare State in Cross-National Perspective," *Journal of Ethnic and Migration Studies*, 36:1–26.

Krivo, Lauren J., Ruth D. Peterson, and Danielle C. Kuhl. 2009. "Segregation, Racial Structure, and Neighborhood Violent Crime," *American Journal of Sociology*, 114:1765–1802.

Krysan, Maria. 2002. "Community Undesirability in Black and White: Examining Racial Residential Preferences through Community Perceptions," *Social Problems*, 49:521–43.

Krysan, Maria and Reynolds Farley. 2002. "The Residential Preferences of Blacks: Do They Explain Persistent Segregation?" *Social Forces*, 80:937–80.

Kukathas, Chandran. 2008. "Anarcho-Multiculturalism: The Pure Theory of Liberalism." In Geoffrey Brahm Levey, ed., *Political Theory and Australian Multiculturalism*. New York: Berghahn Books.

Kumlin, Staffan and Bo Rothstein. 2008. "Minorities and Mistrust: The Cushioning Impact of Social Contacts and Institutional Fairness," Quality of Government Institute, Universit of Gothenburg (Sweden) Working Paper Series 2008:18, available at www.qog.pol.gu.se/working_papers/2008_18_Kumlin_Rothstein.pdf.

2010. "Questioning the New Liberal Dilemma: Immigrants, Social Trust and Institutional Fairness," *Comparative Politics*, 43:63–80.

Kymlicka, Will. 2007a. *Multicultural Odysseys*. Oxford: Oxford University Press.

2007b. "Testing the Liberal Multiculturalist Hypothesis: Normative Theories and Social Science Evidence," *Canadian Journal of Political Science*, 43:257–71.

2010a. "Ethnic, Linguistic, and Multicultural Diversity of Canada." In John C. Courtney and David E. Smith, eds., *The Oxford Handbook of Canadian Politics*. New York: Oxford University Press.

2010b. *The Current State of Multiculturalism in Canada and Research Themes on Canadian Multiculturalism 2008–2010*. Ottawa: Department of Citizenship and Immigration, available at www.cic.gc.ca/english/resources/.../multi-state/section2.asp.

La Ferrara, Eliana and Angelo Mele. 2005. "Racial Segregation and Public School Expenditure," unpublished paper, Bocconi University (Italy), available at http://ideas.repec.org/p/cpr/ceprdp/5750.html.

Lancee, Bram and Jaap Dronkers. 2008. "Ethnic Diversity in Neighborhoods and Individual Trust of Immigrants and Natives: A Replication of Putnam (2007) in a West-European Country," presented at the International Conference on Theoretical Perspectives on Social Cohesion and Social Capital, Royal Flemish Academy of Belgium for Science and the Arts, Brussels, May.

In press. "Ethnic, Religious and Economic Diversity in the Neighbourhood: Explaining Quality of Contact with Neighbours, Trust in the Neighbourhood and Inter-ethnic Trust for Immigrant and Native Residents," *Journal of Ethnic and Migration Studies*, available at www.eui.eu/Personal/Dronkers/English/diversity.pdf.

LaPorta, Rafael, Florencio Lopez-Silanes, Andrei Schleifer, and Robert W. Vishney. 1997. "Trust in Large Organizations," *American Economic Review Papers and Proceedings*, **87**:333–8.

Laurence, James. 2009. "The Effect of Ethnic Diversity and Community Disadvantage on Social Cohesion: A Multi-Level Analysis of Social Capital and Interethnic Relations in UK Communities," *European Sociological Review*, DOI:10.1093/esr/jcp057, available online at www.esr.oxfordjournals.org.

Laurence, James and Anthony Heath. 2008. *Predictors of Community Cohesion: Multi-level Modelling of the 2005 Citizenship Survey*. London: Communities and Local Government, available at www.communities.gov.uk/documents/communities/pdf/681539.pdf.

Leigh, Andrew. 2006. "Trust, Inequality and Ethnic Heterogeneity," *Economic Record*, **82**:268–80.

Letki, Natalia. 2008. "Does Diversity Erode Social Cohesion? Social Capital and Race in British Neighbourhoods," *Political Studies*, **56**:99–106.

Levey, Geoffrey Brahm. 2008. "Multicultural Political Thought in Australian Perspective." In Geoffrey Brahm Levey, ed., *Political Theory and Australian Multiculturalism*. New York: Berghahn Books.

Lichter, Daniel T. 1985. "Racial Concentration and Segregation Across U.S. Counties, 1950–1980," *Demography*, **22**:603–9.

Lieberson, Stanley. 1981. "The Impact of Residential Segregation on Ethnic Assimilation," *Social Forces*, **40**:52–7.

Lindbom, Anders. 2001. "Dismantling the Social Democratic Welfare Model? Has the Swedish Welfare State Lost Its Defining Characteristics?" *Scandinavian Political Studies*, **24**:171–93.

Linden, Anna-Lisa and Goran Lindberg. 1991. "Immigrant Housing Patterns in Sweden." In Edward D. Huttman, ed., and Wim Blauw and Juliet Saltman, co-editors, *Urban Housing Segregation of Minorities in Western Europe and the United States*. Durham: Duke University Press.

Liska, Allen E., Mitchell B. Chamlin, and Mark D. Reed. 1985. "Testing the Economic Production and Conflict Models of Crime Control," *Social Forces*, **64**:119–38.

Loomis, Jeff. 2006. *Privatizing Community: The Growth of Private Resident Associations*. Calgary, Alberta: Federation of Calgary Communities, available at www.calgarycommunities.com/FCCServices/.../RAResearchReport.pdf.

Lopez, Mark. 2000. *The Origins of Multiculturalism in Australian Politics 1945–1975*. Melbourne: Melbourne University Press.

Loury, Glenn. 1977. "A Dynamic Theory of Racial Income Differences." In P. A. Wallace and A. Le Mund, eds., *Women, Minorities, and Employment Discrimination*. Lexington, MA: Lexington Books.

Lyall, Sarah. 2006. "In Britain, efforts to engage Muslims sputter," *International Herald Tribune* (August 19–20), 6, available at http://www.nytimes.com/2006/08/18/world/europe/18iht-muslims.2532373.html.

MacLennan, Hugh. 1945. *Two Solitudes*. Toronto: Duell, Sloan and Pearce.

Mahoney, John and Constance M. Pechura. 1980. "Values and Volunteers: Axiology of Altruism in a Crisis Center," *Psychological Reports*, 47:1007–12.

Malik, Kenan. 2011. "Assimilation's Failure, Terrorism's Rise," *New York Times*, Washington edition (July 7):A21.

Manning, Alan and Sanchari Roy. 2007. "Culture Clash or Culture Club? The Identity and Attitudes of Immigrants in Britain." Center for Economic Performance, London School of Economics, Discussion Paper 790, available at cep.lse.ac.uk/pubs/download/dp0790.pdf.

Mansbridge, Jane. 1999. "Altruistic Trust." In Mark Warren, ed., *Democracy and Trust*. New York: Cambridge University Press.

Månsson, Jonas and Mikael Olsson. 2009. "An Analysis of Labor Market Attainment in Sweden among its Post-war Immigrants from Estonia, Latvia, Lithuania and Poland," available at www.eale.nl/Conference2009/Programme/.../add101678_ReSvKbPeAE.pdf.

Markus, Andrew. 1988. "How Australians See Each Other." In The Committee to Advise on Australia's Immigration Policies, *Immigration: A Commitment to Australia, Consultants' Reports*. Canberra: Australia Government Publishing Service.

2010. *Mapping Social Cohesion2010: the Scanlon Foundation Surveys Summary Report*, available at http://www.globalmovements.monash.edu.au/socialcohesion/.

Markus, Andrew and Jessica Arnup. 2009. *Mapping Social Cohesion: The 2009 Scanlon Foundation Surveys*, available at: http://www.globalmovements.monash.edu.au/news/documents/Social%20Cohesion_full%20report_FINAL.pdf.

Markus, Andrew and Dharmalingam, Arunachalam. 2007. *Mapping Social Cohesion: The Scanlon Foundation Surveys*, available at www.scoa.org.au/.../387423_72752_Mapping%20Social%20Cohesion%202007.pdf.

Markus, Andrew, James Jupp, and Peter McDonald. 2009. *Australia's Immigration Revolution*. Crows Nest, Australia: Allen and Unwin.

Marschall, Melissa and Dietlind Stolle. 2004. "Race and the City: Neighborhood Context and the Development of Generalized Trust," *Political Behavior*, 26:126–54.

Marsden, Peter V. 1987. "Core Discussion Networks of Americans," *American Sociological Review*, 52:122–31.

Martin, Michael E. 2007. *Residential Segregation Patterns of Latinos in the United States, 1990–2000: Testing the Ethnic Enclave and Inequality Theories*. New York: Routledge.

Mason, Andrew. 2010.. "Integration, Cohesion and National Identity: Theoretical Reflections on Recent UK Policy," *British Journal of Political Science*, 857–74

Massey, Douglas S. 1996. "The Age of Extremes: Concentrated Affluence and Poverty in the Twentieth Century," *Demography*, 33:395–412.

2007. *Categorically Unequal: The American Stratification System*. New York: Russell Sage Foundation.

Massey, Douglas S. and Nancy A. Denton. 1993. *American Apartheid: Segregation and the Making of the Underclass*. Cambridge: Harvard University Press.

Masters, Roger D. 1989. *The Nature of Politics*. New Haven: Yale University Press.

Matuszeski, Janina and Frederick Schneider. 2006. "Patterns of Ethnic Group Segregation and Civil Conflict." Unpublished paper, Harvard University, available at isites.harvard.edu/fs/docs/icb.topic637173.files/Matuszeski_061003.pdf.

Maxwell, Rahsaan. 2006. "Muslims, South Asians and the British Mainstream: A National Identity Crisis?" *West European Politics*, 29:736–56.

2009. "Caribbean and South Asian Identification with British Society: The Importance of Perceived Discrimination," *Ethnic and Racial Studies*, 8:1449–69.

McClelland, Katherine and Erika Linnander. 2006. "The Role of Contact and Information in Racial Attitude Change among White College Students," *Sociological Inquiry*, 76:81–115.

McCloskey, Herbert and John Zaller. 1984. *The American Ethos: Public Attitudes toward Capitalism and Democracy*. Cambridge, MA: Harvard University Press.

McKenzie, Barbara. 1948. "The Importance of Contact in Determining Attitudes Toward Negroes," *Journal of Abnormal Social Psychology*, 43:417–41.

McPherson, Miller, Lynn Smith-Lovin, and James M. Cook. 2001. "Birds of a Feather: Homophily in Social Networks," *Annual Review of Sociology*, 27:415–44.

Menadue, John. 2003. "Australia Multiculturalism: Successes, Problems, Risks." In Leonie Kramer, ed., *The Multicultural Experiment: Immigrants, Refugees, and National Identity*. Sydney: Macleay Press

Messick, David M. and Marilynn B. Brewer. 1983. "Solving Social Dilemmas: A Review." In L. Wheeler and P. Shaver, eds., *Review of Personality and Social Psychology*. Beverly Hills: Sage Publications.

Miguel, Edward and Mary Kay Gugerty. 2005. "Ethnic Diversity,. Social Sanctions, and Public Goods in Kenya," *Journal of Public Economics*, 89:2325–68.

Mirza, Munira, Abi Senthilkumaran, and Zein Ja'far. 2007. *Living Apart Together: British Muslims and the Paradox of Multiculturalism*. London: Policy Exchange, available at http://www.policypointers.org/Page/View/5265.

Modood, Tariq. 2007. *Multiculturalism*. Cambridge, UK: Polity Press.

2008. "South Asian Assertiveness in Britain." In S. Koshy and R.Radhakrishnan, eds., *The South Asian Diaspora*. Oxford: Oxford University Press.

Mogahed, Dalia. 2007. "Beyond Multiculturalism vs. Assimilation: Gallup World Poll," available at www.gallup.com/se/File/128162/londonbrieffull041307.pdf.

Morales, Laura and Alfonso Echazarra. 2010. "Does the Residential Concentration of Immigrants Change the Political Landscape? An Analysis of Immigration-related Diversity and Political Culture in Spain." Presented at the ESRC Seminar Series on The Social and Economic Foundations of Ethnic Minority Political Representation, Manchester University, Manchester, UK, January.

Morgan, Kathleen O'Leary and Scott Morgan with Rachel Boba. 2009. *City Crime Rankings 2008–2009: Crime in Metropolitan America*. Washington, DC: CQ Press.

Morrill, R. L. 1975. "The Negro Ghetto: Problems and Alternatives." In Ceri Peach, ed., *Urban Social Segregation*. London: Longman.

Mosle, Sara. 2000. "The Vanity of Volunteerism," *New York Times Magazine* (July 2):22–7, 40–56.

Murdie, Robert A. and Lars-Erik Borgegard. 1998. "Immigration, Spatial Segregation and Housing Segmentation of Immigrants in Metropolitan Stockholm, 1960–95," *Urban Studies*, 35:1869–88.

Murdie, Robert and Sutama Ghosh. 2010. "Does Spatial Concentration Always Mean a Lack of Integration? Exploring Ethnic Concentration and Integration in Toronto," *Journal of Ethnic and Migration Studies*, 36:293–311.

Musterd, Sako. 2003. "Segregation and Integration: A Contested Relationship," *Journal of Ethnic and Migration Studies*, 29:623–41.

Myrdal, Gunnar. 1964. *An American Dilemma: The Negro Problem and Modern Democracy*. New York: McGraw Hill. Originally published in 1944.

National Multicultural Advisory Council. 1999. *Australian Multiculturalism for a New Century: Towards Inclusiveness*. Canberra.

Nesslein, Thomas S. 2003. "Markets versus Planning: An Assessment of the Swedish Housing Model in the Post-War Period," *Urban Studies*, 40:1259–82.

New Jersey Office of State Planning. 1988. *Populations Trends and Projections*. December. Technical Reference Document 88–44, available at http://www.nj.gov/state/planning/docs/populationprojections120188.pdf.

Norwood, Christopher. 1975. *About Paterson*. New York: Harper Colophan.

Offe, Claus. 1999. "Trust and Knowledge, Rules and Decisions: Exploring a Difficult Conceptual Terrain." In Mark Warren, ed., *Democracy and Trust*. Cambridge: Cambridge University Press.

Oliver, J. Eric. 2001. *Democracy in Suburbia*. Princeton: Princeton University Press.

O'Neill, William L. 1986. *American High: The Years of Confidence, 1945–1986*. New York: Free Press.

Orfield, Gary. 2009. *Reviving the Goal of an Integrated Society: A 21st Century Challenge*. Los Angeles: The Civil Rights Project/Proyecto Derechos Civiles at UCLA.

Orr, Larry, Judith D. Feins, Robin Jacob, Erik Beecroft, Lisa Sanbonmatsu, Lawrence F. Katz, Jeffrey B. Liebman, and Jeffrey R. Kling. 2003. *Moving to Opportunity: Interim Impacts Evaluation*. Washington: Department of Housing and Urban Development.

Ottaviano, Gianmarco I. P. and Giovanni Peri. 2005. "The Economic Value of Cultural Diversity: Evidence from U.S. Cities," *Journal of Economic Geography*, 6:9–44.

Ouseley, Sir Michael. 2001. *Community Pride Not Prejudice – Making Diversity Work in Bradford- the Ouseley Report*. Coventry, UK: Institute of Community Cohesion, Futures Institute, available at http://resources.cohesioninstitute.org.uk/Publications/Documents/Document/Default.aspx?recordId=98.

Page, Susan. 2010. "Western Cities Fare Best in Well-being Index," *USA Today*, available at http://www.usatoday.com/news/nation/2010–02–15-cities_N.htm#table.

Parekh, Bhiku. 2002. *The Future of Multiethnic Britain: The Runnymeade Trust Commission on the Future of Multi-Ethnic Britain*. London: Profile Books.

N.d. "What Is Multiculturalism?" available at www.india-seminar.com/1999/484/484%20parekh.htm.

Peach, Ceri. 1996. "Does Britain Have Ghettos?" *Transactions of the Institute of British Geographers*, New Series, 21:216–35.

1998. "South Asian and Caribbean Ethnic Minority Housing Choice in Britain," *Urban Studies*, 35:1657–80.

2005. "The Mosaic Versus the Melting Pot: Canada and the USA," *Scottish Geographical Journal*, 121:3–27.

Pennant, Rachel. 2005. "Diversity, Trust, and Community Participation in England," Findings 253, Home Office, Research Development and Statistics Directorate, United Kingdom, available at http://homeoffice.gov.uk/rds/pubintro1.html.

Pettigrew, Thomas F. 1986. "The Intergroup Contact Hypothesis Reconsidered." In Miles Hewstone and Rupert Brown, eds., *Contact and Conflict in Intergroup Relations*. Oxford: Basil Blackwell.

1998. "Intergroup Conflict Theory," *Annual Review of Psychology*, 49:65–85.

Pettigrew, Thomas F. and Linda R. Tropp. 2006. "A Meta-Analytic Test of Intergroup Contact Theory," *Journal of Personality and Social Psychology*, 90:751–83.

2011. *When Groups Meet: the Dynamics of Intergroup Contact*. Philadelphia: Psychology Press.

Pew Forum on Religion in Public Life. 2009. *Mapping the Global Muslim Population : A Report on the Size and Distribution of the World's Muslim Population*. Washington: Pew Research Center, available at http://pewforum.org/Mapping-the-Global-Muslim-Population.aspx.

2011. "The Future of the Global Muslim Population: Projections for 2010–2030," available at http://pewforum.org/The-Future-of-the-Global-Muslim-Population.aspx.

Pew Research Center. 2007. *Muslim Americans: Middle Class and Mostly Mainstream*. Washington: Pew Research Center, available at http://pewresearch.org/pubs/483/muslim-americans.

Phan, Mai B. 2008. "We're All in This Together: Context, Contacts, and Social Trust in Canada," *Analyses of Social Issues and Public Policy*, 8:23–51.

Phan, Mai B. and Raymond Breton. 2009. "Inequalities and Patterns of Social Attachments in Quebec and the Rest of Canada." In Jeffrey G. Reitz, Raymond Breton, Karen Kisiel Dion, and Kenneth L. Dion. 2009. *Multiculturalism and Social Cohesion: Potentials and Challenges of Diversity*. New York: Springer.

Phillips, Deborah. 1998. "Black Minority Ethnic Concentration, Segregation and Dispersal in Britain," *Urban Studies*, 35:1681–1702.

2010. "'Minority Ethnic Segregation, Integration and Citizenship: A European Perspective," *Journal of Ethnic and Migration Studies*, 36:209–25.

Phillips, Deborah and Valerie Karn. 1991. "Racial Segregation in Britain: Patterns, Processes, and Policy Approaches." In Edward D. Huttman, ed., and Wim Blauw and Juliet Saltman, co-editors, *Urban Housing Segregation of Minorities in Western Europe and the United States*. Durham: Duke University Press.

Phillips, Trevor. 2005. "Sleepwalking to Segregation." Speech given to Manchester Council for Community Relations, September 22. Available at www.humanities.manchester.ac.uk/socialchange/research/social-change/summer-workshops/documents/sleepwalking.pdf.

Phinney, Jean S., John W. Berry, Paul Vedder, and Karmela Liebkind. 2006. "The Acculturation Experience: Behaviors of Immigrant Youth." In John W. Berry, Jean S. Phinney, David L. Sam, and Paul Vedder, eds., *Immigrant Youth in Cultural Transition*. Mahwah, NJ: Lawrence Erlbaum Associates.

Pikkety, Thomas and Emmanuel Saez. 2004. "Income Inequality in the United States, 1913–2002," available at elsa.berkeley.edu/~saez/piketty-saezOUP04US.pdf.

Porter, J. R. and R. E. Washington. 1993. "Minority Identity and Self-Esteem," *Annual Review of Sociology*, 19:139–61.

Portes, Alejandro and Patricia Landolt. 1996, "The Downside of Social Capital," *The American Prospect*: 26:18–21.

Potter, David M. 1954. *People of Plenty*. Chicago: University of Chicago Press.

Poulsen, Michael, Ron Johnston, and James Forrest. 2004. "Is Sydney a Divided City Ethnically?" *Australian Geographical Studies*, 42:356–77.

Putnam, Robert D. 1993. *Making Democracy Work: Civic Traditions in Modern Italy*. Princeton: Princeton University Press

2000. *Bowling Alone*. New York: Simon and Schuster.

2007. "*E Pluribus Unum*: Diversity and Community in the Twenty-first Century The 2006 Johan Skytte Prize Lecture," *Scandinavian Political Studies*, 30:137–74.

Quillian, Lincoln and Mary E. Campbell. 2003. "Beyond Black and White: The Present and Future of Multiracial Friendship Segregation," *American Sociological Review*, 68:540–66.

Racial Residential Segregation Measurement Project. N.d . "Residential Segregation: What it is And How We Measure It," Population Studies Center, University of Michigan, available at http://enceladus.isr.umich.edu/race/seg.html.

Rahn, Wendy M. and John E. Transue. 1998. "Social Trust and Value Change: The Decline of Social Capital in American Youth, 1976–1995," *Political Psychology*, 19:545–66.

Reeskens, Tim and Marc Hooghe. 2009. "Is Local Ethnic Diversity Harmful for Social Capital?" presented at the 5th General Conference of the European Consortium for Political Research, Potsdam, Germany, September.

Reitz, Jeffrey G. and Rupa Banerjee. 2007. "Racial Inequality, Social Cohesion, and Policy Issues in Canada." In Keith Banting, Thomas J. Courchene, and F. Leslie Seidle, eds., *Belonging? Diversity, Recognition, and Shared Citizenship in Canada*. Montreal: Institute for Research in Public Policy.

Reitz, Jeffrey G., Raymond Breton, Karen Kisiel Dion, and Kenneth L. Dion. 2009. *Multiculturalism and Social Cohesion: Potentials and Challenges of Diversity*. New York: Springer.

Resnick, Philip. 2005. *The European Roots of Canadian Identity*. Peterborough, Ontario: Broadview.

Rice, Gareth. 2011. "Is There a Fionnish 'Progressive Dilemma?'," Helsinki *Times* (May 12–18):2.

Rice, Tom W. and Brent Steele. 2001. "White Ethnic Diversity and Community Attachment in Small Iowa Towns," *Social Science Quarterly*, 82:397–407.

Rocha, Rene R. and Rodolfo Espino. 2009. "Racial Threat, Residential Segregation, and the Policy Attitudes of Anglos," *Political Research Quarterly*, 62:415–26.

Rodriguez, Juan. 2006. "Racial and ethnic disparities in income, education and home ownership persist and may be growing," *Diversity News* (November 17) available at http://diversityjobs.com/news/racial-and-ethnic-disparities-in-income-education-and-home-ownership-persist-and-may-be-growing/.

Rokeach, Milton. 1973. *The Nature of Human Values*. New York: Free Press.

Rosenbaum, James E. 1991. "Black Pioneers – Do Their Moves to the Suburbs Increase Economic Opportunity for Mothers and Children?" *Housing Policy Debate*, 2:1179–1213.

Rosenbaum, James E., Susan J. Popkin, Julie E. Kaufman, and Jennifer Rusin. 1991."Social Integration of Low-Income Black Adults in Middle-Class White Suburbs," *Social Problems*, 38:448–61.

Rosenstone, Steven J. and John Mark Hansen. 1993. *Mobilization, Participation, and Democracy in America*. New York: Macmillan.

Rotenberg, Ken J. and Carrie Cerda. 1994. "Racially Based Trust Expectancies of Native American and Caucasian Children," *Journal of Social Psychology*, 134:621–32.

Rothstein, Bo. 2000. "Trust, Social Dilemmas, and Collective Memories: On the Rise and Decline of the Swedish Model," *Journal of Theoretical Politics*, 12:477–99.

Rothstein, Bo and Eric M. Uslaner. 2005. "All for All: Equality, Corruption, and Social Trust," *World Politics*, 58:41–72.

Rothwell, Jonathan. 2010. "Trust in Diverse, Integrated, Cities: A Revisionist Perspective," Brookings Institution, available at http://ssrn.com/abstract=1358647.

Rosenblum, Nancy L. 1998. *Membership and Morals*. Princeton: Princeton University Press.

Sachs, Jeffrey D. and Andrew M. Warner. 1997. "Natural Resource Abundance and Economic Growth," Harvard University Center for International

Development. Available at http://www2.cid.harvard.edu/Warner's%20Files/Natresf5.pdf.

Salée, Daniel. 2007. "The Quebec State and the Management of Ethnocultural Diversity: Perspectives on an Ambiguous Record." In Keith Banting, Thomas J. Courchene, and F. Leslie Seidle, eds., *Belonging? Diversity, Recognition, and Shared Citizenship in Canada*. Montreal: Institute for Research in Public Policy.

Savelkoul, Michael, Maurice Gesthuizen, and Peer Scheepers. 2011. "Explaining Relationships Between Ethnic Diversity and Informal Social Capital Across European Countries and Regions: Tests of Constrict, Conflict and Contact Theory." *Social Science Research*, 40: 1091–1107.

Schoenfeld, Eugen. 1978. "Image of Man: The Effect of Religion on Trust," *Review of Religious Research*, 20:61–7.

Schierup, Carl-Ulrik and Aleksandra Ålund. 2011. "The End of Swedish Exceptionalism? Citizenship, Neoliberalism and the Politics of Exclusion," *Race and Class*, 53:45–64.

Scruggs, Lyle A. and James P. Allan. 2008. "Social Stratification and Welfare Regimes for the 21st Century: Revisiting the Three Worlds of Welfare Capitalism," *World Politics*, 60:642–64.

Sharkey, Patrick. 2009. *Neighborhoods and the Black-White Mobility Gap*. Washington: Economic Mobility Project of the Pew Charitable Trusts. Available at www.economicmobility.org/assets/pdfs/PEW_NEIGHBORHOODS.pdf.

Simeon, Richard. 1977. *Must Canada Fail?* Montreal: McGill-Queens University Press.

Simpson, Ludi. 2004. "Statistics of Racial Segregation: Measures, Evidence and Policy," *Urban Studies*, 41:661–81.

Smiley, Donald V. 1980. *Canada in Question: Federalism in the Eighties*, third ed. Toronto: McGraw-Hill Ryerson.

Smith, Tom W. 1997. "Factors Relating to Misanthropy in Contemporary American Society," *Social Science Research*, 26:170–96.

Sniderman, Paul M. and Thomas Piazza. 1993. *The Scar of Race*. Cambridge: Harvard University Press.

Sonderskov, Kim MaNnemar. 2011a. "Explaining Large-n Cooperation: Generalized Social Trust and the Social Exchange Heuristic," *Rationality and Society*, 23:51–74.

2011b. "Does Generalized Social Trust Lead to Associational Membership? Unravelling a Bowl of Well-Tossed Spaghetti," *European Sociological Review*, 27:419–34.

Soroka, Stuart N., John F. Helliwell, and Richard Johnston. 2007. "Measuring and Modelling Interpersonal Trust." In Fiona M. Kay and Richard Johnston, eds., *Social Capital, Diversity, and the Welfare State*. Vancouver: University of British Columbia Press.

Soroka, Stuart N., Richard Johnston, and Keith Banting. 2007. "Ties that Bind? Social Cohesion and Diversity in Canada." In Keith Banting, Thomas J. Courchene, and F. Leslie Seidle, eds., *Belonging? Diversity, Recognition, and Shared Citizenship in Canada*. Montreal: Institute for Research in Public Policy.

Soss, Joe and Lawrence R. Jacobs. 2009. "The Place of Inequality: Non-participation in the American Polity," *Political Science Quarterly*, 124:95–125.

Statistics Sweden. 2008. *Beskrivning av Sveriges Befolkning 2008* (in Swedish), available at http://www.scb.se/Pages/PublishingCalendarViewInfo____259923.aspx?publobjid=9315.

Stein, Robert M., Stephanie Shirley Post, and Allison L. Rinden. 2000. "Reconciling Context and Contact Effects on Racial Attitudes," *Political Research Quarterly*, 53:285–303.

Stolle, Dietlind. 1998. "Bowling Together, Bowling Alone: The Development of Generalized Trust in Voluntary Associations," *Political Psychology*, 19:497–526.

Stolle, Dietlind and Allison Harrell. 2009. "Social Capital and Ethno-Racial Diversity: Learning to Trust in a Diverse Society." Presented at the Workshop on Diversity and Democratic Politics: Canada in Comparative Perspective, Queens University, Kingston, Ontario, Canada, May 7–8.

Stolle, Dietlind, Soeren Petermann, Karen Schoenwaelder, and Thomas Schmitt with Joe Heywood. 2011. "Consequences of Immigration-related Diversity on Social Integration and Social Cohesion – bringing Contact Back In." Presented at the European Consortium for Political Research General Conference, Reykjavik, Iceland, August.

Stolle, Dietlind, Stuart Soroka, and Richard Johnston. 2008. "When Does Diversity Erode Trust? Neighborhood Diversity, Interpersonal Trust and the Mediating Effect of Social Interactions," *Political Studies*, 56:57–75.

Stolle, Dietlind and Eric M. Uslaner. 2003. "The Structure of Trust in Canada." Presented at the 2003 Biennial Meetings of the Association for Canadian Studies in Canada, November, Portland, OR.

Szulkin, Rysard and Jan O. Jonsson. 2007. "Ethnic Segregation and Educational Outcomes in Swedish Comprehensive Schools." *Stockholm University Linnaeus Center for Integration Studies Working Paper* 2007:2, available at http://swopec.hhs.se/sulcis/abs/sulcis2007_002.htm.

Tagliabue, John. 2011. "A Swede by Any Other Name. In Fact, Many Swedes." *New York Times* (February 1):A8.

Taher, Abul. 2007. "Minorities Feel More British than Whites," *Sunday Times* (February 18), available at http://www.timesonline.co.uk/tol/news/uk/article1400803.ece.

Taylor, Marylee C. 1998. "How White Attitudes Vary with the Racial Composition of Local Populations: Numbers Count," *American Sociological Review*, 63:512–35.

Tehara, Auvniet K. 2010. "Moving Beyond a "Samosa and Sari" View of Multiculturalism: Whiteness and Canadian Identity," available at http://www.thedashingfellows.com/moving-beyond-a-quot-samosa-and-sari-quot-view-of-multiculturalism-whiteness-and-canadian-identity/5783.

Tilbury, Farida. 2007. "The Retreat from Multiculturalism: the Australian Experience." Presented at the Conference on Pluralism, Inclusion and Citizenship, 3rd Global Conference, Interdisciplinary.net, Salzburg, available at http://www.inter-disciplinary.net/ati/diversity/pluralism/pl3/Tilbury%20paper.pdf.

Timberlake, Jeffrey M. 2000. "Still Life in Black and White: Effects of Racial and Class Attitudes on Prospects for Residential Integration in Atlanta," *Sociological Inquiry*, 70:420–45.

Tocqueville, Alexis de. 1945. *Democracy in America*, vol. 2. Translated by Henry Reeve. New York: Alfred A. Knopf. Originally published in 1840.

Tolsma, Jochem, Tom van der Meer, and Maurice Gesthuizen. 2009. "The Impact of Neighbourhood and Municipality Characteristics on Social Cohesion in the Netherlands," *Acta Politica*, 44:286–313.

Tonkin, Richard and Robert Rutherfoord. *Citizenship Survey 2007/08: Questions*. London: Citizenship Survey Team Race, Cohesion and Faith Research Unit Communities and Local Government, 2008. Available at http://www.data-archive.ac.uk/doc/5739%5Cmrdoc%5Cpdf%5C5739us erguide.pdf.

Trivers, Robert L. 1971. "The Evolution of Reciprocal Altruism," *Quarterly Review of Biology*, 46:35–57.

Trondman, Mats. 2006. "Disowning Knowledge: to Be or Not to Be 'The Immigrant' in Sweden," *Ethnic and Racial Studies*, 29:431–51.

Trovato, Frank and Zheng Wu. 2005. "Changing Composition of Canada's Population: Aboriginal and Minority Groups." Prepared for the SSHRC Cluster Workshop on Population Change and Public Policy, London, Ontario, February.

Trudeau, Pierre Elliott, Robert L. Stanfield, David Lewis, and Réal Caouette. 1971. "Announcement of Implementation of Policy of Multiculturalism Within Bilingual Framework," *House of Commons Debates* (October 8):8545–8, available at http://www.abheritage.ca/albertans/speeches/trudeau.html.

UNI (Uniting Canada) 1991. *Spicer Commission: Citizen's Forum on Canadian Unity*, available at http://www.uni.ca/initiatives/spicer.html.

Uslaner, Eric M. 1993. *The Decline of Comity in Congress*. Ann Arbor: University of Michigan Press.

2000. "Is the Senate More Civil Than the House?" in Burdett Loomis, ed., *Esteemed Colleagues: Civility and Deliberation in the Senate*. Washington, DC: Brookings Institution.

2001. "Volunteering and Social Capital: How Trust and Religion Shape Civic Participation in the United States." In Paul Dekker and Eric M. Uslaner, eds., *Social Capital and Participation in Everyday Life*. London: Routledge.

2002. *The Moral Foundations of Trust*. New York: Cambridge University Press.

2007a. "Tax Evasion, Trust, and the Strong Arm of the Law," in Nicholas Hayoz and Simon Hug, eds., *Trust, Institutions, and State Capacities: A Comparative Study* (Bern: Peter Lang AG., 2007), pp. 17–50.

2007b. "Trust and Risk: Implications for Management," in Michael Siegrist, Heinz. Gutscher, and Timothy. C. Earle (eds.), *Trust in Cooperative Risk Management: Uncertainty and Scepticism in the Public Mind* (London: Earthscan, 2007), pp. 73–94.

2008a. *Corruption, Inequality, and the Rule of Law*. New York: Cambridge University Press.

2008b. "Where You Stand Depends Upon Where Your Grandparents Sat: The Inheritability of Generalized Trust," *Public Opinion Quarterly*, 72:1–14.

In press. "Does Diversity Drive Down Trust?" In Per Selle and Sanjeev Prakash, eds., *Civil Society, the State and Social Capital: Theory, Evidence, Policy*. London: Routledge.

Uslaner, Eric M. and Mitchell Brown. 2005. "Inequality, Trust, and Civic Engagement," *American Politics Research*, 31:868–94.

Valentova, Marie and Guayarmina Berzosa. 2010. "Attitudes Toward Immigrants in Luxembourg – Do Contacts Matter?" CEPS Instead Working Paper 2010–20. Available at http://econpapers.repec.org/paper/irscepswp/2010–20.htm.

van der Meer, Tom and Jochem Tolsma. 2011. "Ethnic Diversity and Its Supposed Detrimental Effect on Social Cohesion: A Review of 56 Unique Empirical Studies." Presented at the European Consortium for Political Research General Conference, Reykjavik, Iceland, August.

Verba, Sidney, Kay Lehman Schlozman, and Henry Brady. 1995. *Voice and Equality: Civic Voluntarism in American Politics*. Cambridge: Harvard University Press.

Vervoort, Miranda, Henk Flap, and Jaco Dagevos. 2010. "The Ethnic Composition of the Neighbourhood and Ethnic Minorities' Social Contacts: Three Unresolved Issues," *European Sociological Review*, DOI:10.1093/esr/jcq029, available at www.esr.oxfordjournals.org.

Wadensjo, Eskil. 2009. "Immigration Policy in Sweden: From Assimilation to Integration and Diversity." Presented at the Conference, "Diversity and Democratic Politics: Canada in Comparative Perspective," Queens University, Kingston, Ontario, May.

Wagner, Ulrich, Oliver Christ, Thomas F. Pettigrew, Jost Stellacher, and Carina Wolf. 2006. "Prejudice and Minority Proportion: Contact Instead of Threat Effects," *Social Psychology Quarterly*, 69:380–90.

Walks, R. Alan and Larry S. Bourne. 2006. "Ghettos in Canada's Cities? Racial Segregation, Ethnic Enclaves and Poverty Concentration in Canadian Urban Areas," *Canadian Geographer*, 50:273–97.

Walmsley, Jim, Alison McIntosh, Kerry Carrington, Michael Bittman, Fran Rolley, and Raj Rajaratnam. 2007. "Social Capital." In Kerry Carrington, Alison McIntosh, and Jim Walmsley, eds., *The Social Costs and Benefits of Migration into Australia*. Armidale, NSW, Australia: Centre for Applied Research in Social Science, available at http://www.immi.gov.au/media/publications/research/social-costs-benefits/.

Walmsley, Jim, Alison McIntosh, and Raj Rajaratnam. 2007. "Produced and Financial Capital – Product Diversity." In Kerry Carrington, Alison McIntosh, and Jim Walmsley, eds., *The Social Costs and Benefits of Migration into Australia*. Armidale, NSW, Australia: Centre for Applied Research in Social Science, available at http://www.immi.gov.au/media/publications/research/social-costs-benefits/.

Waters, Mary C. 2009. "Comparing Immigrant Integration in Britain and the US." Prepared for the Harvard Manchester Initiative on Social Change, available at www.ageofobamabook.com/papers/waters.pdf.

Watson, Tara. 2009. "Inequality and the Measurement of Racial Segregation by Income in American Neighborhoods," National Bureau of Economic Research Working Paper 14908, available at http://www.nber.org/papers/w14908.

Weeks, John. 2005. "Inequality Trends in Some Developed OECD Countries," DESA Working Paper No. 6, Centre for Development Policy and Research at the School of Oriental and African Studies (SOAS), University of London, available at www.un.org/esa/desa/papers/2005/wp6_2005.pdf.

Weiner, David A., Byron F. Lutz, and Jens Ludwig. 2009. "The Effects of School Desegregation on Crime," National Bureau of Economic Research Working Paper 15380, available at http://www.nber.org/papers/w15380.

Weinreb, Arthur. 2010. "Australia Introduces New Multiculturalism Policy," available at http://www.suite101.com/content/australia-introduces-new-multiculturalism-policy-a348269.

Whitehead, Tom. 2009. "Labour wanted mass immigration to make UK more multicultural, says former adviser," *Daily Telegraph* (October 23), available at http://www.telegraph.co.uk/news/uknews/law-and-order/6418456/Labour-wanted-mass-immigration-to-make-UK-more-multicultural-says-former-adviser.html.

Wilkes, Rima and John Iceland. 2004. "Hypersegregation in the Twenty-First Century," *Demography*, **41**:23–36.

Williams, Robin M., Jr. 1947. *The Reduction of Intergroup Tensions*. New York: Social Science Research Council.

Jr. in collaboration with John P. Dean and Edward A. Suchman. 1964. *Strangers Next Door: Ethnic Relations in American Communities*. Englewood Cliffs, New Jersey.

Wilner, Daniel M., Rosabelle Price Walkley, and Stuart W. Cook. 1955. *Human Relations in Interracial Housing: A Study of the Contact Hypothesis*. New York: Russell and Russell.

Wilson, William Julius. 1987. *The Truly Disadvantaged: The Inner City, the Underclass, and Public Policy*. Chicago: University of Chicago Press.

Wirth, Louis. 1927. "The Ghetto," *American Journal of Sociology*, **33**:57–71.

1938. "Urbanism as a Way of Life," *American Journal of Sociology*, **44**:1–24.

Woolever, Cynthia. 1992. "A Contextual Approach to Neighbourhood Attachment," *Urban Studies*, **29**:99–116.

Wu, Zheng, Christopher M. Schimmele, and Feng Hou. 2009. "Racial Diversity and Sense of Belonging in Urban Neighborhoods." Presented at the Annual Meetings of Canadian Population Society, Ottawa, May.

Wuthnow, Robert. 1991. *Acts of Compassion*. Princeton: Princeton University Press.

1999. "Mobilizing Civic Engagement: The Changing Impact of Religious Involvement." In Morris Fiorina and Theda Skocpol, eds., *Civic Engagement in American Democracy*. Washington: Brookings Institution.

Yamigishi, Toshio and Midori Yamigishi. 1994. "Trust and Commitment in the United States and Japan," *Motivation and Emotion*, **18**:129–66.

Zhou, Min. 1997. "Social Capital in Chinatown." In Lois Weis and Maxine S. Seller, eds., *Beyond Black and White: New Voices, New Faces in the United States Schools*. Albany, NY: State University of New York Press.

Zick, Andreas, Beatte Kupper, and Andreas Hovermann. 2011. *Intolerance, Prejudice, and Discrimination: A European Report*. Berlin: Friedrich Ebert Stiftung Forum, available at http://www.uni-bielefeld.de/ikg/zick/ZicketalGFEengl.pdf.

Zubrinsky, Camille L. and Lawrence Bobo. 1996. "Prismatic Metropolis: Race and Residential Segregation in the City of the Angels," *Social Science Research*. 25:335–74.

Index